Joseph Shield Nicholson

A Treatise on Money And Essays on Monetary Problems

Second Edition

Joseph Shield Nicholson

A Treatise on Money And Essays on Monetary Problems
Second Edition

ISBN/EAN: 9783744731812

Printed in Europe, USA, Canada, Australia, Japan

Cover: Foto ©Suzi / pixelio.de

More available books at **www.hansebooks.com**

A TREATISE ON MONEY

AND

ESSAYS ON MONETARY PROBLEMS

A

TREATISE ON MONEY

AND

ESSAYS ON MONETARY PROBLEMS

BY

J. SHIELD NICHOLSON, M.A., D.Sc.

PROFESSOR OF POLITICAL ECONOMY IN THE UNIVERSITY OF EDINBURGH

SOMETIME EXAMINER IN THE UNIVERSITIES OF CAMBRIDGE, LONDON, AND VICTORIA

SECOND EDITION
Revised and Enlarged

LONDON

ADAM AND CHARLES BLACK

1893

PREFACE TO THE SECOND EDITION

In the present edition I have included six new essays — IX. to XIV. inclusive—and I have to express my obligation to the proprietors of the various journals in which they first appeared for their kindness in allowing me to republish them.

Since the first appearance of this work the problems treated have become of more and more practical importance, and the literature of the subject has grown in a corresponding degree. India has just revolutionised her currency, and the United States has repealed the Sherman Act. The *Report of the Gold and Silver Commission* (1888) and the *Report of the Committee on Indian Currency* (1893) contain a mass of valuable information and a clear statement of principles. Dr. Soetbeer's learned and judicial bibliography on Gold and Silver Coinage (1892)* has given students an unrivalled source of reference.

To prevent misapprehension, I may state that the object of this volume is twofold. In the first place, I

* *Litteraturnachweis über Geld und Münzwesen* (Berlin, 1892).

have tried in the *Treatise on Money* to give the leading
principles in an intelligible and popular form; and
secondly, I have attempted to apply these principles
to some actual problems, especially those embraced in
what is called the Silver Question.   I have throughout
indicated as carefully as possible the cases in which
my own opinions differ from those generally received,
and on this ground I venture to hope that the work
may prove useful to the various parties engaged in the
present controversies on currency.   It would be a
great mistake to suppose that the combatants can be
divided simply into Mono-metallists and Bi-metallists.
Of both there are several species: witness the discus-
sions on the recent legislation of India and the United
States.   Fortunately the chance of an ultimate compromise or agreement is much greater through this
very diversity of opinion.   If all the Bi-metallists were
to insist on the universal adoption of the old ratio, and
all the Mono-metallists on the universal adoption of a
gold standard pure and simple, reconciliation would be
impossible.   Already an agreement has almost been
established on one point of fundamental importance,
namely, that some solution must be attempted.

J. SHIELD NICHOLSON.

UNIVERSITY OF EDINBURGH,
    November 1893.

PREFACE TO THE FIRST EDITION

IN the spring of 1886, the Directors of the *Wholesale Co-operative Society* requested me to write for their Annual an essay on Money, suitable for the industrial classes. I gladly took advantage of this request to recast the general principles of monetary science, and I thought the best way to make the theories popular and intelligible was to indicate their bearing upon questions of present interest. In doing so, however, I took the greatest pains to point out where any conflict of opinions arose: my object was not conversion but instruction. This was the original form of the present *Treatise on Money*, but many corrections have been made, and the last two chapters have been entirely rewritten.

The second part of the volume consists of a number of essays, differing widely in character, but all dealing with present monetary problems. This description applies even to the essay on "John Law and his System," for it was never more necessary than at present to show the connection between credit and

metallic money, and there has never been a better
example in the whole range of financial history than
" the system " *par excellence.*

In the paper on " One-Pound Notes for England,"
a definite scheme for their issue, with the special
object of restoring the gold coinage, is proposed.

The essay on " The Effects of Great Discoveries of
the Precious Metals" is mainly historical; but the
bearing on some aspects of the present controversy
is obvious.

Next in order come two addresses in which the
subject of " International Bi-metallism" is treated in
a somewhat popular manner.

The short paper on the " Stability of the Fixed
Ratio" is a statistical illustration of a well-known
theory.

The essay on " The Measurement of Variations in
the Value of the Monetary Standard" deals with an
extremely difficult statistical problem.   The general
method is original,* and the practical form of it may
be useful as a supplement to other methods also
confessedly imperfect with the statistics at present
available.

I venture to call special attention to the last essay
in the volume,† on the " Causes of Movements in
General Prices."   It was commenced more than two

---

* Compare Mr. Edgeworth's learned memorandum, presented to
the British Association. September 1887.

† Essay VIII. in the present edition.

years ago, and has been completed with my examination before the Currency Commission fresh in my mind. The first part contains a brief critical exposition of all the principal causes which have been assigned for the recent fall in prices, and the conclusion is that several of these causes—*e.g.* improved methods of production, on which much stress is sometimes laid—are indeterminate in their action, and, at any rate, of minor importance.

It is, however, the concluding portion of this essay which will, I hope, provoke most criticism. It contains, I believe, the first complete statement of the various modes in which gold prices, silver prices, and the ratio between gold and silver may theoretically interact, with the consequent effects on international trade. One of these possible modes is of great interest at the present time, as it shows that the fall in gold prices may be the direct effect of the prior depreciation of silver. The general analysis, however, indicates several other possible cases, and only facts can decide whether this particular solution is correct.

J. SHIELD NICHOLSON.

The University,
Edinburgh. *February* 1888.

CONTENTS

PART I

A TREATISE ON MONEY

CHAPTER I

DIFFICULTIES IN THE STUDY AND PRACTICAL IMPORTANCE OF THE SUBJECT

CHAPTER II

FUNCTIONS OF MONEY

CHAPTER III

MATERIAL MONEY AND REQUISITES OF GOOD COINAGE

CHAPTER IV

GRESHAM'S LAW AND TOKEN COINS

CHAPTER V

THE QUANTITY OF MONEY AND GENERAL PRICES

CHAPTER VI

EFFECTS OF CREDIT OR "REPRESENTATIVE MONEY" ON PRICES

CHAPTER VII

INFLUENCE ON THE GENERAL LEVEL OF PRICES IN ANY ONE COUNTRY OF THE GENERAL LEVEL OF PRICES IN OTHER COUNTRIES

CHAPTER VIII

EFFECTS ON GENERAL PRICES OF THE USE OF BOTH GOLD AND SILVER AS STANDARD MONEY

PART II

ESSAYS ON MONETARY PROBLEMS

I

PART I

A TREATISE ON MONEY

CHAPTER I

§ 1. *The difficulty of getting clear ideas.*—It seems desirable at the outset to warn the reader that, although this treatise on the principles of monetary science is intended to be elementary and introductory, the subject is in its nature difficult, and, in spite of its having been treated by many writers celebrated for their clearness of thought and distinctness of language, has not yet received a form which can be considered easy reading. The difficulties presented are of two kinds.

In the *first* place, there is the difficulty of getting clear ideas and attaching accurate and definite meanings to the words employed. People are apt to imagine that because they are familiar with the use of the words money, pound sterling, exchange, bank-note, etc., they are equally familiar with the things and processes and ideas which the words stand for. As a consequence, they do not think it necessary to strain the attention and couple what seems easy reading with hard thinking, and, according to the degree of their self-esteem, they come to the conclusion either that the subject is one which no one can understand with any amount of reading, or one which every one can understand without any reading at all.

§ 2. *The difficulty due to the complexity of facts.*— The *second* difficulty inherent in the subject depends upon matters of fact, and the need for statistics and experience to give body to the abstract ideas and general propositions of the theory. Even the most zealous student is apt to become bewildered when he finds authorities of equal standing opposed to one another on problems of great practical urgency, and feels inclined to conclude that there are no settled principles in the whole subject. This conflict of opinions, however, often arises simply from the fact that there is not sufficient evidence on which to base a certain conclusion—just as in medicine the best doctors may disagree, or in war the best generals, although no one would deny the vast progress in modern times of the art of healing or the art of destruction. It must be remembered, also, that the public only hears of the conflicts between the experts in any subject and of the struggles in making the next advance; as soon as a controversy is settled it passes from the newspaper or periodical to the text-book.

Only those who take the trouble to compare the monetary policy of successive historical periods can form any idea of the extraordinary progress made in the theory and practice of this branch of finance.

This progress, as in other practical sciences, has consisted in overcoming difficulties of both the kinds just noticed. On the one side ideas and general principles have been made clear and intelligible, and on the other large stores of facts and figures have been brought to bear on their practical application. It is to what may be regarded as well established that the following pages will be mainly devoted, and if matters of controversy are introduced, the leading opinions on both sides will be stated, and the reader left, like a British jury, in his own person to form his own conclusions on the facts and opinions advanced.

§ 3. *Importance of general study of money in a country with popular government.*—I have thought it necessary to emphasise and explain the nature of the difficulty of the subject, partly with the view of showing the need for hard thinking in some cases, and a suspension of judgment in others until sufficient evidence has been obtained, but principally on account of its great importance to the industrial classes in a community with popular government. If it is once generally believed that questions of currency can be decided off-hand by popular votes, the way becomes open for great national calamities.

At the same time, however, when questions of changes in monetary policy arise, they cannot be left to the decision of a few authorities without appeal to the people. It is hardly possible to make any change of this kind without producing a certain conflict of interests, and all history proves that it is not wise for any class to leave its interests entirely in the hands of representatives drawn from another. In many

cases, no doubt, the conflict of interests between
capital and labour, for example, or landlords and
tenants, or traders and consumers, is more apparent
than real ; but in some cases of vital importance the
divergence of interests is fundamental.

In the exchange of services and commodities, as a
rule, both parties to the exchange gain, but in mere
monetary changes what one gains another must lose.
If, for instance, owing to a change in the currency,
there is a general rise in prices, debtors will gain at
the expense of creditors ; a farmer with a long lease
at a fixed rent will gain from a rise in prices and the
landlord will lose—the one will obtain a greater and
the other a less share than before in the general
wealth of the community.

§ 4. *Enormous power for evil in currency regulations possessed by Governments, illustrated from English
history.* — The enormous power for evil which a
Government possesses in effecting changes in currency
has received more than one startling illustration in
our own history. "It may be doubted," says Mac-
aulay, speaking of the state of things which rendered
necessary the recoinage of 1696, "whether all the
misery which had been inflicted on the nation in a
quarter of a century, by bad kings, bad parliaments,
and bad judges, was equal to the misery caused in a
single year by bad crowns and bad shillings. The
evil was felt daily, and almost hourly, in almost
every place and by almost every class : in the dairy
and on the threshing-floor, by the anvil and by the
loom, on the billows of the ocean and in the depths
of the mine. Nothing could be purchased without

dispute. Over every counter there was wrangling from morning to night. The workman and his employer had a quarrel as regularly as the Saturday came round. No merchant would contract to deliver goods without making some stipulation about the quality of the coin in which he was to be paid. Even men of business were often bewildered by the confusion into which all pecuniary transactions were thrown. The simple and the careless were pillaged without mercy by extortioners whose demands grew even more rapidly than the money shrank. The labourer found that the bit of metal which, when he received it, was called a shilling, would hardly, when he wanted to purchase a pot of beer or a loaf of rye-bread, go so far as sixpence. Where artisans of more than usual intelligence were collected in great numbers, as in the dockyard of Chatham, they were able to make complaints heard and to obtain some redress; but the ignorant and helpless peasant was cruelly ground between one class which would give money only by tale (counting) and another which would only vote it by weight."

Professor Thorold Rogers, in his interesting work entitled *Six Centuries of English Work and Wages*, often calls attention to the importance to the industrial classes of a sound system of currency. "The monetary history of all countries," he writes, "is full of instances which illustrate the rapidity with which people fall into the delusion that high prices, due to over-issues of paper, the coinage of an over-valued metal, or to excessive speculation, are evidences of prosperity. Our English Parliament, in the present

century, endorsed the follies of Vansittart and repu-
diated the truths which were announced by the Bullion
Committee and Lord King. But the issue of base
money is rapidly and irremediably mischievous. It
affects all except those who are quick at measuring
the exact extent of the fraud, and by turning the base
coin into an article of traffic, can trade on the knowledge and skill which they possess. To the poor, and
indeed to all who live by wages and fixed salaries, it
is speedily ruinous. The effect of the base money of
Henry VIII. and Edward VI., though it lasted only
sixteen years, was potent enough to dominate in the
history of labour and wages from the sixteenth century
to the present time, so enduring are the causes which
influence the economical history of a nation.'

§ 5. *Evils of bad currency in France during the
Revolution.*—Nor must it be supposed that the evils
of bad currency have been inflicted on nations only
by despots and irresponsible Governments. The most
glaring example of the violation of sound principles of
currency recorded in history is the issue by the
Government of the great French Revolution of the
inconvertible notes called *assignats.* " It was constantly
urged," says A. D. White in his work on *Paper Money
Inflation in France,* "that if any nation could safely
issue paper money France was now that nation; that
she was fully warned by a severe experience; that she
was now a constitutional Government controlled by
an enlightened, patriotic people—not, as in the days
of the former issue of paper money, an absolute
monarchy controlled by politicians and adventurers;
that she was able to secure every franc of her paper

money by a virtual mortgage of a landed domain of vastly greater value than the entire issue; that with men like Bailly, Mirabeau, and Necker at the head, she could not commit the financial mistakes and errors from which France had suffered when at the head stood John Law and the Regent and Cardinal Dubois." Deluded by these arguments, the issues were made, with fatal consequences to French industry. " What the bigotry of Louis XIV. and the shiftlessness of Louis XV. could not do in nearly a century, was accomplished by thus tampering with the currency in a few months. Everything that tariffs and custom-houses could do was done. Still, the great manu-factories of Normandy were closed; those of the rest of the kingdom speedily followed, and vast numbers of workmen in all parts of the country were thrown out of employment. In the words of the most brilliant apologist for French Revolutionary states-manship—'Commerce was dead—betting took its place.'"

§ 6. *Difficulties in radical changes in currency, but such changes sometimes necessary.*—It would require many large volumes to describe the magnitude of the evils which different nations, from the earliest times down to our own day, have suffered from ill-regulated currencies. So much have some Socialist writers been impressed by these evils and by other difficulties which arise even in the best monetary systems, that they have tried to formulate schemes in which the use of money would be entirely forbidden: with them money itself is, in the fullest meaning of the expres-sion, the root of all evil.

Other writers, again, who have given much attention to the subject, have been so much impressed with
the evil consequences of any disturbance of a nation's
system of currency, that they are opposed to all
changes if during a moderate length of time the
system has worked at all well.   In a recent paper,
Mr. Giffen has endeavoured to show that the functions of Government regarding money should be
reduced to a minimum, and he writes in the most
despairing tone of human fallibility.   " To obtain the
action of Governments you have to submit the discussion to tribunals of a very peculiar description,—
to Parliaments which are full of people who have no
intellectual interest in the subjects, and no qualification of any sort or kind for dealing with them ;
and to constituencies electing the members of Parliament who are still more unfit, and who have little
conception of the nature of the problems to be
discussed, and no means whatsoever of forming
practical conclusions upon them—who are, in fact,
likely to be bewildered and confused if a Government
makes a change of any kind in respect of the standard
money."

It may certainly be conceded to Mr. Giffen that
very strong reasons ought to be adduced before any
great change in a monetary system can be recommended ; but the conditions of industry have varied
so rapidly, such enormous changes have taken place
even during the last fifty years, that it is quite possible that a system of currency which acted well
enough in former times may at present require some
modification.   It would certainly be a most remark-

able thing if, when economic institutions of every
kind have been remodelled, when vital changes have
taken place in the production and distribution of
wealth, when remote nations have become more
closely knit together by commerce than were cities of
the same country fifty years ago, when the whole
industrial world has been almost revolutionised, no
change whatever in currency, which is the very life-
blood of industry, should be necessary or desirable.

§ 7. *The subject of money is in its nature difficult,
but not obscure or mysterious—it requires, like mathematics, hard thinking and regular advance.*—And if
any change is requisite, the scheme proposed ought to
be of a nature which can be made intelligible to the
people interested. Bare authority will not be accepted
in these days; and after all, the fundamental principles of money may be understood by any person of
ordinary capacity who will devote a little trouble, and
who is not too proud to begin at the beginning. To
say that a subject is difficult is not to say that it is
obscure, or unintelligible, or mysterious, or demanding
some peculiar, rare native gift. Mathematics is a
difficult study—even arithmetic, although now part
of a compulsory education, is not easy; but mathematical reasoning is eminently clear and distinct. So
it is with money: the principles of the subject,
although in one sense the most difficult, are also the
clearest and most intelligible in economic science.
Those who find the practical problems at present
agitating the public mind difficult of comprehension
and apparently insoluble, would look on them with
very different eyes if they had made a systematic

study of the elements of monetary science. "There is much," says Professor Jevons, "to be learnt about money before entering upon those abstruse questions which barely admit of decided answers. In studying a language, we begin with the grammar before we try to read or write. In mathematics we practise ourselves in simple arithmetic before we proceed to the subtleties of algebra and the differential calculus. But it is the grave misfortune of the moral and political sciences that they are continually discussed by those who have never laboured at the elementary grammar or the simple arithmetic of the subject. Hence the extraordinary schemes and fallacies every now and then put forth."

CHAPTER II

FUNCTIONS OF MONEY

§ 1. *Definition of money.*—A good deal of discussion has taken place as to the proper definition of the term "money," and it must not be thought that, because no particular definition has been generally adopted by economists, therefore the discussion has been wasted. The great use of definitions is to lay bare the meanings of the terms employed, to clear up the ideas for which they stand, and thus to get rid of all ambiguities; but it is a matter of comparatively small importance whether different writers use the same word in precisely the same sense when, either from their definition at the outset or from the context, the meaning is plain.

As regards money, for example, some writers may include and some exclude bank-notes, and other forms of credit, but no harm is done provided the functions of notes, cheques, etc., are properly described. There is, however, considerable danger in laying down, at first, hard-and-fast definitions, and then deducing general laws, and applying these laws to particular cases without due consideration.

In the sequel we shall see that by far the most important proposition laid down respecting money is that, other things being the same, its value depends on its quantity—that if the quantity of money is increased, the value of each particular piece is diminished. Now, if we were to lay down at the outset a definition of money which included convertible bank-notes, and were then to argue, in accordance with the proposition just noticed, that an increase of bank-notes would lower the value of money, we might happen to speak the truth, but unless many more circumstances were taken into account we should only speak the truth by accident. Yet reasoning of this kind prevailed in making the most important law ever made affecting the paper currency of this country. As it happens, it is generally admitted that this Act, passed in 1844, has on the whole worked well, or, at any rate, has done no great harm; but it is more satisfactory when Acts of Parliament succeed on the grounds on which they were ostensibly passed, and not for reasons which were not considered. It would be out of place to discuss the Act in question at this stage; I have only mentioned it to show the danger of being misled by words. Opinions are divided on the real merits of the Act, but no one now will defend the reasoning with which it was supported by its promoters.

I shall not attempt to give a short and simple definition of money, because it seems to me that the meaning of the term must vary according to circumstances. An illustration will make this quite clear.

What is meant in the money articles of the news-
papers by the supply of money and the demand for
money? Every one knows it is not merely coin or
notes of the Bank of England, but they would have
some difficulty in explaining what else ought to be
included. The important thing, however, for our
present purpose, is not to decide what is the most
appropriate meaning to give to the term "money,"
but to describe certain functions of the industrial
world which are generally briefly spoken of as being
performed by money.

§ 2. *Money as a medium of exchange.*—First of all,
then, let us consider money as *a medium of exchange*,
and its importance in this capacity. "It is easy to
imagine, even in a primitive society, the inconveniences of pure barter. The griefs of the bootmaker
wanting a hat, who found many who had hats but
did not at the time want boots, and many men who
wanted boots badly enough but were quite as ill off,
temporarily or permanently, respecting hats, have
been related by every writer on money" (Walker).
But what is not so often attended to is the ever-
increasing importance, with the growing complexity of
industrial societies, of a universal medium of exchange:
it becomes, as division of labour is extended, not merely
a convenience in distributing the finished product,
but an actual necessary of production. Let any one
consider the vast series of operations necessary to provide for the maintenance in our days of the family of
an unskilled labourer; or, better still, let him glance
over the list of occupations of the people as given in
the census reports, in which he will find hundreds of

names to which he can attach no meaning whatever.* Without some common medium of exchange, it would be absolutely impossible under our present industrial system to carry on the manufactures and commerce of the country. The only conceivable alternative would be governmental control of the most elaborate kind pervading every home, involving in itself an enormous waste of time and labour. Without a complete revolution in the conditions of society, a medium of exchange is indispensable. Production rests on division of labour, and division of labour involves easy and prompt exchange, which, again, involves a common medium. Money in this sense is as essential to the interchange of commodities as language to the interchange of ideas, and in the last resort the exchange of commodities is for the most part the exchange of the services through which they are made. Thus money, in the sense of a common medium of exchange, is necessary in order to exchange all kinds of labour, from the highest to the lowest.

In these days we are so familiar with this universal medium, with this alchemist's stone which turns everything into gold—land and labour, the fleeting wealth of the present and the stored wealth from the past— that it is difficult for us to realise the state of a nation in which custom took the place of contract, and the mass of the people lived practically without money. There can be no doubt that during the Middle Ages the commutation of various services and labour dues into

---

* The Census Report for 1881 states that it was found necessary, in order to classify the different employments returned, to make a small dictionary.

money equivalents was the principal factor in the industrial progress of that period. The break-up of feudalism, the independence of the towns, the abolition of serfdom, and the growth of commerce, are all largely due to the substitution of money payments resting on contracts in place of services founded on law and custom. So far from being an evil, during this period at any rate, the extension of the use of money as a medium of exchange was the means of effecting great social reforms, and there can be little doubt that progress was retarded largely by the deficiency of the precious metals, and especially the dearth of silver.

The Socialists, who look on money as an engine by which the rich torture the poor, will find in many instances that, on the contrary, it has been the greatest benefactor of labour. We have a modern instance of the benefits of money payments in the state of things which led to the passing of the Truck Acts. Every one knows that the worst mode in which a workman can be paid for his labour is in a quantity of the commodity which he makes or assists in making—in cider, for example, as was the custom in some places in England.

§ 3. *Money as a measure of values.*—Necessarily involved in this function of money as a medium of exchange is its function as *a measure of values.* It is useless to convert all things and services into terms of money as a medium of exchange unless this is done at certain rates. What we want to know in any given case is not the bare fact that by means of money exchanges can be effected between one commodity and ten thousand others, but we want some *measure* of the rates of exchange.

Now it is quite possible that the *actual* medium of exchange adopted may not be itself the measure in which values are expressed—it may itself be measured by some other standard. In this country at the present time the standard unit of value is the sovereign, which consists of a definite amount of gold and alloy fixed by Act of Parliament. Consequently all values in this country are measured in pounds and parts of pounds. But although the sovereign is the standard unit, it is by no means the exclusive medium of exchange. We use not only silver and bronze, but paper as the actual medium.

The important point to observe, however, is that all these substances used as actual means of exchange are measured in terms of the sovereign either as multiples or submultiples. Wages, according to the quality of the labour, the times of payment, etc., are paid sometimes in pence, sometimes in shillings, sometimes in bank-notes, sometimes in cheques; but the standard measure is the sovereign, and the values of the pence, shillings, notes, or cheques depend on their relation to the sovereign.

It is extremely important to distinguish between the actual medium and the measure of reckoning. In some parts of Scotland the rent paid for land depends on the prices of certain kinds of agricultural produce; in effect, we may suppose that the rents consist nominally of so much corn. But they would not be actually paid in corn. Instead of the rents depending on the prices of a few agricultural products, they might depend on the prices of a hundred different articles. That would be just as if the farmer stipulated to pay certain quantities of these articles in different proportions. In this way the unit of value would be very complex, but the payment would never be made in all these articles.

We see, then, that the two functions of money already noticed are not necessarily performed by the same thing: we may measure in terms of one thing and pay in terms of another, but the two functions are equally necessary to an industrial society, and are mutually dependent. The medium of exchange would be useless unless measured in terms of the standard, and the measure would be useless unless some common medium of giving effect to it practically is adopted. A person who has something to sell—whether labour, or land, or produce—wants to know not only that his commodity bears a certain proportion in value to the commodities of other sellers—that is, he not only wants his commodity measured as the others are measured, but he wants some medium by which he can make as many purchases of these commodities as his article entitles him to obtain.

§ 4. *Money as a standard for deferred payments.*— So far nothing has been said of the element of *time*. We have spoken of exchanges being effected and the values of commodities being measured without any reference (except by way of illustration) to deferred payments, or payments extending over a long period. It is this consideration, however, which constitutes the greatest difficulty, both practical and theoretical, in choosing a standard unit of value as the basis of

money. At any particular time, or, rather, to effect
any single set of exchanges, we might measure the
values of all commodities by any one of them—say
corn—write down their values in terms of corn on
bits of paper, and exchange accordingly. In some
Socialistic schemes it has been proposed to issue
labour-tickets against commodities or services, and
everything being expressed in terms of so much
labour, exchanges might be made on this basis. But
a little reflection would show that there would be
much difficulty in taking an hour's labour as the
unit of value over a long period, because all kinds of
changes might occur in the efficiency, or intensity, or
hardship of the labour; and the same kind of difficulty arises with whatever standard is chosen.

§ 5. *Contracts for long periods.*—Under our present
system we must find some means of overcoming uncertainty in the interpretation of contracts : the whole
of industry rests on an endless series of contracts,
which ought to admit of a definite interpretation.
Now it is quite easy to lay down that our unit of
value, our chosen standard, shall consist of a certain
weight of a certain specified substance of a certain
quality, and if we only wanted our unit as a measure
of weight or of fineness, no more would be required.

But the difficulty is this: We want our unit to
measure, not weight, or qualities, or capacities, or colours,
but *values*. We may, by choosing any substance whatever, capable of exact measurement and definition, avoid
in one sense any uncertainty in the interpretation of
contracts ; but we do so in a purely artificial and useless
manner unless other changes are taken into account.

To discover what these other requisites are, let us take an example of deferred payments. A farmer takes a farm on a nineteen years' lease at so many pounds, say £1000 a year. There will be no doubt about the meaning of the contract. He must either pay exactly every year the thousand sovereigns, or give some document or other which will enable the receiver to obtain on demand that number of pounds sterling. In making this agreement, supposing the bargain was the result of competition, the farmer would have taken into account not only how much the land would yield of various kinds of produce, but also the prices he would expect on the average to obtain, as also the prices he would have to pay for the various expenses of production, for labour, machines, manures, etc. Suppose, now, that at the end of ten years, owing to any cause whatever, the prices of produce have fallen very greatly, and also that the price of labour and the materials of production have not fallen equally, the result will be that he cannot really afford to pay the same rent as before, and he will be inclined to argue that Government should release him from his contract, because it was entered on with the expectation that prices would on the average have remained steady. The example just taken is essentially the case of many farmers at the present time. And they may very plausibly argue that if they are compelled to pay their rents they will be ruined, that the land in the process will be exhausted, that their successors will not have the same experience, and allege other inconveniences to the nation at large. This is not the place to consider whether this

plea should be urged on the Government or on the
landlords, but of the hardship to the farmers there can
be no doubt.

Let us take another example, also of a practical
kind. The Indian Government engages the services
of a highly trained body of men, and promises to
pay them a certain number of rupees. There is no
doubt as to the meaning of the rupee in its material
shape. It is a certain weight of a certain quality of
silver. Suppose at the time the bargain is made ten
rupees go to a sovereign, then the savings of Indian
servants remitted home will command that rate so
long as it lasts; but it is equally clear that if the
value of the rupee sinks to a shilling, for purposes of
remittance they will lose half the value of their salaries.

One more example on a larger scale. The Government of this country has to pay more than twenty
millions sterling of interest on the National Debt.
To do so it must levy taxes. If, reckoned in money,
the taxable wealth of the country has become much
less, so much more heavy must the taxation be to
make these payments. ·

§ 6. *Importance of comparative stability of value in
money.*—It is clear from these examples that "money"
is required not only as a medium of exchange and a
measure of values, but as a standard for deferred payments. So long as contracts into which time enters
as an element are expressed in terms of money, it is
necessary that the standard adopted should possess
comparative *stability of value.* It is at this point that
one of the most serious difficulties of the subject arises,
for it is now universally admitted in works on political

economy that any such thing as a commodity with absolute stability of value is unattainable. The best way to see this is to consider the causes on which the value of any commodity depends.

§ 7. *Meaning of terms "demand" and "supply."*— Stated in the most general terms, and in the form most familiar to the industrial world, value may be said to depend on demand and supply. Both of these words, however, familiar as they are, require some further explanation. What do we really understand by *demand?* It is quite clear that we do not simply mean desire to possess, for, roughly speaking, it may be said that human desires are insatiable—that everybody desires everything. It is obviously not in this vague sense that we can properly speak of there being no demand for commodities of various kinds—for food, clothes, houses, and luxuries. There are, at any rate, always "poor about our gates," who not only desire but very urgently need those very things for which the commercial papers tell us there is no demand.

Precisely the same difficulty occurs in regard to *supply.* All manufacturers would be delighted to supply many times as much of their articles as they actually do if they could only find purchasers. The explanation is found in introducing a phrase which must always be understood. Both demand and supply mean demand and supply *at a price*, and the peculiarity of both is, that in general they vary with the price, but in opposite directions. As a general rule it may be laid down that, other things being equal, if the price of an article falls relatively to that of others, the demand increases.

This is a law which has received striking illustration from the history of taxation. Impose a tax of a very onerous amount, and instead of increasing the revenue you may kill the revenue altogether; whilst, on the other hand, the progressive diminution of a tax, by increasing the demand, may also increase the revenue obtainable.

As regards supply, the general rule is, that if there is a rise in the price an additional supply will be forthcoming. If, for example, the price of coal rises, a great stimulus is given to coal-mining; labour and capital are directed to this industry, and there is a great increase in the supply.

§ 8. *Law of demand and supply.*—We see, then, that the demand and supply of any article both vary according to price—both depend upon price: how, then, can we say that price depends on demand and supply? The solution is found in what J. S. Mill called the "equation between demand and supply," which may be expressed in the following form. In any market, competition will take place between sellers on one side and buyers on the other, until such a price is arrived at that the quantity demanded at that price is equal to the quantity offered. Any increase in the competition of buyers will tend to raise the price, and the rise in the price will drive the poorest and least eager of the competitors from the circle of demanders; whilst, on the other hand, the same rise will tend to induce dealers who had been withholding their stocks to come forward.

It will be seen, then, that everything depends

on competition; * and this disposes of an objection
by the late Professor Cairnes, who said that all J. S.
Mill's boasted equation amounted to was, that in
any market the quantity bought at a price was precisely equal to the quantity sold at that price, which
was no doubt quite true, but also quite useless. But
the point of J. S. Mill's argument is, that competition
is the moving force according to which the price rises
and falls, and the quantities offered or demanded are
increased and diminished.

If, now, we push the analysis further, and ask,
On what does competition depend? we have thrust
upon us at once a variety of causes. Amongst these,
undoubtedly the most important are the various
conditions of supply. Some things are absolutely
limited, and this class consists by no means simply
of such commodities as are indicated by the stock
example of old pictures. The land of a whole
country, and equally the areas of particular districts
and towns, are strictly limited. It must be remembered, also, that many things which could be increased
if only time were allowed, may be wanted immediately. Take, for example, the food-supplies of any
industrial area. No doubt this country could raise a
much greater supply of food within its own borders,
but in case of a great war, or other cause of cessation
of imports, there would certainly be famine prices.

* For the purposes of this treatise it was not thought advisable
to push the analysis of value further. The writer fully admits the
importance of considering the conception of *final utility* and the
case of *monopoly* (cf. Note on Value in his edition of the *Wealth of
Nations*, p. 107).

There are, however, other commodities which can be indefinitely increased at very short notice, and no one would give fancy prices for existing stocks of cloth if by waiting a few weeks an abundant supply could be obtained. It is not necessary for the present purpose to go into further detail. The point which is essential to the argument is, that one important factor in determining value is the conditions of supply, and these conditions are subject to variation, as regards most articles, with every change in the methods of production.

The conditions affecting demand are equally important, and also subject to variation. A rise in the price of any article will probably lead to an increase in the demand for convenient substitutes, and, with the progress of civilisation, the wants and desires of people are constantly changing. Whether, then, we look to a simple market and temporary prices, or to the annual consumption of a great nation, we find abundant reasons for expecting constant changes in relative values. It is, then, quite clear that we cannot in strictness say that any single commodity is capable of possessing stability of value. For value means, in the last resort, exchange value; and any commodity we like to choose will, in the lapse of a very short time, fetch more of one article and less of another.

§ 9. *Is comparative stability of value in money attainable?*—Are we, then, to suppose that the search for a kind of money which will possess stability of value is an idle quest, and that as regards stability of value every article will be equally unsuitable? This would obviously be unjustifiable. A little reflection will show that, for practical purposes, we may get for a considerable time a much greater comparative stability in some things than in others. In some things the annual production compared with the total amount in use may be small, and the demand may be fairly constant—that is, not subject to sudden changes in fashion or (to express it more generally) in desire. A commodity of this kind would be properly said to be more stable in value than an article in which these qualities were wanting.

Thus, although we cannot find any substance for our standard money, a given quantity of which will always possess the same purchasing power over each and every commodity, we may find that one substance will over a term of years have a much more uniform power of purchasing things in general than is the case with other substances. "Things in general" is, of course, a vague and rather uncertain expression, but it is perhaps the best obtainable. For practical purposes, however, we only require a particular class of things. An agricultural labourer, for example, if he wishes to compare the purchasing power of his wages with those in other times and places, will be able to make a tolerably just comparison by taking a very few commodities; and if he can lay by a few pounds he will be satisfied with the stability of value of money, provided they enable him to obtain about the same amount of the articles of his habitual consumption as when he made his saving.

Unless some stability of value of the kind indicated were attainable in money, the world would be put to very great inconvenience. This has been illustrated only too often in history by the criminal, or at best ill-considered, action of Governments in artificially changing the value of the standard. It is, at any rate, perfectly certain that a coin of a uniform weight and fineness is in all respects more steady in value, or represents a more constant purchasing power, than one which is subjected to wilful debasement or diminution. And if, instead of metal, paper is exclusively used for money, and the issues are not most carefully regulated, the fluctuations in value will be still greater and more detrimental.

§ 10. *A tabular standard of value.*—We have now examined the three most important functions of what is briefly spoken of as money. Every industrial society requires a common medium of exchange, a general measure of values, and a standard for deferred payments; and there can be no doubt that it will be much more convenient if these three requisites are found united in, or rather conjoined with, the standard money of a nation. It has, however, already been pointed out that it is not necessary that the actual medium of exchange should itself be the money of account or measure of values, and in the same way it is not necessary that contracts for long periods should be made, as they are usually at present, in terms of definite quantities of the standard money.

This is especially noteworthy at a time when the general movement in prices is downwards at an uncertain rate. It may, then, be worth while to describe briefly what is known as the "tabular standard," of which the reader will find a more detailed account in

A TABULAR STANDARD 29

the excellent manual of Professor Jevons on *Money*
(pp. 327-333), to which reference has already been
made. The following passages will, perhaps, suffice
to show the essentials of the scheme: "To carry
Lowe's and Scrope's plans (published in 1822 and
1833 respectively) into effect, a permanent Government Commission would have to be created, and
endowed with a kind of judicial power. The officers of
the department would collect the current prices of
commodities in all the principal markets of the kingdom, and by a well-defined system of calculations
would compute from their data the average variations
in the purchasing power of gold. The decisions of
this Commission would be published monthly, and
payments would be adjusted in accordance with them.
Thus, suppose that a debt of £100 was incurred upon
the 1st July 1875, and was to be paid back on
1st July 1878; if the Commission had decided in
June 1878 that the value of gold had fallen in the
ratio of 106 to 100 in the intervening years, then
the creditor would claim an increase of 6 per cent
in the nominal amount of the debt. . . . The difficulties in the way of such a scheme are not considerable. It would no doubt introduce a certain complexity into the relations of debtors and creditors,
and disputes might sometimes arise as to the date
of the debt whence the calculations must be made.
The work of the Commission, when once established
and directed by Act of Parliament, would be little
more than that of accountants acting according to
fixed rules. Their decisions would be of a perfectly
bonâ fide character, because, in addition to their

average results, they would be required to publish periodically the detailed tables of prices upon which their calculations were founded, and thus many persons could sufficiently verify the data and the calculations. Fraud would be out of the question."

It will be observed that, according to this scheme, there would be no change in the actual currency; the only object would be to give a more definite meaning to contracts for deferred payments by taking into account changes in the purchasing power of the sovereign. Recently the plan in question has received strong support from Professor Marshall. I quote from a paper furnished by him to the Royal Commission on the Depression of Trade (Third Report, Appendix C, p. 33): "A perfectly exact measure of purchasing power is not only unattainable, but even unthinkable [that is, taking into account the varying wants and resources of industrial societies]. The same change of prices affects the purchasing power of money to different persons in different ways. For one who can seldom afford to have meat, a rise of one-fourth in the price of meat, accompanied by a fall of one-fourth in that of bread, means a rise in the purchasing power of money. His wages will go further than before; while to his richer neighbour, who spends twice as much on meat as on bread, the change acts the other way. The Government would, of course, take account only of the total consumption of the whole nation; but even so, it would be troubled by constant changes in the way in which the nation spent its income. The estimate of the importance of different commodities would have to be recast from time to time."

§ 11. *Index numbers.*—The form in which the problem of a general rise or fall in prices is most often presented to the public is in the calculation of what are termed "index numbers"; and, in fact, the tabular standard is simply an official index number. We may take as an example the index numbers which for many years have been adopted in the annual commercial review of the *Economist* newspaper. According to this method, the average prices of a number of selected articles were determined for a period of six years (1845-50), and each of these prices per unit taken was reckoned at 100. Thus we might get a pound, or a yard, or a gallon, as the original unit, but the price per unit is in every case 100. Now, suppose changes occur in prices, then the corresponding change is marked by the addition to or subtraction from this 100 of the necessary percentages. In general, we find movements in opposite directions, and the resultant or general movement is determined by simple addition of the new index numbers, as they are called. Thus, if, as in the *Economist*, 22 articles are taken, the addition of the original initial index numbers would be 2200. If at any time the aggregate index numbers amount to more than 2200, a general rise in prices is said to have taken place; if they amount to less, there is a general fall. It is quite clear that the calculation is very rough, and must always be used with caution. For example, if the index numbers showed a general rise, it would not do without further examination to say that the same money wages would purchase less commodities for the use of labourers, for it might happen that the particular articles consumed by labourers had fallen in price on the whole.

§ 12. *Movements in index numbers in recent years.*—It may be interesting to notice the principal movements in the index numbers of the *Economist* since their adoption, when, as explained, the total index number of 22 commodities reckoned at 100 each was 2200. A fluctuating rise, with occasional relapses in particular years, took place up to 1864, when the index number was 3787. This is equivalent to saying that on the articles taken there was an average rise of about 72 per cent. (It must, however, be remembered this very high number is largely due to the exceptional price of cotton, owing to the American Civil War.) From 1864 to 1871 there was a fluctuating fall in prices, the index number in the latter year being 2590. Then a rise took place, the numbers in 1872-3-4 being respectively 2835, 2947, 2891. Thus, in these years of inflation, as they are often termed, though there was a rise of about 31 per cent on the original index number of 1845-50, there was a still greater fall from the number of 1864. From 1874 there has been a steady and rapid decline, until we find, on 1st January 1886, the aggregate index number is only 2023, which is lower than the original number, and than that of any subsequent year.*

---

* For a criticism on the general method of index numbers, compare the Essay on "Variations in the Value of the Monetary Standard" (p. 256). By far the best monograph on the whole subject is that furnished by Mr. F. Y. Edgeworth to the British Association, September 1887.

It is this very remarkable fall in prices which is at present exciting so much attention, and which has been the principal cause of the appointment of the Royal Commission on Currency. I have dwelt at some length on this aspect of the subject, because it is not only the most difficult of the functions of money to understand, but has very serious practical consequences. I am not inclined to think that the use of a general official index number, however carefully it was constructed, would be likely, at any rate for many generations, to be commonly adopted as the basis of contracts, even for a long term of years. It is all very well to talk of getting rid of the speculative element, say in rents, but human nature is on the whole so buoyant and confident, that this is precisely the element an enterprising farmer would wish to retain. At the same time, however, I think it must be admitted that the idea is a very fruitful one, and is capable of less perfect but more practical applications in the shape of varieties of the "sliding scale." If there is any likelihood of a fall in prices during the next ten years, being on the same scale as in the last ten, undoubtedly a great many contracts must be readjusted to the change in the purchasing power of the standard money.

CHAPTER III

MATERIAL MONEY AND REQUISITES OF GOOD COINAGE

§ 1. *Early forms of money.*—It is necessary, however, before attempting to explain the causes of these movements in general prices, to return to the simple elements of the subject, and to consider what substances are best adapted to serve for money, or to fulfil these various money functions. We are so much accustomed to regard gold and silver as money *par excellence*, that we are apt to forget the number and variety of materials which have been used at different times. If space permitted, a historical survey would show that what are termed the precious metals may be regarded as "survivals of the fittest" in the struggle for existence of a great variety of substances.

"It is entirely," as Professor Jevons says, "a question of degree what commodities will, in any given society, form the most convenient currency." I give a few examples, chiefly derived from this writer's work on *Money*. In the hunting stage of societies skins have very commonly been used, and this is the explanation of the verse in Job (ii. 4): "Skin for

skin; yea, all that a man hath will he give for his
life." The transition from skins to leather was
natural, and leather money is said to have been used
in many ancient nations. Even in quite recent times,
in the trade of the Hudson's Bay Company with the
North American Indians, furs long formed the medium
of exchange. In the pastoral stage, when the principal
wealth of the society consisted of herds, we find cattle
used as a measure of value, and it is said that *pecunia*,
the Latin term for money, is derived from *pecus*,
cattle.

In the agricultural state corn came into use as
money, and is said still to form the medium of exchange in some remote parts of Europe, whilst at
different times and places olive-oil, tobacco, tea, dried
fish, salt, and straw mats have been used. Iron, tin,
lead, and copper were also tried at a higher stage of
development, but in the great majority of cases all
other materials for standard money have given place
to gold and silver; and during the last twelve years
in the Western world an attempt has been made to
make gold the sole standard.

§ 2. *Qualities of good metallic money.*—An enumeration of the various qualities good metallic money
should possess will explain this gradual exclusive
adoption of gold and silver. The substance should
be generally acceptable on its own account if it is to
serve as a medium of exchange, and no metals are
more sought after on their own account than these
two. There can be no doubt in our own times that
the consumption of gold, especially for the arts, has
enormously increased, and is one of the most im-

portant factors to be taken into account in considering
the effects of the "scarcity of gold," of which more
will be said presently. It is well known also that one
of the best signs of the prosperity of India is a large
importation of gold, not for use as money, but as
treasure or ornaments.

Other qualities of good metallic money which
require little explanation, and which are eminently
possessed by gold and silver, are *portability*, which
again is closely connected with great value in small
bulk; *durability*, so that no deterioration takes place
by saving, and a minimum of wear and tear in use;
uniformity of parts, so that equal weights, however
large or small, shall have the same value; *divisibility*,
which is implied in the quality just mentioned; and
finally, what Professor Jevons calls *cognisability*, or
such characteristics that the purity of the metal may
be easily recognised, and that it may be conveniently
coined. Taking all these qualities together, gold and
silver are certainly the best metals for money; and
it may be noticed that gold is too valuable in proportion to its weight to be used for very small, just as
silver is hardly valuable enough for very large sums.

§ 3. *Connection of these qualities with the functions of
money.*——It is hardly necessary to explain the connection between these qualities of money and its
primary functions as a measure of value and medium
of exchange; but, as has been shown above, in the
progress of society, stability of value becomes of more
and more importance, and in this respect it is essential
that the supply should keep even pace with the demand if that is possible. The great durability of gold

and silver, and the care taken of them in consequence
of their value, render the supply in the hands of man
very large compared with the annual produce of the
mines.   At present the proportion of the annual to
the total supply is probably not much more than one
to fifty.*   As we shall see presently, the greatest
sources of fluctuations are on the side of demand.   At
any rate, there can be no doubt that these metals are,
in respect of comparative stability of value, superior to
any others.

§ 4. *Coinage of money.*   "*What is a pound?*"—In
the list of qualities mentioned as desirable in metallic
money, it will be remembered that the last was
cognisability.   At first, after gold and silver were
generally adopted, the risk of being defrauded by
inferior quality or adulteration was left entirely to the
receiver of the metals; in fact, they circulated between
the inhabitants of the country simply as merchandise, just as at present between different countries.
Very early, however, it began to be recognised that
there would be great convenience if pieces of the
metal were certified by authority to be of certain
weights and fineness; and accordingly, coinage has
always been one of the first industrial functions that
Governments have undertaken.

At the time of the Domesday survey in England
(1086) every important town had, as part of its
privileges, the right to a mint.   It is probable, both
from the analogy of other cases and the particular
evidence to hand, that the profits of the king or

* The statistics as to the total amount of gold and silver in the
hands of man are of course extremely vague.

feudal lord acted at least as powerfully as the
interests and convenience of the subjects in the
institution of coinage, and it is certainly noteworthy
how surely and steadily the nominal weight diminished
in reality. At the same time, however, in the interests of historical truth, it must be observed that in
most cases (until the reign of Henry VIII.) the lowering of the weight of the standard coins was only the
legal expression of an accomplished fact (through law-
ful and unlawful wear and tear). The purity of the
standard silver was never tampered with except by
the first Defender of the Faith.

The following is an interesting passage from a
speech of Sir Robert Peel in the debate on the Bank
Charter Act, May 6, 1844, in which he asked his
famous question—"What is a pound?" "What is
the meaning," he said, "of the pound according to the
ancient monetary policy of this country? The origin
of the term was this: In the reign of William the
Conqueror a pound weight of silver was also the
pound of account. The 'pound' represented both
the weight of metal and the denomination of money.
By subsequent debasements of the currency a great
alteration was made, not in the name, but in the intrinsic value of the pound sterling; and it was not
until a late period of the reign of Queen Elizabeth
that silver, being then the standard of value, received
that determinate weight which it retained without
variation, with constant refusals to debase the standard
of silver, until the year 1816, when gold became the
exclusive standard of value."

It was in this year that the Coinage Act was

passed, which, though since repealed, was in substance re-enacted by the Coinage Act of 1870. According to this Act, the coinage of gold bullion of standard value is executed in England (nominally) without cost to the owner, and without limit as to amount. In practice, however, it is usual for the owner of gold bullion to take it to the Bank of England, which is bound by law to buy any amount of gold at the rate of £3 : 17 : 9 per ounce of standard gold. The bank is authorised to charge £3 : 17 : 10½ per ounce to the Mint, the difference (1½d. per ounce) being its remuneration for trouble incurred, while, as the owner of the bullion is thus able to convert it immediately into money, he finds the transaction profitable, as he saves the loss of interest from delay. The charge on coining gold bullion is thus about $\frac{1}{6}$ per cent practically.

§ 5. *The Mint price of gold.*—It will be seen, then, that what is termed the Mint price of gold is a very different thing from other prices. In all essentials, all that is meant by the Mint price is that a certain amount of gold, mixed with a definite proportion of alloy to harden it, is coined into a certain number of gold coins of a given denomination. The old way of expressing this in the Mint indentures was that twenty pounds' weight, troy, of standard gold are to be coined into 934 sovereigns and one half-sovereign. If, then, any one foolishly complains that the Mint price of gold is fixed, the real meaning of his complaint is that the weight of the sovereign is fixed.

Sometimes a difficulty is felt in reconciling this fixity in the price of gold with the constant fluctua-

tions in the value of gold. The difficulty arises from
the fact that the exchange values of all other commodities are reckoned in terms of gold coins, but there
is not even an apparent contradiction in saying that
an ounce of gold will make a fixed number of coins,
whilst these coins will exchange for a variable amount
of other commodities.

§ 6. *The value of gold.*—It is important, however,
to observe that by business men the phrase "value of
gold" is sometimes used, as is always the case in the
writings of political economists, in the sense of exchange value or purchasing power, but more often
with quite a different meaning—namely, as equivalent to the rate of interest, and especially the Bank
of England minimum rate; in other words, they mean
by the value of gold, the price paid for the use of a
certain sum for a certain period.

At a later stage it will be necessary to explain that
the rate of interest—the rate at which traders can
discount their bills, or otherwise obtain advances—
often has an important effect on the prices of commodities. A very high rate may cause a fall in prices,
and a low rate may in some cases cause a rise; but
the two things are absolutely distinct, and it is quite
possible, and indeed common, to have a low rate of
interest with a low level of prices—that is to say, a
low value of gold in the sense of interest, and a high
value in the sense of purchasing power.

To summarise: The Mint price of gold depends on
the weight of the sovereign as fixed by law, whilst
the exchange value of gold means its purchasing
power over other things; so that, if the general level

of prices is low, that means the value of gold is high—its purchasing power is great ; whilst, if the level of prices is high, conversely the value of gold is low.

§ 7. *Possible difference between the Mint price and the market price of gold.*—It is, however, quite possible that, although the Mint price of gold is fixed in the manner described, the market price of that metal might in certain circumstances rise above the Mint price. This could not happen so long as the standard gold money is the actual circulating medium, and also is in reality of the same weight and fineness which by law it ought to be. But if the actual currency, whether by fraud or by the act of the Government, or by natural wear and tear, becomes of less than its nominal value, then the market price of gold reckoned in these inferior coins will rise in proportion to the inferiority.

In the same way, if inconvertible paper money is the actual currency, the market price of gold reckoned in these notes may rise to any height above the Mint price. The nature and magnitude of the evils which result from depreciation of the coinage may be gathered from the passages already quoted in the introduction to this subject. It must be observed that the ultimate result is the same whether the debasement is caused by natural wear and tear, by individuals "garbling" the coins, or by the Government making light issues. It is quite possible, however, that if the coins have gradually become light by ordinary wear and tear, they may for a long time circulate at their nominal value side by side with coins of full weight more recently issued. It is certain, however, that if the deterioration goes on, at some point it will be suddenly recognised; the good coins will be melted and exported, and the whole of the actual currency will become, and be recognised as, depreciated in value.

§ 8. *Bad state of English gold coinage.*—It is, perhaps, not generally known, though the fact has long been familiar to experts, that the gold currency of England is at present in a very unsatisfactory state, and that, unless something is done in the way of restoration, the depreciation must soon be taken into account practically, with very injurious consequences to the industry of the nation. So long ago as 1869, Professor Jevons ascertained, by a careful and exhaustive inquiry, that $31\frac{1}{2}$ per cent of the sovereigns and nearly one-half of the ten-shilling pieces were below the legal limit. Since that date matters have certainly got much worse, and an attempt was made by Mr. Childers, in 1884, to provide a remedy. The urgency of the reform in itself was generally recognised, but the particular scheme announced did not find favour, and was obliged to be withdrawn.

Without going into details, it may be mentioned that the essence of the plan was to withdraw all the light coins, then to make the sovereigns of full weight by abstracting from the half-sovereign a certain amount of gold, this coin being thus reduced to the level of "token" currency, as it is termed. Before giving an account of this species of money, something more must be said of the manner in which the standard coin may become depreciated, and the difficulties in providing a remedy for the evil.

CHAPTER IV

GRESHAM'S LAW AND TOKEN COINS

§ 1. *Gresham's Law and defective coins.*—What is now generally known as Gresham's Law, in honour of Sir Thomas Gresham (founder of the London Royal Exchange), who clearly perceived its truth in the reign of Queen Elizabeth, briefly stated, declares that bad money drives good money out of circulation, whilst good money cannot drive out bad. "At first sight," as Professor Jevons remarks, "there seems something paradoxical in the fact that when beautiful new coins of full weight are issued from the Mint the people still continue to circulate in preference the depreciated ones. . . . In all other matters everybody is led by self-interest to choose the better and to reject the worse: but in the case of money, it would seem as if they paradoxically retain the worse and get rid of the better." The solution of the difficulty is found in the fact that the object for which the bad money is used is simply to effect exchanges and to pay debts, and so long as the money is accepted by the payee, the payer has no further care. Indeed it is for the interest of the payer to pay in the cheapest or worst coins obtainable and acceptable.

Suppose that in any country the coinage, which for simplicity may be assumed to consist of gold only, has become to a large extent much below the nominal standard of weight and fineness. Now let the Government issue a large number of new coins of full value. Obviously under these circumstances, unless the old coinage is effectively withdrawn, no debtor, if he is guided solely by what is called "enlightened self-interest," will be so foolish as to pay his debts with new coins when he might sell them to the bullion dealer, for melting or exportation, for a larger number of the old coins, which, so long as they are actual currency, would answer his purpose equally well. Even if all debtors were as sensitive, moral, or fearful as the repentant sinners who send "conscience money" to the Chancellor of the Exchequer for taxes evaded, there would always be a number of criminals who would be only too glad to make a living by picking and culling and garbling the coinage. This is a species of criminality which it is extremely difficult to detect, and experience shows that there is not much use in imposing heavy penalties when detection is uncertain.

§ 2. *How Gresham's Law operates.*—Before making practical deductions, however, from Gresham's Law, the peculiar manner in which this law operates must be carefully recognised. It is quite possible, as the present state of our gold coinage shows, that the mere force of habit will be sufficient to keep light coins in use at their nominal value.

With a certain level of prices, a certain quantity of currency of some kind is required by the country at large for the purposes of internal trade. The great majority of people have no means of practically testing the coins which they receive, and creditors will, as a rule, take the coin put into their hand, even if it is obviously light, and trust to passing it again, rather than reject it, and wait for payment. Shopkeepers in particular are not likely to refuse "ready money" of a very inferior kind if they imagine it will be taken by some rival.

If the Government were obstinately to refuse to make new issues of gold coins, and the bad money were limited, then, in accordance with a principle which will presently be explained, there is, theoretically, no limit to the actual depreciation, whilst nominally the coins remain at *par* value, and pass as such. Practically, however, in this case, a stimulus would be given to the illicit manufacture of inferior coins. It will be observed to what a large extent the effective operation of Gresham's Law may depend on breaking the laws of the land; but it does not operate entirely in this manner now, because the laws against the exportation of gold coins have been repealed.

§ 3. *History of token coins.*—The proviso noticed above, as to the limitation of issues by the Government, naturally leads to the consideration of "token" coinage. "Token" coins may be defined in a preliminary manner as coins the nominal value of which as money is avowedly greater than their value as metal, even if the cost of coinage is taken into account. They are essentially bank-notes of a very low denomination, and generally placed under peculiar

restrictions. The subject may be best introduced
by a slight historical sketch derived mainly from
Boyne's *Tokens of the Seventeenth Century* and Burn's
account of the London tradesmen's tokens in the
Beaufoy Cabinet.

From the earliest times the small coinage of
England was of silver. Silver money was coined as
low in value as the penny, three-farthings, half-
penny, and farthing. A silver three-farthing piece
was struck in the reign of Queen Elizabeth (1561),
which is interesting as explaining a passage in Shakespeare, though the poet, with his usual disregard of
anachronisms in his historical plays, throws back the
usage of the coin of Elizabeth to the reign of John.
On the coin in question, beside the queen's head is
a rose, and in the play—*King John,* Act i. Scene 1
—Faulconbridge is made to say, satirically, of his
brother—

> "My face so thin,
> That in mine ear I durst not stick a rose,
> Lest men should say—'Look, there three-farthings goes!'"

It may be added, that in Shakespeare's time there was
a custom of putting a natural rose behind the ear or
in the head-dress.

These coins were at first standard coins, and it is
easy to see that the silver coin of a penny or three-
farthings, and still more one of a farthing, would be
very inconvenient in size and easily lost. Besides
this, these small coins do not seem to have been
coined in sufficient abundance for the purposes of
trade; and accordingly, the great want of halfpence
and farthings in the reign of Elizabeth compelled the

almost general use of private "tokens" of lead, tin, and, it is said, of leather. These issues took place, much to the inconvenience of poor people (for the issuers often refused to change the tokens for goods or sterling money), up to the year 1613, when the king (James I.) granted, for a consideration, the monopoly of striking copper farthings to Lord John Harington.

On the accession of Charles I. the patent for the coinage of farthings was renewed. "The privilege was greatly abused by the patentees, who issued them in *unreasonable* quantities, and at a merely nominal intrinsic value. They encouraged the circulation by giving twenty-one shillings in farthings for twenty shillings in silver; by this means many unprincipled persons were induced to purchase them, and would *force five, ten, and even twenty shillings'* worth of them at a time on all with whom they had dealings. In a short time not only the city of London, but the whole kingdom, and especially the counties adjacent to the metropolis, were so burdened with them, that in many places scarcely any silver or gold coin was left, the currency consisting entirely of farthing tokens."

The patentees were not content with the profits obtained in the home country, but forwarded large parcels of their farthing tokens to the American colonies; but the Old Pilgrim Fathers were not to be taken in in this manner, and it is grimly recorded of Massachusetts—"March 4th, 1634, at the General Court at New Town, brass (or copper) farthings were forbidden, and *bullets* were made to pass for farthings."

In England, however, the accumulation of the patent farthings in the hands of small tradesmen caused them so great a loss from the refusal of the patentees to exchange them, that in 1644, in consequence of the public demand, they were suppressed by the House of Commons, which ordered that they should be surcharged from money raised on the patentees' estates. It appears that by this Act the royal tokens were suppressed, and at any rate the decapitation of the king five years later "annulled for ever all disputes between the patentees of the farthing token and the public." The Crown had throughout been the greatest delinquent, and had plundered the poor most mercilessly. The whole affair, to all who were engaged or named in it, remains one of indelible disgrace. After the death of the king, the old practice of private issues was resorted to—the tokens being made of lead, brass, and copper. In Mr. Boyne's work detailed descriptions of 9466 tokens are given, and probably more than twenty thousand different kinds were in use from 1648-1672.

§ 4. *Abuses of private tokens.*—The necessity for small change, and the abuses which arise from the use of private tokens, are graphically described in an old print of 1671 in the following passages: "The number of those whose bowels yearn for their daily bread before they can earn a penny to buy it, do eminently exceed all the rest of the people in any nation, and their extreme poverty makes them incapable of paying if trusted, so that to keep them from farthings, and such small exchanges, were to starve three-quarters of the people, and withal to break, and so in fine to starve, all those multitudes of petty retailers who sell only these poor all necessaries for life. This necessity enforceth those retailers, for want of a publique allowed token, to make tokens of pence, halfpence, and farthings, and therein, as in all else, to grind the faces of the poor by wholly refusing, or at best giving but what they please for their own late-vented tokens." Evelyn, in his *Diary*, speaks of the tokens issued by every tavern " passable through the neighbourhood, though seldom reaching further than the next street or two." It is easy to see, without further details, that the issue of private tokens, though at first made to supply a public convenience, had become a public nuisance.

§ 5. *Principles of good token coinage.*—The historical references just given show, in the first place, that the attempt by the Crown to make a revenue from token farthings by issuing, or allowing to be issued, excessive quantities, had resulted in a great evil : the sterling full-value coin had been driven from circulation, and the tokens had become practically worthless. The only quality of good money they possessed was probably a certain uniformity.

On the suppression of these royal tokens, the issues by private people had to some extent provided the small change needed, but only to some extent, because there was no uniformity, and the circulation only extended over a very small area—" the next street or two."

Thus, by sad experience, the people of this country had forced upon them the true principles of regulating the issues of small change. To secure uniformity,

and to make the medium of exchange general, it was
necessary for Government to undertake the coinage
itself. At first, in defiance or in ignorance of
Gresham's Law, it was thought sufficient to utter a
number of new silver coins of the value of one penny
and twopence " for the smaller traffic and commerce,"
but these coins were hoarded, and the private issues
were continued for the vast profit made from them.
At last it came to be understood that the proper plan
was to make the small coins of nominal value only,
to suppress private issues, to strictly limit the issues
by Government, and to make them legal tender only
for a limited amount.

§ 6. *Present system of token coins in this country.*—
Under the system at present in force in this country
both the silver and the bronze coins are royal tokens,
the former being legal tender up to forty shillings,
and the latter to twelve pence. The metallic value
of the bronze is not more than one-quarter of its
nominal value, and at present the silver is at least 30
per cent below its professed value. It must not, however, be thought that this difference between the
nominal and real value is an injury to the persons
using the coins. So long as the coins pass current
for what they profess to be,—so long as a debt of two
pounds can be paid by forty shillings, and a debt of
one shilling by twelve pennies,—there can be no
injury. It is quite true that the Mint makes a profit
on the coins actually issued, but it does not attempt
to force the issues, and to all intents and purposes the
small coins are the same as convertible bank-notes of
the same value.

Quite recently an example on a small scale of the injury inflicted by the use of private tokens has been forthcoming in London. Large quantities of French bronze coins, of about the same size and appearance as the English pennies and halfpennies, were put in circulation. Some people took them, and then they found that they could not pass them. No one who in the course of trade would get large quantities could afford to do so. Brewers and others, by an arrangement with the Mint, may return their English coppers, but obviously the English Mint cannot take at their nominal value foreign tokens. If that were possible, in a short time the country would be flooded with foreign bronze, as in the time of Charles I. with token farthings. Accordingly, the importation of these coins has been stringently prohibited.

§ 7. *Shape, etc., of coins.*—It may naturally occur to the reader who is mindful of the cynical view of human nature on which Gresham's Law rests, that a very profitable industry to a clever criminal would be the manufacture of bronze and silver coins, which in weight and quality were exactly like those issued by the Mint. It is to obviate this danger that the coins are made in such a manner as to require the use of elaborate machinery, whilst, of course, at the same time heavy penalties are imposed in case of detection. Thus the device and shape of the coins are by no means matters of indifference. It may be remarked also, though the observation applies even more to coins of standard quality than to token coins, that the shape and device ought to be such as to render the wear and tear a minimum, and to reveal any tampering in the way of clipping. The milled edges on coins are difficult to make uniformly, and prevent unlawful reduction by paring. It is, however, obvious that if the token coins are allowed to be in circulation till they are worn quite smooth, fraudulent manufacture will be more easy.

§ 8. *Difficulties of keeping coins at full value.*—We are now in a position to see more clearly the meaning of, and the difficulties in the way of, keeping the standard coin at its full value. Any one, as was shown above, can get gold coined into sovereigns and half-sovereigns practically free of charge, and any gold imported must undoubtedly be coined before it can be used for currency. If, however, a large quantity of the coins actually used are much below the standard, the evil will naturally spread, for there is a direct encouragement to artificially reduce the good coins, and at any rate they will always be chosen for export.

As the law stands at present, it is illegal either to give or receive coins below the proper value; but as Mr. Childers pointed out in introducing his scheme, this would logically involve the carrying about by every person of apparatus to test any coins he may receive. This is clearly impracticable, and the law is in most cases a dead letter. Even the banks have large accumulations of light-weight gold. The Bank of England, however, and Government Offices, only receive the gold coins at their full weight, and cases are on record in which as a consequence people have been mulcted of large sums.

The practical difficulty is to meet the expense of

restoring the coinage, and to make the restoration in an equitable way and without encouragement to fraud. Obviously if the Bank of England offered to receive during a lengthy period all coins at their nominal value, giving full-weight coins in return, a great encouragement would be given to "sweating" or otherwise lightening the coins of full weight as they were issued, as well as those which happened to be in circulation.

Again, as regards the expense, it would clearly be unfair to make the last holder responsible, owing to the letter of the law; and yet, so long as no practical inconvenience is felt, the Chancellor of the Exchequer would have a difficulty in making taxation for the purpose popular, to say nothing of the danger of fraud as just described. I shall return to this subject in connection with one-pound notes, the consideration of which properly comes at a later stage.

CHAPTER V

THE QUANTITY OF MONEY AND GENERAL PRICES

§ 1. *Meaning of appreciation and depreciation of gold and silver.* — This examination of money as the mechanism of exchange may now be left for what constitutes the most difficult and contentious part of the subject—viz. the connection between money and prices; in other words, the causes which determine the value of money, which is the same thing, as we said, as the general level of prices.

I take this opportunity of explaining a term which is often used in a very confusing manner—*the appreciation of gold.* When we speak of the appreciation of gold, what we mean is, that in the countries using gold as the standard money, the general level of prices has become lower; in other words, that a given gold coin or a certain weight of standard gold will purchase more commodities—or conversely, that commodities will bring fewer pieces of gold.

Accordingly, it is unmeaning to speak of the general fall in prices being *caused* by the appreciation of gold; the two expressions in countries with free mintage of gold currency mean precisely the same thing. We often use the term *depreciation* of gold in two senses. We may refer to a depreciation, through loss in weight or purity, of a gold currency; or we may mean the converse of the appreciation just described—that is, by depreciation we may understand a fall in the value of gold compared with commodities.

Some light may perhaps be thrown on the expressions by considering the way in which they are properly used as regards silver. In countries such as England, where gold is the standard and silver is only used in limited quantities as token coinage, silver has a price just like any other commodity. For the first seventy years of this century this price—for reasons afterwards to be given—was about 60d. per ounce troy, but latterly it has fallen as low as 42d. This fall in the gold price of silver constitutes the depreciation of silver.

At the same time, it is often pointed out that in India, where the standard currency is silver, no depreciation, but rather appreciation, of silver relatively to commodities has taken place. This is using the terms in the same sense as when applied to gold.

§ 2. *General and relative prices.*—To pass, however, from the question of words to the question of facts, our present problem is to explain the causes which govern *general* movements in prices, or which determine the changes in the exchange value of money. As has already been pointed out in connection with "index numbers," from 1850, to go no further back, great changes have taken place in the general level of prices, and we ought to be able to discover the causes of these changes. More than this, we ought to be able to explain in a general way the causes which must always be in operation.

First of all, in order to avoid a common source of confusion, it may be well to explain that our problem is the determination of *general* prices, and not, as at an earlier stage of this inquiry (chap. ii. § 8), the changes in the *relative* values of commodities reckoned in prices. It is easy to see how, from causes affecting some particular article, that article may have fallen or risen in value; and similarly, through the whole range of commodities, we may discover causes which have made some to rise and others to fall. If, however, we find that, apart from these relative changes, a *general* change in the level has occurred, it is natural to conclude that this is due either to causes primarily affecting the standard by which prices are determined, or to causes of a very wide-reaching character affecting commodities. It cannot be too often insisted on that the real meaning of the value of money is its value as compared with things in general—that is, its value as determined by the general level of prices.

§ 3. *In explaining general prices, it is necessary to begin with a simple case, or a " hypothetical market."*— Now, under the present conditions of industry and exchange, the causes which lead to general movements of prices are exceedingly complex and various, and in order to understand them it is necessary to begin with the simplest case, and then gradually to introduce the less obvious, though equally effective, causes of movement. I would then beg the reader to get rid, as far as possible, of all the notions he may have formed of the causes of the actual movements in prices in recent years in the complex industrial world of to-day, and, in order to isolate and examine the most important cause of all, to take up an attitude of observation in what, for fault of a better term, may be called a "hypothetical market."

The phrase is suggestive of unreality, but no more so than the suppositions or hypotheses constantly made in physics and mathematics, of bodies perfectly rigid, smooth, or without weight, or of lines without breadth, or of points without parts or magnitude.

Let the following, then, be assumed as the laws and conditions of our market : (1) No exchanges are to be made unless money (which, to be quite unreal and simple, we may suppose to consist of counters of a certain size made of the bones of the dodo) actually passes from hand to hand at every transaction. If, for example, one merchant has two pipes but no tobacco, and another two ounces of tobacco but no pipe, we cannot allow an exchange of a pipe for an ounce of tobacco unless money is used. Credit and barter are alike unknown. (2) The money is to be regarded as of no use whatever except to effect exchanges, so that it will not be withheld for hoarding ; in other words, it will be actually in circulation. (3) Let it be assumed that there are ten traders, each with one kind of commodity and no money, and one trader with all the money (100 pieces) and no commodities. Further, let this moneyed man place an equal estimation on all the commodities.

Now let the market be opened according to the rules laid down ; then all the money will be offered against all the goods, and every article being assumed

of equal value, the price given for each will be ten
pieces, and the general level of prices will be ten.   It
will be observed, in this operation, each piece of money
changes hands only once—it passes, namely, from the
moneyed man to the respective traders.   It is perfectly
clear, under these suppositions, that if the amount of
money had been 1000 pieces the general level would
have been 100 pieces per article, and if only ten pieces
the price per article would have been one piece only.
Under these very rigid assumptions, then, it is obvious
that the value of the money varies exactly and inversely
with the quantity put in circulation.   If the merchant
with the "money" had sacks full of dodo counters, the
value of each would be very small reckoned in goods,
perhaps not equal to the thousandth part of a pipe of
tobacco, for example.

§ 4. *Illustration of the effects of the quantity of
money from the French assignats.*—We have in this
way isolated a cause which is in the actual world of
commerce, though often hidden and overshadowed,
always present, and of the greatest consequence.   As I
am quite aware that the practical man naturally
distrusts abstract reasonings, and considers them as
impalpable as ghosts which he can see through, I
hasten to support with hard facts the position that, at
any rate, one most important factor in determining the
general level of prices in a country is the quantity of
money in circulation.

I will take, first, as the nearest approximation to an
unreal state of things such as was assumed, a state of
things which ought never to have occurred.   I allude to
the issues of the *assignats*, or inconvertible notes, of the

French Revolution, the general evil consequences of which have already been noticed. I quote a few sentences, taken almost at random, from the work of Mr. White. "Towards the end of 1794 there had been issued 7000 millions in *assignats;* by May 1795, 10,000 millions; by the end of July, 16,000 millions; by the beginning of 1796, 45,000 millions, of which 36,000 were in actual circulation." "At last a paper note, professing to be worth £4 sterling, passed current for less than threepence in money." It is to be noticed that this tremendous depreciation took place in spite of the law imposing penalties on those who gave or received the paper at less than its nominal value, at first of six years in irons, then of twenty years, and finally punishing with death investments of capital in foreign countries.

§ 5. *Fallacy of notes " representing " property.*—This is the most glaring but by no means the only example of the depreciation of inconvertible notes, and it has at last come to be perfectly understood that the only possible way of preventing or lessening the depreciation is to strictly limit the issues. The very meaning of the term inconvertible is that the note cannot be exchanged on demand against standard metallic money, and consequently the only limit to issues is found in the will of the issuers. The French asserted, at first, that since their notes "represented" property, as indeed at first they were supposed to do, being professedly assignments of public land, they could never become depreciated.

Now this argument is only good so far as it implies some kind of limitation of the issues. But it would be quite as effective and rational to make the issues " represent " so many stars in the firmament, or the ages of so many ladies, or anything whatever limited in number or amount. If by representation is not meant convertibility on demand into some valuable commodity, the only thing that determines the value is their quantity compared with the work to be done by them. It may, perhaps, be advisable to repeat that, although the depreciation of the notes is usually reckoned as against gold in the standard metallic money, it implies necessarily a general rise in prices of all commodities to the extent of the depreciation.*

§ 6. *Illustration from the Bank Restriction in England.*—Another example, though happily of a less startling character than that just noticed, is furnished by the suspension of cash (metallic) payments by the Bank of England during the period known as the Bank Restriction—"the dark age of currency." The Government, being engaged in the vast continental wars in which Napoleon was the ruling spirit, were afraid that all the specie would be drained from the country, and none be left for military operations. Accordingly, in 1796, the Bank of England was

---

* The rise in prices would theoretically be greater than is indicated by the depreciation of the notes compared with gold. For as gold is withdrawn from circulation and thrown on the bullion market, it will tend to fall in value—in other words, gold itself will be to some extent depreciated. Conversely, on the resumption of specie ¦payments, the demand for gold may cause a relative appreciation—that is to say, prices will fall to a lower level than was indicated by the premium on gold. Practically, however, both effects are generally not great, owing to gold being an international commodity.

restrained from paying out specie against its notes
—that is, the notes became inconvertible. This
lasted practically about twenty-three years, and during
this period the notes became depreciated. In 1814
the average price of gold reckoned in notes had risen
to £5 : 4s. instead of £3 : 17 : 9, and general prices
had risen accordingly. The Bank of England directors,
when examined as to the plan they had adopted in
making issues, gave answers which, as Mr. Bagehot
has said, have become classical by their nonsense.
They imagined that the quantity of notes issued had
nothing to do with their value, provided only that
they were issued in the usual course, on good banking
securities, at a minimum interest of 5 per cent. By
this plan they did indeed, to some extent, limit the
issues, but not enough, as the event proved. The
only perfectly safe plan with inconvertible issues is
to restrict them as soon as ever the market price of
bullion rises above the Mint price.

§ 7. *Further illustrations of the effects of the quantity
of money.*—Further illustrations of the fundamental
importance of the quantity of money in the determination of its value (or the general level of prices)
are furnished in the case of the precious metals,
though here, as we shall see presently, the operation
of the quantity is, in the modern world at least, not
so exclusively overpowering. The decline of the
Roman Empire was largely due to a deficiency of the
circulating medium, which was remitted in payment
of taxes in large quantities to Rome and the central
cities of the empire. As a consequence, whilst in the
provinces prices ruled low, and the miserable taxpayer

would give any amount of wealth for coins, in the centre of the empire, where money was abundant, prices were high. It is necessary to add, for the benefit of those who may see quotations in historical works of Roman prices, that the Romans had early acquired the art of debasing their money—a method of reducing its value and raising the level of prices next in efficacy and injurious consequences to the excessive issues of inconvertible paper.

We have in the times of the Middle Ages a constant dearth of the precious metals, and consequently a low level of prices. Under the Tudors a great rise occurred, which illustrates in a twofold manner the effects of increasing the quantity of money. In the first place, under Henry VIII. and Edward VI. the currency was debased, and thus artificially increased in amount, and next it was naturally increased by the great discoveries of the precious metals in America, especially the celebrated silver mines of Potosi. The rise in prices, occurring as it did in an irregular manner, attracted much attention and produced much social disturbance, and even at that time a few keen minds detected the true cause.

Coming to the present century, we find on reference to the index numbers already quoted an uncommon rise in prices between 1850-64, during which period the great discoveries of gold in Australia and California largely increased the supply of that metal; and there can be little doubt that this fall in the value of gold, as indicated by the general rise in prices, was caused mainly by the increase in the quantity of metallic money. The great fall which has since

occurred in prices is at any rate coincident with a
gradual falling off in the gold supply and the use of
gold in place of silver, thus increasing the amount of
commodities to be moved or transactions to be effected
by gold.

§ 8. *Influence and meaning of rapidity of circulation.*—It is time, however, to abandon this excursion
into the realm of historical facts, which was undertaken to give substance to the "airy nothings" of
abstract reasoning, and to return to our "hypothetical market," with its dodo counters and one-idea'd
traders.

Let us assume as before that no exchanges are
possible without money passing, that one merchant
has all the money (100 pieces), and that ten have
commodities of equal value; but instead of the
merchant with the money wishing for all the commodities equally, let us suppose that he only wants
the whole of number one, whilst number one requires
that of number two, and so on up to the ninth
merchant, who wants the commodity of number ten,
who wants the dodos. In this case each article will
be exchanged once, but the money will pass from hand
to hand ten times, and the price of each article will be
100 instead of 10 as before.

We now see, under these circumstances, with the
same quantity of money and the same volume of
transactions, the level of prices is ten times as great
as before, and the reason is that every piece of money
is used ten times instead of once. This frequent use
of money is what is generally called rapidity of circulation, but Mill's phrase, "efficiency of money,"

is perhaps more suggestive of the meaning intended. The whole argument may be put in a sentence which only requires a little thinking out to become quite clear : *The effect on prices must be the same when, in effecting transactions, one piece of money is used ten times, as when ten pieces of money are used once.*

§ 9. *Practical illustration of rapidity of circulation.* —The reader may, perhaps, rebel against this abstract manner of stating the case, but the object, as before, is to isolate one cause and to be sure of having the conditions the same.

But the truth I am anxious to convey may be seen, though not so clearly and forcibly, by taking the common facts of trade. It surely is quite obvious that, with a certain level of prices, ready-money transactions may be carried on with a small amount of money if it circulates rapidly, whilst, if the circulation is sluggish, more will be required. And practically, this is the same thing as saying that prices may be varied either by increasing the quantity of money or by increasing the rapidity of circulation—*i.e.* the number of times each piece is used. The reason for taking, in this case, a hypothetical market of a simple kind is, that if we take a whole country for a certain period of time (say a year), it is difficult to estimate the rapidity of circulation, and we are misled by considering changes in the volume of trade and the effects of barter and credit, which require, in order to be properly understood, a separate investigation.

§ 10. *Influence on general prices of the volume of trade.*—We are then still a long way from an adequate and complete account of the causes affecting general prices in a great industrial country, even after allowing for rapidity of circulation as well as for quantity of money. As regards the number of transactions or the volume of trade, a glance at our supposititious market will show us that an increase in the transactions, or in the work to be done by the money, must have the same effect as a diminution in the quantity of money, the transactions remaining unchanged.

Again, looking to the ordinary course of trade, it ought to be clear that if the commerce and population of the world are increased, so that the amount of ready-money transactions is doubled, then so far, unless the quantity of money is equally increased, there must be a proportionate fall in prices. This is practically a very important consideration.

There can be no doubt that, after the great discoveries of the precious metals in the sixteenth and the nineteenth centuries, the rise of prices would have been much greater but for the enormous increase in the volume of trade.

It follows too, from this consideration, that, other causes affecting prices remaining the same, any increase in the volume of trade by the extension of commerce to new countries must, in exact opposition to the popular view, result not in a rise but in a fall of prices, unless these new countries happen to produce the precious metals in greater abundance than their commerce requires.

§ 11. *Influence of barter on general prices.*—In the abstract presentation of the argument, so far, it has been assumed that money must pass from hand to hand at every transaction—in other words, that there is no barter; and it is only on this supposition that the level of prices is exactly proportioned to the quantity and rapidity of circulation of the money. "And this requires us to observe"—I quote from Professor Walker (*Money*, p. 64)—"that in the view of those who hold that money acts as a measure of value, it performs this function in respect of a vast bulk of commodities where it is not called on to become a medium of exchange. It is its use as a medium of exchange which determines its value, yet its value so determined becomes the means of estimating values without reference to actual exchanges. It costs nothing to measure values in this sense; it costs something to exchange them. It requires the actual use of money for a longer or shorter space of time to effect those double exchanges which we call buying and selling, but the prices resulting from such exchanges may be applied to far greater bodies of wealth without the use of money. For example, a farmer sells a cow to be sent to the city for beef. It is only in the actual sale that money is used, but he takes the price—the money value—thus determined as the means of estimating the value of his herd; and so does the Government in taxing him; so, also, do his neighbours in deciding how much of a man he is. . . . It will be observed that every time a barter transaction is substituted for [ready money] buying and selling, the demand for money is thereby diminished and its value thereby lowered (the supply remaining the same), while the higher prices of commodities which result from the sales actually effected by the use of money are carried over in estimation to the commodities remaining unsold, or to those whose transfer is accomplished by a direct exchange of goods for goods. And conversely, just so far as sales for money are substituted for barter transactions, the demand for money being thereby increased, the value of money rises, and the lower prices which result are carried over in estimation to the commodities directly exchanged or remaining in store."

§ 12. *Influence on general prices of the use of the precious metals for other purposes besides coinage.*— So much, then, for the effects of barter; and omitting for the present the most difficult and intricate inquiry into the effects of credit, we may advance a step nearer the reality of the modern world by taking into account the fact that metallic money—for the present purpose we will say gold money—instead of being counters of dodo's bones or inconvertible paper, is made from a substance which is highly prized for various purposes in the arts and manufactures, and which is only obtained from the mines with a considerable expenditure of capital and labour.

If gold were no longer used for coinage, it would probably still possess a very high value as a commodity. People would still prefer gold ornaments of all kinds to those made of any other metal. I may mention that the ancient Egyptians, as their mummies reveal, used gold for stopping teeth, and since their time numberless new uses have been found for gold. It follows, therefore, that in practice,

instead of " money " being offered as we at first supposed against commodities regardless of its value for
other purposes, if the value of gold coins became very
low there would be a tendency to melt them down to
use in other ways.

An illustration will make this clear. If five gold
sovereigns would only purchase five small loaves and
two or three fishes, a man would be much more ready
to cause them to be melted for a gold watch than if
they would purchase a house full of luxuries. In
fact, as in other things, a fall in the value of gold
as a commodity increases the quantity demanded. To
take a practical case: Great gold discoveries, by increasing the quantity of gold money, will so far tend
to make prices rise; but the rise will not be quite as
great as it otherwise would be, because the use of gold
for the arts will be stimulated by its fall in value,
and thus the quantity available for coinage will be
diminished.

It follows, then, that although in some aspects of
the question it is useful to emphasise the function of
money as a mere medium of exchange, because there
has often been a tendency to confuse money with
the wealth which it measures and exchanges, it would
be an error to neglect altogether the use of gold for
other purposes, especially if, in addition to those indicated, we consider also hoarding.

§ 13. *Influence on general prices of the cost of production of the precious metals.*—There is, however, apart
from this absorption and diffusion, a much more direct
and powerful check on the rise in gold prices to be
found in the conditions of supply; for in the value of

gold, as in other things, it is necessary to consider supply as much as demand.

Unlike the issues of tokens or inconvertible notes, in which the quantity depends on the will of Governments, the quantity of gold money can only be increased at considerable cost. Mines which are very productive and easily worked only furnish part of the annual supply; and, on the other hand, a certain portion is yielded by mines which it only just pays to work, and which, to adopt classical economic language, are on the "margin of cultivation," and yield their supplies under the most unfavourable circumstances.

What, then, speaking generally, are the limiting conditions which determine whether gold-mines of a certain productivity will be worked—omitting, of course, irrational and spasmodic speculation? Clearly, the conditions are to be found in the expenses of working compared with the yield.

These expenses obviously vary with the general level of prices. If prices are high, the wages of labour, the cost of implements and machinery, and the expenses of transport, will also be high, and therefore the gold produced will yield a smaller profit than if prices were low; and if the expenses of working, owing to a further rise in prices, become still greater, the profit must become still smaller— and if the rise of prices continues, must vanish. It follows, then, that every rise in general prices tends to check production from the mines, whilst every fall, by rendering a diminution of expenses possible, tends to increase and extend production. It will thus be seen *that the cost of production of gold only operates on general prices by increasing or diminishing the annual supply, and thus affecting the quantity in use.*

§ 14. *Effects of the durability of the precious metals.* —If, now, it be remembered that the durability of gold is very great, and that of the annual supplies a large part is required for the arts and for simply maintaining and restoring the gold coins actually in circulation, it will be seen that, under present circumstances, when the average annual supply is less than £22,000,000, whilst the gold coinage of the civilised world is estimated (roughly) at £800,000,000, the influence of the yearly fluctuations in production must be very small.*

This is a point which requires the strongest emphasis, as even so clear a thinker as J. S. Mill has been led into the error of over-estimating the effects of this element. In one sense, indeed, the cost of production of gold is certainly the most important cause affecting its value, but only in the sense of imposing a limit on a rise in prices, or a fall in the value of the metal. If gold could be produced very cheaply by a kind of alchemy, there would be hardly any limit to the rise in prices; but, seeing that the quantity of gold is only one element in governing prices, and cost of production only one element affecting this quantity, it is a gross error to say, as Mill does, that " the value of gold depends, apart from temporary fluctuations, on its cost of production."

---

* The statistics, as before observed, are very uncertain, but the argument rests on the annual production *relatively* to the total mass, and there can be little doubt that it is very small.

For, to take only one other cause, the volume of trade, it is clear that, although the annual supply of gold was increasing, and the cost of production diminishing, if the volume of trade was increasing at a much greater rate, the value of gold would rise, or, in other words, general prices would fall.

It is easy to see the way in which the error arose. It was observed quite correctly that the value of gold coins must on the average be equal to the value of the same weight of gold bullion. But the next step in the argument was a mistake of effect for cause; for it was supposed that if we only determined the value of the bullion, we should in that way determine the value of the coins into which it could be made. It was then argued that gold bullion was simply a commodity, and that its normal value depended on its cost of production. Herein lay the mistake. Rightly understood, the general level of prices rests on many causes, and this general level of prices determines the exchange value of gold coins — in fact, that is the very meaning of their value — whilst the value of the coins determines the value of the bullion.

Cost of production can only affect the value of any article through supply, and its effect is very different in case of a durable commodity like gold, which is only slowly worn by being used, and in the case of one such as corn, of which the greater part of the annual supply is consumed in a year, though, of course, it may be allowed that so far the difference is only one of degree.

CHAPTER VI

EFFECTS OF CREDIT OR "REPRESENTATIVE MONEY" ON PRICES

§ 1. *Great use of credit substitutes for money in England.*—It is, however, at the stage of the inquiry now reached, in which it becomes necessary to examine the effect of credit on prices, that the greatest difficulties in connection with the value of money arise. The importance of this element may, perhaps, be best seen by considering what would be the effect on prices if, in a country such as modern England, the conditions first assumed in our "hypothetical market" actually prevailed, and if money in the shape of coins were necessary in every transaction. It is almost impossible to picture to the mind what would be the extent of the fall in prices, but some idea may be formed by taking into account a few well-known facts.

In the first place, it is very unusual for coin to be used at all in wholesale transactions. In the *Statistical Journal* for September 1865, Sir John Lubbock published some particulars concerning the business of his bank during the last few days of

1864. Transactions to the extent of £23,000,000 were effected by the use of credit documents and coin, and the proportions per cent were as follows: Cheques and bills of exchange, 94·1; Bank of England notes, 5·0; country bank-notes, ·3; and actual coin only ·6. That is to say, of business transactions to the amount of £23,000,000, a very little more than ½ per cent were effected by means of coin, and only a little above 5 per cent by credit documents, which are supposed to represent coin directly.

The "clearings" of the Banker's Clearing House in London, in which the reciprocal obligations of the banks are balanced, exceed £6,000,000,000 sterling per annum, and these form part only of the total payments of the whole country, whilst it has been calculated that the whole value of the metals employed in the currency is less than £140,000,000.

§ 2. *Influence of credit on general prices shown by reference to commercial crises.*—The way in which changes in credit at once produce changes in general prices is illustrated by the phenomena which precede and follow commercial crises. We get, as a rule, in the first place, an excessive use of credit instruments of various kinds, accompanied by a great rise in prices. All sorts of paper, which in less confident times would not be looked at, are used as a basis of buying and selling. But the competition of those who buy on credit, so long as that credit is accepted, obviously affects the demand for commodities, and raises prices just as much as when ready money is offered. A person whose cheque will be taken in payment can bid as effectively as one who brings a bag of money, and in times of inflation and confidence the banks will advance directly or indirectly on all kinds of securities.

Thus, in the period of the culmination of a commercial fever, the amount of "representative money" is largely increased, and with this increase there is an inflation of prices. As soon, however, as the contraction of credit sets in, the bankers make wry faces over credit documents not of the first class, and there is a sudden diminution in the representative money and a great fall in prices. So great is the effect of credit, even in the dullest times, that there is a tendency for people to rush to the other extreme in estimating the influence of the precious metals, and to consider the quantity of metallic money as of the very slightest effect in governing general prices, and thus the exchange value of money.

§ 3. *All credit ultimately rests on a metallic basis.*— It seems at first sight that, just as there is no limit to the rise in prices due to the issue of inconvertible paper, except the will of the Government in limiting the issues, so also there is no limit to the creation of credit substitutes for coin, except the will of bankers, traders, and merchants. It is well then to state, in the most emphatic manner, that the whole of this vast superstructure of credit must rest on a metallic basis, and if this basis is cut away, the whole structure would fall.

Let us consider the way in which, in England, this metallic basis imposes a limit—though an elastic one—on the rise in prices. In the first place, the banks themselves are built up on gold foundations. It has been said that if all the banks at the same moment were obliged to meet their obligations in actual coin, they would just be able to pay 4d. in the pound; but if this is true, it is equally true to say that, small as 4d. seems, still if, as a body, they only kept 2d. per pound in reserve, they would be unable to conduct their business.

In this country, more than in any country, the economy in the use of gold has reached a marvellous development. Every bank is obliged to keep a small amount of "till" money, but its real reserve is usually lodged with the Bank of England. We have, as a matter of fact, as Mr. Bagehot's *Lombard Street* shows in the most forcible manner, a *one-reserve* system.

A banker who has a sufficient balance at the Bank of England to meet any drain at all likely to be made upon his bank, thinks, and thinks rightly, that he has his reserve quite safe, and yet, as a rule, there is not gold enough in the Bank of England available to meet these bankers' balances if all drawn at once, for the Bank of England itself, being a bank, lends its deposits. But the directors of the bank are fully aware of the limits imposed upon them by the necessities of having a sufficient reserve, and they speedily check these advances, and take steps for attracting gold from abroad when the gold at their disposal falls below a certain point.

In order to understand the nature of the credit institutions of this country, it is most important to form a clear idea of the position and functions of the Bank of England, which is the heart of the circulating

system. These functions, rights and obligations may
be described as partly legal and partly customary.
The governor and directors of the Bank are, in the
world of commerce, like the Prime Minister and
his Cabinet in the world of politics—they have to
observe the letter of the law and the spirit of the
constitution.

§ 4. *The Bank Charter Act of* 1844.—So far as
the law is concerned, it is practically settled by the
famous Bank Charter Act of 1844. Seeing that
many miles of print have been devoted to the merits
and demerits of this Act, it may be thought impossible to discuss it profitably in a few lines. As my
object, however, is mainly descriptive, and not critical,
the task is not hopeless.

In the first place, it must be observed that the Act
says nothing, paradoxical as it may seem, of what is
generally understood by banking—nothing, for example, as to the kind of securities on which advances
may be made, of the proportion of reserve to liabilities,
of the method of fixing the rate of interest, or of the
kind of business which the Bank may undertake. In
fact, the Act may be best described as is done by
Macculloch. " In dealing with the Bank of England,
Sir Robert Peel adopted the proposal previously made
by Lord Overstone, for effecting a complete separation
between the issuing and banking departments of that
establishment, and giving the directors full liberty to
manage the latter at discretion, while they should have
no power whatever over the other."

Thus the main object of the Act was to regulate
the issues of bank-notes, and the plan adopted was as

follows :* "The notes of the Bank of England in circulation for some years previously to 1844 rarely amounted to £20,000,000, or sunk so low as £16,000,000. And such being the case, Sir Robert Peel was justified in assuming that the circulation of the Bank could not in any ordinary condition of society, or under any mere commercial vicissitudes, be reduced below £14,000,000. And the Act of 1844 allows the Bank to issue this amount upon securities of which the £11,015,000 she has lent to the public is the most important item. Inasmuch, however, as the issues of the provincial banks were at the same time limited in amount [also determined by their average circulation during three months before the passing of the Act], and confined to certain existing banks, it was further provided, in the event of any of these banks ceasing to issue notes, that the Bank of England might be empowered by order in council to issue upon securities two-thirds and no more of the notes which such banks had been authorised to issue. [Under this condition the total secured issue of the Bank has been increased to £15,750,000.†] *But for every other note which the issue department may at any time issue over and above the maximum amount (£15,750,000) issued on securities, an equal amount of coin or bullion must be paid into its coffers.* And hence, under this system, the notes of the Bank of England are rendered really and truly equivalent to gold, while their immediate conversion into that metal no longer depends, as it previously did, on the good faith, the skill, and the prudence of the directors."

---

* Macculloch's *Commercial Dictionary*—Article " Bank."

† This amount has recently been still further increased to £16,450,000.

The position of the Bank in respect of its note-issues is well described by a former governor as follows: "The issue department is out of our hands altogether. We are mere trustees under the Act of Parliament to see that these securities are placed there and kept up to that amount; and in no case can any (ordinary) creditor of the Bank touch that which is reserved for a note-holder. We are in that respect merely administrative; we are trustees to hold that amount in the issue department, and our banking department has a totally separate function, which has no relation whatever to the issue department."

§ 5. *Practical illustration of the working of the Bank Act.*—The practical effect of these regulations may be illustrated by an example which happily is historically purely fictitious. Suppose the directors of the Bank of England had used the deposits of the public or of other banks with them in an imprudent manner, and locked them up in securities of various kinds which had become unrealisable on demand. Suppose next that the depositors draw to an unusual amount on the Bank, and the Bank has not a sufficient reserve to meet these demands in the banking department.

Now, although the depositors might be perfectly willing to accept Bank of England notes in payment of their claims—and for all internal trade, at least, they would answer the purpose equally well—the Bank has no power to issue these notes. It may be that £20,000,000 of gold is lying idle in the issue department against notes already in circulation: the Bank cannot use this gold to pay away nor as a

foundation of further issues. The example is fictitious
so far as the management of the deposits of the Bank
of England is concerned, but in three great commercial crises since the Act was passed it has been
suspended.

This suspension of the Act requires a word of
explanation. It did not mean that the notes were
rendered inconvertible, as was the case at the beginning of the century during the period of the bank
restriction already alluded to, for although the Act
was suspended, any one who wished could take notes
to the Bank and get gold in exchange: it simply
meant that in case of need the banking department
might issue additional notes to its customers on
security. It is worth noticing that the principle of
this Act has recently been adopted to regulate the
Imperial Bank of Germany, with a modification suggested by the experience of England in commercial
crises.

The German Bank may issue notes not backed by
gold to a certain fixed amount, and in case of need it
may issue notes on securities beyond this sum, on payment to Government of a tax of 5 per cent on the
additional issues. The Act is thus self-suspensory,
instead of requiring, as in England, the direct intervention of the Government, which afterwards receives
Parliamentary sanction.

§ 6. *Bank of England notes are simply a convenient
form of currency.*—Bank of England notes are thus,
in ordinary circumstances, simply and solely a convenient form of currency, the gold which they represent
being in the vaults of the Bank instead of in the

pockets of the people. But this gold is held solely against the notes, and cannot be used for ordinary banking purposes. Every week the Bank of England issues an account in which the affairs of the two departments are kept distinct. Any one who refers to one of these accounts, as published in the *Economist*, for instance, will see that the reserve in the banking department is for the most part held in notes. The account, for example, for the week ending December 14, 1887, states that the total value of the notes issued was £35,401,930, of which £16,200,000 were issued in the manner described above against Government debt and other securities, and the remainder, £19,201,930, against gold bullion. In the banking department we have as assets Government and other securities to the extent of about £33,000,000, notes to the amount of about £12,000,000, and gold and silver coin about £1,250,000. This last sum must be considered as "till" money in coin, but coin for the Bank of England notes would be obtained from the issue department.

§ 7. *One-pound notes used in Scotland and Ireland, and recommended for England.*—Under the present law, no bank in England can issue notes for sums under £5, whilst in Scotland and Ireland notes for £1 may be issued by the authorised banks, under similar restrictions as to holding gold for issues above a certain amount. The fact that these £1 notes, although strictly convertible, have to a large extent supplanted gold sovereigns as currency, seems to show that, in the opinion of the people of Ireland and Scotland, they are found to be a more convenient form of currency. One way, then, of restoring and maintaining the gold coinage in England would be to issue £1 notes, and to allow the Bank of England to issue a sufficient amount *not* against gold to pay for recoining the old sovereigns and half-sovereigns. This plan would leave untouched the principle of the Act of 1844, except by changing the limit of issues not against gold from £16,200,000, as at present, to, say, £20,000,000. All the gold withdrawn from circulation would be kept in reserve against the notes in the issue department, but it would be reckoned at its full weight value. Space will not allow me to give further details of the scheme.*

§ 8. *Not only bank-notes but all forms of credit substitutes rest on a gold basis.*—The brief examination of the Bank Act of 1844 just made shows clearly enough that at any rate the bank-notes rest on a gold basis definitely fixed by law; but in the exchange of commodities in all wholesale transactions, and even to a large extent in the retail trade, other forms of representative money play an important part, and in these cases the connection with gold is neither so definite nor so obvious.

Any explanation of an adequate kind would involve a more complete account of banking and the money market than can be attempted in this place, but the reader who wishes for a lucid, popular, and sound exposition of the subject may be confidently recommended to read Mr. Bagehot's *Lombard Street: A Description of the Money Market.* He will there

* I give full details of this scheme in a paper read before the British Association at Birmingham, September 1886. See p. 152.

6

find ample illustration of the general proposition laid
down above, that all credit in this country rests on
gold, and ultimately on the gold held in the issue
department of the Bank of England against the notes
held in the banking department.

"In consequence," says Mr. Bagehot, after a preliminary survey of the system, "all our credit system
depends on the Bank of England for its security. On
the wisdom of the directors of that one joint-stock
company it depends whether England shall be *solvent
or insolvent*. This may seem too strong, but it is not.
All banks depend on the Bank of England, and all
merchants depend on some banker. If a merchant
have £10,000 at his banker's, and wants to pay it
to some one in Germany, he will not be able to
pay it unless his banker can pay him, and the
banker will not be able to pay him if the Bank of
England should be in difficulties and cannot produce
his reserve."

One other passage may be quoted : "We see, then,
that the banking reserve of the Bank of England—
some ten millions on an average of years now, and
formerly much less—is all which is held against the
liabilities of Lombard Street; and if that were all,
we might well be amazed at the immense development of our credit system—in plain English, at the
immense amount of our debts payable on demand,
and the smallness of the sum of actual money which
we keep to pay them if demanded. But there is
more to come. Lombard Street is not only a place
requiring to keep a reserve—it is itself a place where
reserves are kept. All country bankers keep their

reserve in London. They only retain in each county town the minimum of cash necessary to the transaction of the current business of that county town. Long experience has told them to a nicety how much this is, and they do not waste capital and lose profit by keeping more idle. They send the money to London, invest a part of it in securities, and keep the rest with the London bankers and the bill-brokers. The habit of Scotch and Irish bankers is much the same. All their spare money is in London, and is invested as all other London money now is; and, *therefore, the reserve in the banking department of the Bank of England is the banking reserve not only of the Bank of England, but of all London; and not only of all London, but of all England, Ireland, and Scotland too.*"

§ 9. *Further limit to the effects of credit by the necessity for cash payments in some cases.*—We have now progressed a long way from our " hypothetical market," and made a corresponding advance towards the many-sided actuality of the practical world. Before proceeding further, however, it must be observed, in considering the limits imposed on a rise in prices due to the expansion of credit, that, however much the use of credit instruments may be extended, there are always a large number of payments which can only be effected by means of " cash."

In England generally, and in Scotland and Ireland, for all sums below £1, wages must be paid in actual coin, and a considerable amount of retail transactions can only be conducted by the same means. Whole-

sale transactions might all be ultimately settled, so
far as our country is concerned, by simple transfers
on the banking accounts of the different merchants,
but smaller payments cannot be met so readily.
Accordingly, if wholesale prices rise, owing to an
expansion of credit, they will soon find a check in
the increased payments which must be made to the
working classes, and the increased demands for currency
in the retail trades.

We are thus, again, brought back to the effect on
the bank reserves as the immediate cause of the
check to the rise in prices. So long as employers of
labour can obtain supplies of currency from the banks,
wholesale prices, and with them wages, may continue
to rise : but as the reserves of the banks are dispersed,
a rise in the rate of interest at which advances can be
made must take place, and a check will be put on the
rise in prices.

CHAPTER VII

INFLUENCE ON THE GENERAL LEVEL OF PRICES IN ANY
ONE COUNTRY OF THE GENERAL LEVEL OF PRICES
IN OTHER COUNTRIES

§ 1. *The general fall of prices in England during
recent years cannot be accounted for by any scarcity of
gold in this country.*—It might, perhaps, be thought
that this investigation of the connection between
money and prices is at length complete. But it is
not so; and a practical problem which is at present
exciting much attention, and to which, in another
connection, reference has already been made, furnishes
a striking illustration of the incompleteness of our
survey. We have already seen that, according to
the *Economist* index numbers, general prices in
England have fallen more than 30 per cent during
the last twelve years; and since Mr. Goschen gave
the authority of his name to the explanation, it has
been very commonly said that the fall is due to the
relative scarcity of gold. We should expect, from the
causes already examined, that if the production of
gold had fallen off whilst the demand for gold had at
any rate not diminished, a fall in general prices would
take place.

But this general argument is met very plausibly
in the following manner. I give, as an example, a
passage from the statement to the Royal Commission
on Trade by Mr. Luke Hansard : " If the fall in prices
in this country is caused by gold itself, that fall must
arise from a scarcity of the metal in circulation and
a scarcity of gold currency for carrying on our daily
transactions, either internally as coin or externally for
export, when it becomes a mere commodity used as
barter the same as any other commodity. Is there
any evidence of a want of metallic currency in this
country, of an insufficient paper currency, or of gold
for export ? I think not."

The answer is supported by statistics. First, as
regards the national circulation—the currency used
in cash transactions—it is pointed out that whilst in
the five years 1870-74 there was a coinage of gold
at the Mint exceeding £32,000,000, in the two suc-
ceeding periods of the same length the coinage was,
from 1875-79, a little over £8,000,000, and from
1880-84 a little under that figure. It is further
stated that " it used formerly to be customary for one
banker to solicit other bankers to take surplus coin
by courtesy, rather than run the risk of having some
few sovereigns cut by paying it into the Bank of
England. [The gold coins are taken by the Bank of
England only by weight.] This still, to some extent,
holds good. But so little demand is there for gold
coin in the country for internal circulation that it is
not uncommon, and is becoming necessary, to pay a
premium or accept a discount from those who have
facilities for paying away large sums. This, I contend,

would not be the case were there any deficient supply
of gold, or were there any such want of it for currency
purposes.   This difficulty in forcing the coin into
circulation again is not to be attributed solely to the
defective state of the coinage, as many of the coins are
of the standard weight."

Again, it is urged that the alleged scarcity has not
operated through the banking reserves of the Bank of
England—the ultimate reserve, as we have seen, of
the country; for, it is said, had this been the case—
had an unusual demand arisen through a foreign
drain—the rate of interest would have been raised in
order to check the export and induce importation.
But we learn that " our rates for advances have been
so low as to offer, if anything, an inducement for
other countries to take gold had they wanted it";
and it is found, as a matter of fact, that from 1874-84,
on balance, the imports of gold into the United Kingdom
have exceeded the exports by about £9,500,000.
" From this fact," the writer states, " and from the
bank rate of discount not showing any markedly
adverse state of the foreign exchanges, I am forced to
the conclusion that there is no scarcity of gold with
us.   Hence it has no agency in causing the recent fall
in prices."

§ 2. *We must look for an explanation of the fall to
foreign countries.*—It will be remarked that throughout
this argument, as to the facts of which there will be
no dispute, the question is constantly regarded from
the point of view of this country alone; and the
answer is, that with the close intercommunication of
markets in these days, this limited view is entirely

insufficient. Without entering into the details of the
theory of foreign trade, it is quite clear that if for
any reason prices had fallen in other countries with
which this country has commercial relations, the fall
must have been reflected to our home markets. It
would plainly be impossible—to take an example of
a particular commodity—to explain the fall in the
price of wheat, without considering the rates ruling in
foreign markets—from America in the West to India
in the East. And in precisely the same way, if general
prices have fallen in other countries owing to the comparative pressure on gold, there will be a corresponding
fall in this country.

§ 3. *General prices will always be adjusted until
there is sufficient currency to effect transactions.*—There
is thus no contradiction whatever between this apparent
abundance of gold in this country and a fall in prices
due to the scarcity of that metal. To make this
quite plain, it is only necessary to reflect on the
connection between gold as an actual means of exchange and as a measure of values, to which at an
earlier stage of the inquiry attention was directed;
and the general law there indicated may now be
stated in a more formal and complete manner as
follows :—

*The measure of values or the general level of prices
throughout the world will be so adjusted that the metals
used as currency, or as the basis of substitutes for currency, will be just sufficient for the purpose.*—We see,
then, that the value of gold is determined in precisely
the same manner as that of any other commodity,
according to the equation between demand and supply.

Competition will go on between those who hold the metal on the one side, and those who wish to obtain it on the other, until such a general level of prices is reached that the quantity demanded at that level is equal to the quantity offered.

Strictly speaking, then, and after making allowance for the temporary difficulties of readjustment, there must always be a sufficiency of gold. If there is not enough to keep prices at one level, prices will fall until there is enough for the new level. It seems probable, for reasons which I have given in another publication, that the process of readjustment to a new level began in the new or undeveloped countries, where the effect of a contraction of currency, credit being in a rudimentary stage, is brought about more rapidly and directly.

§ 4. *Two ways in which prices in any one country are directly affected by the monetary conditions of other countries.*—There are, then, to resume the general argument, two modes in which prices in any particular country depend on the monetary conditions of the rest of the world. *In the first place*, the world requires to keep up a certain level of prices, a certain amount of gold as actual circulating medium, and if there is not enough in any area, prices must fall in that area. But in these days the fall would be at once telegraphed, and other markets would be influenced.

Secondly, the great national banks require, in order to support the credit superstructure of their respective countries, a certain proportion of metallic reserve to liabilities. The proportion, as Mr. Bagehot has so well explained, varies according to circumstances, but there is a minimum which may be regarded as the danger point. If, for example, the Bank of England finds its reserve rapidly diminishing, and there seems a probability of further and possibly uncertain calls, it at once raises its rate of discount. Those who wish to get accommodation from the Bank can only do so at this higher rate. As a consequence they will, in the first place, try other banks, but under our one-reserve system any such pressure caused by foreign demands must fall on the Bank of England, and in the last resort the market rate must follow the Bank rate.

These high rates in a country where the margin of profits is very small, and where the discount of bills is carried on to an enormous extent, must act as a break upon trade, and prices will fall. We might find then that prices in England fell below the level of prices in other countries owing to scarcity of gold in this form, due, in the first place, to foreign demands.

In whatever manner the subject is regarded, it thus becomes clear that the general level of prices in any one country depends on causes beyond the power of that country to control, and a fall in prices cannot be explained without a wide survey. Those who assert that the relative scarcity in gold, the falling off in its production, and the exceptional demands for currency purposes, and similar causes, cannot have caused a fall in prices in this country, because here there is abundance of gold for the existing level of prices, are guilty of the same kind of fallacy as a man who should suppose that the ship cannot sink because there is no leak in the particular cabin in which he happens to sleep. To change the simile—in these days one body politic may catch low prices from another, as readily as one body physical may catch fever.*

* For an elaboration of the argument in this chapter, see the Essay on the "Causes of Movements in General Prices," p. 286.

CHAPTER VIII

EFFECTS ON GENERAL PRICES OF THE USE OF BOTH GOLD AND SILVER AS STANDARD MONEY

§ 1. *Warning to the reader of differences of opinion on the Silver Question.*—It is time now to complete, so far as the limits of this inquiry allow, the enumeration of the causes affecting general prices, by taking into account one more circumstance which, for the sake of simplicity in the argument, has hitherto been omitted. I have spoken sometimes of the precious metals and sometimes of gold, and I propose at this point to consider the effects of the fact that for standard currency—that is, for their unlimited legal tender—some nations use gold, some silver, and some both. I have elsewhere given my views on what is termed the silver question, in its practical and political aspects, and in this place I am only concerned to explain the general theory of this subject in such a manner as to make the controversy intelligible.

§ 2. *The meaning of bi-metallism.*—In any country or group of countries forming a monetary union, bi-metallism implies that both as regards coinage and legal tender, gold and silver are on precisely the same footing. It is not the mere use of both metals for currency, but the use of both as standard money, which constitutes the essence of bi-metallism. It can only lead to confusion to say that bi-metallism exists *de facto* everywhere, on the ground that in all countries silver is used at any rate for token money; for the relations of token money and standard money to prices are essentially different, and the difference may be expressed in the following general principle: *The quantity of standard money, other things remaining the same, determines the general level of prices, whilst, on the other hand, the quantity of token-money is determined by the general level of prices.* The qualifying phrase, "other things remaining the same," refers to the various conditions already enumerated which also operate on general prices. The difference may also be expressed by saying that a standard metal is coined in unlimited quantities when brought to the mint, but that token money is issued only in limited quantities, according to the wants of the community, at the discretion of the authorities. There is, for example, no reason why very great discoveries of silver should cause the issue of one extra sixpence in this country, but similar discoveries of gold would be sure to cause an increase in the amount of gold coined.

§ 3. *The necessity of a fixed ratio between gold and silver in a bi-metallic system.*—It is conceivable that a Government might coin both metals on the same conditions, receive both on equal terms in payment of taxes, and constitute both equally legal tender, and yet at the same time allow the ratio of one metal to the other to vary according to the market price of the two metals, or according to proclamation from time to time. When, however, it is remembered that cash payments are effected not in bullion but in coins, it will be apparent that much inconvenience would arise if the relative value of the gold and silver coins were constantly changing. Consider, for example, the common case of getting change for a sovereign, or, still better, the frauds to which the poor and ignorant would be liable. Accordingly, nations which have adopted bi-metallism practically have always issued their coins at a ratio which was intended to be fixed and unalterable.

§ 4. *Consequences of the adoption of fixed ratio bi-metallism by one country.*—Suppose, for the sake of illustration, that England alone were to adopt bi-metallism at such a ratio of gold to silver that the gold in a sovereign was precisely equal in value to the silver in twenty shillings. Under this supposition silver could be minted to any extent, and used for the payment of debts in the same way as gold at present. But now assume that, owing to some change in the demand for, or the supply of, silver abroad, the market ratio varied from the legal ratio in such a manner that the silver in twenty shillings was no longer equal in value to the gold in a sovereign. In these circumstances Gresham's Law (cf. chap. iv.) would at once come into operation. No one would be willing to pay his debts in gold when, by first selling his gold for silver, he could obtain more than twenty shillings for his sovereign. Thus either the silver would actually

drive the gold from circulation, or else the gold
would command an *agio* (or premium), just as it
does compared with depreciated inconvertible notes.
It follows, then, that either the country would become
really mono-metallic on a silver basis, or else that
practically, in all large operations at any rate, the
ratio would become variable.

It must be observed also, in the case assumed, that
other nations would be likely to send their silver to
this country. So long as the bi-metallism existed in
full operation, any depreciation of silver abroad would
cause it to be sent to its best market. It is not true
to say that silver could be taken to the bi-metallic
mints and directly exchanged against gold, but it is
easy to see that so long as the bi-metallic country
possessed any gold and acted on bi-metallic principles,
silver could always indirectly obtain gold at the fixed
ratio price; for a foreigner could send silver (say) to
London, and draw against his remittances, and sell his
bill for gold.

At the same time, however, it may be suggested
that the mere existence of bi-metallism in any great
country would have a steadying effect on the gold price
of silver in other places, just as the London quotations
of many stocks and commodities govern quotations in
other markets. Such is alleged to have been the
effect of the existence of bi-metallism in France for a
period of seventy years in this century; and certainly,
as a matter of fact, the market ratio fluctuated within
very narrow limits in spite of the enormous gold discoveries about 1850 and a number of other important
commercial and financial changes.

The steadiness in the price of silver during this long period need not, however, be ascribed wholly to the existence of partial bi-metallism, for so long as some nations used gold and some silver, and preserved their respective standards, the ratio would clearly remain more steady than could be the case when suddenly the mintage of silver as standard money was abandoned by several countries.

§ 5. *International bi-metallism.*—If, however, it be granted that one country alone could not effectively maintain a fixed ratio between gold and silver, and keep both metals in circulation as standard money, it may still be maintained that, if the principal commercial nations were to simultaneously adopt bi-metallism at the same fixed ratio, no disturbance of that ratio could take place. I have in another place * elaborated this argument, and need only state here the principal positions. It rests essentially on what is known as the *compensatory action* of the double or (to adopt a better term) the joint standard. To illustrate this theory, suppose that all the great commercial nations have adopted bi-metallism in the manner suggested; and next suppose, if it is possible, that silver, for example, suddenly becomes cheaper, reckoned in gold, than it ought to be according to the ratio. This would, as explained in the last section, at once bring into play Gresham's Law, and the silver would tend to drive the gold from circulation. But then the crucial question arises: Whither would this gold go, and whence would the silver be obtained to take its place? It is main-

---

* Essay on the " Stability of a Fixed Ratio between Gold and Silver under International Bi-metallism," p. 247.

tained that as the gold was thrown upon, and the silver withdrawn from, the bullion market, the former would fall and the latter rise in value, and thus that the ratio would be restored. In fact, it is argued by those who rely most on this compensatory action of the double or joint standard, that the ratio never could be disturbed, and the argument is really a *reductio ad absurdum*.

On the other side it is maintained, following the contention of Lord Liverpool, that all rich nations naturally prefer gold as their standard. Consequently, if all the great commercial nations adopted bi-metallism, and yet at the same time they really preferred gold as the principal money, it may be thought that a premium on gold would arise. In support of this view it has been urged that no bank would, in the light of recent experience, and merely in reliance on the *theory* of international bi-metallism, run the risk of keeping a large reserve of silver. Again, it is said that Governments would prefer gold to silver for their war chests, and also that gold would be hoarded or converted into plate, rather than be passed at what might appear too low a value compared with silver.

Sometimes, however, the objections to international bi-metallism are based (as for example by Professor Nasse)* on the dangers which the banks, and consequently the Governments of the bi-metallic nations, would undergo, from the fact that the discredited and disliked silver would be paid into the banks and would

---

* See Essay in *Schönberg's Handbuch*, vol. i. p. 279. This essay is, perhaps, the best statement yet made on the mono-metallic side and well deserves translation.

not be withdrawn, and thus that the whole credit system of the civilised world would rest on an insecure foundation.

Finally, it is objected that with conventional bi-metallism, in which silver was presumably over-valued, a stimulus would be given to the production of silver, and relatively a check placed on the production of gold. Such a stimulus and check, however, could operate but very slightly on mines which yielded any rent (for it may be assumed that they are worked at full pressure), and the difference in the annual supply due to this cause would thus be very small in amount compared with the total stock.

I shall not attempt in this place to decide on the relative merits of these conflicting arguments. It may not, however, be out of place to observe that the logical conclusion to the argument that all the more highly civilised nations naturally prefer gold, would seem to be that they will all attempt to adopt the gold standard. If the argument has any force at all, it certainly applies with far greater cogency to the United States or France at the present day than to England at the time when Lord Liverpool wrote. But the probable consequences of any attempt to make the gold standard universal may be expressed in the words of Mr Goschen, at the Conference at Paris in 1878. " If, however, other States were to carry on a propaganda in favour of a gold standard and of the demonetisation of silver, the Indian Government would be obliged to reconsider its position, and might be forced by events to take measures similar to those taken elsewhere. *In that case the scramble to get rid of*

*silver might provoke one of the gravest crises ever under-
gone by commerce.*"

§ 6. *The effects of changes in the relative value of
gold and silver on the general level of prices in gold-
using and silver - using countries respectively.* — The
sentence just quoted from so eminent a financial
authority as Mr Goschen, naturally leads to an inquiry
as to the manner in which such a grave crisis could
arise. Since Adam Smith destroyed the mercantile
system, with its fetish of a favourable monetary
balance, popular opinion, which is ever liable to run
from one extreme to the other, has been inclined to
exaggerate the position that money is in general not
the end but the medium of exchange. No one now
will deny the truth so clearly stated by John Law,
nearly a century before the *Wealth of Nations* became
famous, in the words: " Money is not the value for
which goods are exchanged, but the value by which
they are exchanged ": but, at the same time, it is
equally false to imagine that changes in money values
only produce nominal effects.

Suppose that, owing to a " scramble for gold " by
Western countries, silver becomes depreciated relatively
to gold, the question arises : What (if any) will be the
effect on general prices in gold-using and silver-using
countries respectively ? The answer depends upon
two lines of argument. In the *first* place, it can
hardly be disputed that, when allowance is made for
the cost of carriage and the remittance of payment, the
price of any commodity reckoned in either standard,
except in the case of transitory market influences,
must be the same in both gold and silver-using

countries (say) in England and India. This adjustment of prices to practical equality has of late become much more ready than formerly, since now most wholesale business is transacted by telegraph. It follows then that, other things remaining the same, if silver falls in value relatively to gold, either silver prices must rise or gold prices must fall, or a movement in both directions must take place. To take an extreme case, assume that silver falls suddenly to half its former value, reckoned in gold. Obviously if Eastern produce were to command the same gold price in London as before, that would mean twice as much silver; and conversely, if Manchester goods were to obtain only the same silver price in Calcutta as before, that would mean only half as much gold. But if the general level of prices in both countries remained the same, Eastern goods would be exported to England in great quantities, whilst the Eastern markets would remain practically closed to English wares. As a natural consequence, the gold price of Eastern goods would tend to fall, owing to the abundant supply, whilst the silver price of English goods would tend to rise, owing to the bareness of the markets. Thus, in time, the two sets of prices must be adjusted, so that the amount of silver which any article of commerce obtains in the East becomes— allowance being made for carriage, etc.—of the same value as the gold which it obtains in the West.

Now, suppose that the adjustment is made entirely by an operation on gold prices—in other words, that the rupee price of Manchester goods, for example, does not rise, and that the gold price of Indian exports

falls. In this case there will be no disturbance of
relative prices in India, everything selling, after
allowing for changes in cost and the like, for the same
silver as before. So far no difference to Indian
interests will arise. The Indian Government, however,
to meet its obligations in gold on this side, will have
to transmit the value of twice as much silver as before,
which will involve twice as much taxation, other
things remaining the same.

In gold-using countries, on the other hand, taking
England as the type, we have supposed that all the
articles of Eastern trade have fallen in their gold price
proportionately to the fall in silver. In this case,
either wages, and all the other elements in the cost of
production of exports to the East, must fall in proportion, or the exportation must cease. Similarly,
as regards articles which compete with exports from
the East (wheat, for example), unless the English cost
of production is lessened, a check will be placed on
production.

If, however, in all the industries which supply
Eastern markets, and in all which compete with
Eastern produce, a fall of prices sets in, and this fall
in turn operates on the various items in the cost of
production (fixed capital, profits, wages, raw material,
etc.), it is necessary, according to the general principles
of industrial competition, that other branches of production should also be affected. In this way, under
the supposition made as to the nature of the adjustment, a fall in the price of silver, reckoned in gold,
may cause a proportionate fall in the general level of
gold prices. This, however, is only one supposition—

for, by parity of reasoning, the adjustment may take place by a rise in silver prices to the full extent of the depreciation, or by a rise in silver prices and a fall in gold prices coincidently. It is, then, of the utmost importance to discover which method of adjustment is most probable.

§ 7. *The general level of gold prices more unstable than that of silver prices.*—It has often been observed by economists, especially since attention has been directed to the recurrence of decennial cycles in trade, that in a highly civilised community—England, for example—the amount of gold used, both for reserve and for circulation, does not vary exactly with the rise or fall in prices,—in other words, that the same quantity of gold will, within certain limits, sustain very different systems of general prices. A reference to the argument in previous chapters on the causes which determine the general level of prices, will at once show that there are several other variable elements besides the quantity of gold. In the same way, in countries in which silver is the standard, we have to consider other elements besides the quantity of silver. Apparently, so long as the general conditions of production and distribution remain the same, the most important of these variable influences is the elasticity of credit; and no demonstration is needed to show that the development of credit is carried to a far higher degree in the gold-using than in the silver-using countries. It follows, then, that so far the level of gold prices is more unstable than that of silver prices.

Again, although there is a tendency to exaggerate

the influence of custom in fixing prices in the East, there can be little doubt that custom operates to a much greater extent there than is the case in the West, so that a diminution of supply which, in the West, might cause a rapid and great rise in prices, might in the East have a much less effect. To take a concrete example, it would be much more easy to raise the price of shirts in this country than of dhooties in India, in response to a rise in raw material.

It thus appears that general prices can only rise over the vast areas of silver-using countries by an actual increase of the circulating medium sufficient to force up the customary rates; and it follows that if silver falls relatively to gold, it is much more probable that gold prices will be forced down than silver prices raised to make the necessary adjustment. It must be remembered that in the East gold is simply a commodity, and to the native mind there is no reason why a rise in the silver price of gold should cause a rise in the price of cotton goods or wheat.

Now it is well known that since 1874 a great fall has occurred in the value of silver compared with gold. Without entering into the causes of this fall, it may be said that some adjustment, in the manner described, of gold and silver prices became necessary. Apparently silver prices have not risen, and gold prices have fallen, as might have been expected, seeing that no great increase in the shipments of silver to the East seems to have taken place. On the question of fact, however, the report of the present Commission will, it may be hoped, speak with authority.

§ 8. *Causes of disturbance in the relative value of gold and silver.*—Seeing, then, that disturbances in the relative values of the two metals are of such consequence, it is important to discover the principal causes of a possible variation. Stated generally, variations can only arise from changes in the conditions of supply or demand. Silver, in the markets of gold-using countries, has a price which will vary with the supply and demand, and a fall in price may arise from an unusual excess of supply or a falling off in demand. A great increase in supply may take place either from great discoveries (or improved processes in working the mines and ores), or from the release of hoards, or from a Government selling silver which it intends to replace with gold. Conversely, a falling off in demand may arise either because Governments require less for their coinage, or because less is required for export. The only element which presents any difficulty is the last: for the demand for export will depend on the balance of indebtedness, which cannot be met except by the actual transmission of silver (that is to say, the balance which remains after other means of remittance are exhausted). Obviously, however, this balance, so far as dependent on commercial transactions, will itself depend partly on the quantities of exports and imports, and partly on the state of prices. But, as was shown above, the state of prices must depend partly on the relative value of gold and silver, and we thus seem to be led into an argument in a circle. If, however, the greater immobility of silver prices be admitted, we escape from the vicious circle, and, in any case, the demand for export is only one element in the demand, and the price of silver may vary from other changes in demand or from changes in supply.

We thus arrive at the position that if silver and gold are left to market influences alone, variations in their relative values are liable to occur, with consequent effects upon prices and commercial transactions. The secondary effects seem of more importance than the mere inconveniences of a fluctuating exchange, though, no doubt, to those actually engaged in trade with silver countries this is a source of annoyance.

§ 9. *Money a proper subject for international agreement.*— It appears, then, that the consideration of this additional factor—namely, the use of both gold and silver as standard money by different countries—has strengthened the conclusion of the last chapter, that the causes of movements in the general level of prices in any one country cannot be explained without a survey which embraces the whole commercial world. Any nation may, of course, choose the metals for its money, and may vary or not the weights and the purity and the denominations of its coins as it pleases, but no nation can be independent of the rest of the world as regards the most important quality of a good system of money—namely, stability of value. Thus, so long as gold and silver form the principal bases on which contracts are made and exchanges take place, every particular nation must consider the monetary conditions of other nations, and a formal definite recognition of this mutual dependence seems the natural outcome of commercial development. Since, however, in this essay I wish to avoid even the

appearance of controversy, I will conclude by
saying that, if it could be effected, every one
would rejoice in a stable international agreement,
but that to some the initial difficulties and the
possible evil consequences seem to outweigh the
probable advantages.

PART II

ESSAYS ON MONETARY PROBLEMS

JOHN LAW OF LAURISTON:

AND

THE GREATEST SPECULATIVE MANIA ON RECORD *

ADDRESS TO THE EDINBURGH PHILOSOPHICAL INSTITUTE, JANUARY 24, 1888†

In the invigorating address ‡ with which Mr. Morley opened the course of lectures for the present session, the most remarkable feature to my mind was the way in which the most brilliant, ingenious, and witty aphorisms of the cynical man of the world were made to appear stale and flat compared with the wisdom of those whose "great thoughts come from the heart." At any rate, all who listened to the address must have been impressed with the fact that, however

---

* I have been much indebted to *Recherches historiques sur le Système de Law*, by E. Levasseur; *Histoire de Law*, by Thiers; Wood's *Memorials of Cramond* and *Life of Law*; the *Mémoires de la Vie privée de Louis XV.*; the account of Law's system in Sir James Steuart's *Political Economy*; and various minor works of Montesquieu and Defoe.

† Some parts were omitted in delivery for want of time.

‡ On "Aphorisms."

coldly and impartially history is written in these days, the heart still warms to the good man struggling with adversity, and pays but listless attention to the brilliant achievements of energy without moral purpose, and intellect without soul.

For my own part, I soon became painfully afraid that, in taking for the subject of my lecture John Law of Lauriston, I had, in one important respect at least, chosen a most uninteresting theme. For, as his earliest biographer puts it, "to his moral character, I am sorry to say, no compliments can be paid": and in support of this statement he quotes the remark of a contemporary that, even before he attained his majority, "he was nicely expert in all manner of debaucheries."

A few facts from his early life will justify and partly explain this judgment.

John Law was born in Edinburgh in April 1671. His father was a goldsmith, an occupation which in those days was more that of a banker of a primitive kind than a craftsman. He amassed a sufficient fortune to buy the estate of Lauriston, but died the next year (1684), and left his son, at the age of fourteen, heir to his estate, and committed to the charge of a prudent but too indulgent mother. The boy was gifted with a handsome person, and became accomplished in all the arts and amusements of society, including tennis and fencing.

Freed from control, he soon began to waste his substance in riotous living. He went up to London about the age of twenty, and celebrated his coming of age by making over the estate of Lauriston to his mother, so as to provide funds for his debts. His next exploit was, at the age of twenty-three, to kill in a duel another man of fashion with whom he had some hot words relating to a married lady. For this affair, after a three days' trial, he was convicted of murder and sentenced to death. On a representation of the case to the Crown, however, he obtained a pardon; but as the relatives of the man who was killed made an appeal, Law was put into prison, and apparently thought it safer to bribe his jailers and escape to the Continent.

He remained abroad about six years, providing the means for his extravagance and pleasures chiefly by gambling.

So far, John Law appears simply as a man of the world, as the world was at the beginning of the eighteenth century. He set off a fine person with handsome dress, and won the hearts of men and women by his brilliant wit and pleasant manner. We have the authority of no less a person than the Professor of Anatomy in the University of Edinburgh of the time, that Mr. Law was one of the easiest, most affable, and best behaved men he had ever seen; and the professor is supported by a crowd of dukes and duchesses. John Law was by no means a needy adventurer, as is too commonly supposed. He was of good family: his father was great-grandson of James Law, Archbishop of Glasgow, and his mother was connected with a branch of the ducal house of Argyll. After his hurried departure to the Continent, as a natural precaution against the possible success of the

appeal against him, he was soon appointed Secretary
to the British Resident in Holland; and some years
before he attained his great celebrity, he married Lady
Catherine Knollys, daughter of Nicholas, third Earl of
Banbury.

Thus John Law had every right to rank as a man
of fashion and a man of honour, which is not indeed
saying very much, comparing our standard with the
standard of his day, but which is saying enough to
show that he was not a cardsharper and swindler, or,
as the French called him after his fall, the "eldest son
of Satan."

But whatever judgment be passed on Law's moral
character—and the popular judgment has certainly
been far too harsh—there can be no two opinions as
to his great financial genius. Having regard to the
circumstances of the time, to the rudimentary condition of monetary science, and to the want of national
experience in credit transactions, he displayed both
wonderful originality and wonderful soundness. It
is not just to test a man's ability by the mere event
of success or failure, which may be largely due to the
action of others beyond his control. John Law's
system certainly ended in the most tremendous
financial collapse on record. But in spite of this
catastrophe, John Law may have been an excellent
financier, just as Napoleon was a great soldier in
spite of Waterloo, and the man who lost his soul to
the devil at a game of chess may have been an excellent
chess-player.

The Bank of England was founded in the year in

which John Law killed Mr Wilson and fled the
country, and the Bank of Scotland was founded in the
next year.

Perhaps the most effective way of bringing before
you the rudimentary state of banking at the time, is
not simply to mention the fact that Bank of England
notes fell considerably below par, but to recall the
main features of a caricature, published after the
failure of Law's great Mississippi Scheme, about
twenty-five years after the foundation of the Bank of
England.   The "Goddess of Shares" is seated in a
beautiful car drawn by the Goddess of Folly. Lest
the car should not roll fast enough, the agents of four
great companies, who are known by their long fox-tails
and cunning looks, turn round the spokes of the wheels,
upon which are marked the names of the several stocks
and their value, sometimes high and sometimes low,
according to the turns of the wheel.   Upon the
ground are the merchandise, day-books and ledgers of
legitimate commerce, crushed under the chariot of
Folly.   All this is simple and natural; but the most
startling thing is to find that those who are drawing
this car of Folly are representatives of great financial
schemes, and that the Bank of England, though a
quarter of a century old at the time, is placed in the
same yoke with the South Sea Bubble.   Imagine the
state of credit in which the Directors of the Bank of
England could be represented as foxes with cunning
looks and long tails, and that noble institution as
trampling upon legitimate commerce!

For the sake of a convenient illustration, I have
abandoned chronology; but at the time the Bank of

England, the first regular bank in the kingdom, was founded, John Law was forced to retire to Holland, and in Amsterdam he found a bank that had been in a flourishing state for nearly a century. The banking, however, which it performed was of the simplest possible kind. Holland was the centre of the world's trade, and it was by trade that she amassed her wealth and became the richest country in Europe. The Dutch traders, however, were much troubled with the defective state of their own coinage, and still more by the circulation of a mass of foreign coins of uncertain value. No merchant could tell exactly what a bill payable in Holland would realise.

The Bank of Amsterdam was instituted to remedy this evil. It would lead me too far from the path of my narrative if I were to describe in any detail the principles on which this bank was founded, and I will confine myself to the idea which so much impressed John Law.

Avoiding technicalities, the essence of the institution may be explained in very few words. The merchants took all sorts of coins to the bank, and the bank gave them credit for the real and not for the nominal value. It is just as if in England the gold coins became so light that the banks were afraid to take them at full value, and only allowed the value by weight. The bank locked up the money, and practically gave the merchants bank-notes representing the money. *

* The Bank of Amsterdam did not actually issue bank-notes in the way practised at present. The precise method of dealing with the bank-credits and bullion, however, is too intricate for consideration in this place. Compare Adam Smith's *Wealth of Nations*, bk. iv. chap. iii., and Sir James Steuart's *Principles of Political Economy*, bk. iv. part ii. chaps. xxxvii.-xxxix.

These bank-notes were bought and sold in order to settle bills, for every one knew that the bank-note represented a certain number of perfect coins. The most curious thing was, that the notes were so much valued that they actually sold for a little more than their nominal value.

It may seem paradoxical to say that a bank-note should ever be worth more than the gold it represents; but again, let me refer to our own light gold coinage for illustration.

Suppose that our banks decide to take the gold only by weight, what would be more natural than for a trader to say, when offered a bag of suspicious-looking coins in payment of a bill, Pay me in notes which the banks must meet in coins of full value; I cannot weigh and test all those coins?

But if many merchants did that at once, and the notes were limited, for a time they would command a premium. People would pay for the extra convenience of a note as they pay now for a post-office order.

To return to the Bank of Amsterdam. It was seen at the time, and it has always been admitted since, that the bank-notes issued by it were in every respect better money than the actual gold and silver coins in circulation. Obviously, so long as the bank retained all its gold, and made no advances at all, so long as it kept to its primary object, its notes were absolutely safe—safer, indeed, than the coin in the possession of the merchant, and in every way they were far more convenient; that is to say, paper money, under certain conditions, was better than metallic money.

It was in Holland that John Law may be said to have matured the leading ideas of his system; and undoubtedly, if not originally due to, they were largely influenced by, his experience in that country. He contrasted Scotland and England with Holland, and found that, whilst all the natural advantages were in favour of the former countries, the trade and wealth of Holland were far superior. The only reason, he thought, must be in the different treatment of industry by Government. So much was he convinced of this, that he wrote: "If Spain, France, or Britain, or any one of them, had applied to trade as early, and upon the same measures, as Holland did, Holland would not have been inhabited."

What, then, were the essential points of difference?

In the answer to this question John Law discovered the elements of his system.

In the first place, he observed that, owing to its banking system, there was in Holland an abundance of money to drive trade, and that credit lent the support of capital to new undertakings, at a very moderate return. In Scotland, on the contrary, trade was fettered, and the development of industry checked, because there was not enough money and credit to give free scope to enterprise.

Accordingly, he thought one of the principal needs of the time was to supply the nation with sufficient money; and as a consequence he has been accused of holding all the errors of the inflationists, and of believing that it was only necessary to flood the country with "counters" (metallic or paper) to bring about prosperity.

There is nothing more dangerous to clear reasoning than to push an analogy to an extreme, and the analogy of " counters " has in recent days probably done much more harm than good. Money is certainly a medium of exchange, and may thus be compared to " counters," but a metaphor does not exhaust all the functions of money and credit.

We shall approach much nearer to the idea in John Law's mind if we suppose, not that he could not distinguish between the real and the nominal wealth of a country, but that he appreciated the difference between a country or city, or even village, with and without a banking system. If it were proposed to establish a branch bank in a new district, it would not savour of practical wisdom to object that money was only " counters "; and it is about as sensible to write down John Law's system as false, under the impression that he did not understand that elementary fragment of monetary science. At any rate, he understood it sufficiently well to write : " Money is not the value for which goods are exchanged, but the value by which they are exchanged; the use of money is to buy goods and silver, whilst money is of no other use "; and Adam Smith himself could not better express this " counters " theory of money.

Next as regards money, John Law observed that in Holland, not only was the paper money better than gold or silver, but that, owing to the preference of people for the paper, the precious metals which it represented remained locked up in the bank and were never demanded. What, then, more natural than to suppose that a paper-money, or at any rate an extensive credit

system, might be formed with some other real security,
such as land, at its back ?   And in modern times, is
not every advance by a bank upon securities of various kinds an example of what Sir James Steuart called
the melting down of wealth into bank-money ?

But apart from the superiority of its monetary
system, John Law imagined that Holland had an advantage over other countries, because she understood
much better the general industrial functions of government, both by way of freedom and by way of control.
Accordingly, we shall find that Law's system, when
fully developed, was, on the one hand, an anticipation
of free trade in the widest sense of the term, involving
the abolition of monopolies and petty restraints and
the repeal of oppressive taxes ; whilst, on the other,
it imposed on the State certain large duties in
industrial organisation, the neglect of which in
modern times has been the principal encouragement
to Socialism.

It was with the view, in the first place, of benefit-
ing his country, by placing the relations of government to industry on a sounder basis, that, soon after
he returned to Scotland, he published his proposal for
a Council of Trade.

The Council of Trade was to have under its control
the whole of the king's revenues, charitable endow-
ments, tithes, and certain specified duties.   This
enormous income, after a certain portion had been
handed over for the use of royalty, was to be employed
for the promotion of industry.   Scotland was then
swarming with beggars, and they were to be compelled

to work; monopolies of various kinds were to be prohibited; duties on imports and exports were to be repealed or reduced; fraudulent bankrupts were to be punished and honest debtors liberated; and in short, the Council of Trade was to carry out a complete scheme of industrial and mercantile reform, on what was a very liberal basis, considering the circumstances of the country at the time.

This proposal, however, came to nothing; and five years later, when about thirty-five years of age, John Law tried to carry out the less ambitious project for the reform of the currency and the extension of credit. With this object in view he published his principal work on *Money and Trade*.

The treatise is written in a vigorous style, and is strictly argumentative. The reasoning is perfectly clear, but often so briefly stated as to be difficult to follow. The design was evidently struck off by the writer at white heat, and under the full conviction that it was perfectly practicable and of the highest national importance. There is not a trace of the prospectus-monger who, to promote his own interest, professes to trade for the public good. Any one who imagines that John Law was simply a projector who deceived a credulous public by flattering, glowing hopes, which he himself knew to be false, cannot do better than glance over the little book on *Money and Trade*. It is from beginning to end a pure piece of political arithmetic, and has no more of the gorgeous visions of speculation than one of Ricardo's tracts on " Currency." In fact, to a person not well versed in economic reasoning, it will be about as entertaining as to a non-mathematical reader a treatise on the differential calculus.

As the scheme was not approved by Parliament, I do not propose to discuss it in detail. The leading idea was to issue bank-notes upon landed security, the amount issued being strictly limited, and the whole management being of the most public character. The reason given was, that at the time there was not sufficient currency in the country to develop its resources, and that the money in use was subject to great and uncertain variations in value. Whether the scheme could ever have worked practically is more than doubtful; but as a piece of theory it is interesting and instructive.

As soon as he found that his proposals for the improvement of the national finance and industry were not likely to be carried out, John Law resumed his old life on the Continent. He visited many of the principal cities in Europe, especially in Italy, and everywhere studied banking and finance, and indulged in gambling and speculation. He first visited Paris in 1708, and became notorious for his high play. It is said that he always took with him to the gambling-table two bags containing gold to the value of several thousand pounds sterling, and was accustomed to play for such high stakes that he used counters to represent his money, to save the trouble of handling the large sums—the counters always being duly honoured at the close of the evening. It was on this occasion that he met the prince who later, as Regent and Duke of Orleans, gave him a field for the development of his system. He made enemies, however, was com-

pelled to leave Paris, and resumed his rambles over
Europe.

By a rare combination of skill and good fortune,
he amassed considerable wealth ; and soon after the
death of Louis XIV., in September 1715, and the
assumption of the Regency by the Duke of Orleans,
he returned to Paris, bringing with him more than
£100,000 sterling.

Between the middle of 1716 and the end of 1720
occurred a series of events of the most astonishing
character, which for a time made John Law the most
powerful man in France and the most celebrated man
in the world.

To understand this extraordinary drama, it is
necessary to grasp both the character of the man and
the state of affairs in France. As for the man, he
may be known by the deeds already noticed. He had
studied finance amongst the phlegmatic Dutch and
the crafty Italians, and had lived a life of pleasure in
the most corrupt courts and cities of Europe. His
manners were pleasing and even enticing, yet he was
quick to resent an injury. Full of resource and un-
tiring in energy, he commanded the respect always
accorded to superior intellectual activity. Thoroughly
convinced of the truth of his own theories, he infected
others with his own enthusiasm. He dazzled the
world with his bold cool-headed gambling, and yet
wrote like a philosopher on the mysteries of value and
money. He had large statesmanlike views on the
industrial policy of nations; but at the same time
he altogether underrated practical difficulties, as if
life were only a game of chance and skill; and he

was prepared to reorganise the industry of a nation or of the world in less time than other men have taken to describe in a book an ideal Utopia.

Such was the man, and by a strange fatality France afforded him a field exactly adapted for the display of his peculiar genius.

France, at the death of Louis XIV., was on the verge of national bankruptcy. The heavy expenditure of the closing years of his reign had only been met by loans contracted at ruinous rates of interest, and by the most burdensome methods of taxation. Every device for raising money had been tried. When no more could be obtained from the people by force, the king resorted to the sale of patents of nobility and of all kinds of offices and monopolies, until Paris was filled with royal officers whose fantastic titles provoked the ridicule of the people. Even public lotteries were practised to such an extent that at last they ceased to be productive. The people became too poor or too hopeless to invest a shilling for the sake of a fortune. About five years before the death of the king, a tenth of the property of every one, from the Dauphin downwards, was exacted; but gradually exemptions crept in, and this new tithe became practically a tax on agriculture and commerce. The coinage was called in, in order that the Government might abstract a certain portion and re-issue at the same nominal value. By an operation of this kind in 1709, the king gained about 23 per cent—that is to say, he practically reduced the weight of each coin by that amount. But the evils caused by the discredit attached to the debased coinage were so great, that in 1713 an edict

was passed to bring it up to the value at which it had
been for nearly fifty years of the flourishing part of
his reign.   Large amounts of promissory-notes on the
part of the State (*billets d'état*) were issued, most of
which did not pass for a quarter of their nominal
value, and some were hardly worth a tenth.

Thus Louis XIV. left to his successor (his great-
grandson), a child of five years, a total debt of $3\frac{1}{2}$
milliards of livres (or about 250 millions sterling at
the proper rate of conversion), a mass of accounts
hopelessly entangled, an empty treasury, a ruined
credit, a people crushed with new taxes that became
every year more unproductive, and a growing expenditure.

All the real power of the State fell into the hands
of the Regent, the Duke of Orleans.   The Parliament
attempted to assert some power, but was speedily and
roughly crushed, and the Duke was, for all practical
purposes, an absolute ruler.   His court became so
hopelessly corrupt that the satirists of the time could
only find fitting parallels in the worst scenes of the
Roman Empire.   The Regent himself indulged in the
grossest debaucheries ; and the day after some of his
saturnalia, in which the very footmen joined, he was
incapable for hours of attending to any serious
business.   One of his mistresses was moved to say
that God had made man's body out of clay, and with
some mud left over, the souls of princes and lacqueys.

Yet even in the muddy soul of the Regent some
grains of pride and honour were left, and he refused
to assent to a complete national bankruptcy.   A
Commission was appointed to examine critically the

obligations of the late king, and to divide them into classes. In the end the national debt was reduced by about one-half, on which interest of 4 per cent was promised. In order to raise funds for present expenses, however, the coinage was again suddenly reduced in real value, in spite of the warnings of experience. The coins which the late king had brought up to their old level were called in and restamped with the new child-king's effigy, and nearly 30 per cent abstracted. It is needless to say that the people, at least the money-dealers, exported their full-weight coins to Holland and other places where they could get them recoined at a cheaper rate.

Such was the state of France when John Law came to Paris to renew his acquaintance with the Regent, who was of course prepared to regard with favour any project that seemed likely to yield money. Law had only to persuade this one man of the probable success of his schemes to ensure full scope for their development, and he lost no time in commencing his work.

In the first act of this great national drama, the principal characters appear in the most favourable light. John Law gives the Regent elementary lessons in banking, and points to the great success of the banks which had already been established in the most flourishing cities of Europe. The Regent learns with a will, and approves of the project for a great national bank; but new to banking and despotism, he takes advice from his counsellors, who, being for the most part of the Polonius order, naturally advise against the scheme.

After much discussion, however, Law was at last

allowed to establish a private bank at his own risk—
the letters patent being dated 2nd May 1716; and
having first, at the humble request of the Parliament,
been naturalised, he commenced operations about June.

The bank was established and conducted on the
soundest principles, and its services soon began to be
appreciated, and John Law proved that bank-notes
representing a fixed amount of gold are far better than
coins, the value of which is being constantly changed
by the Government. His notes were promises to pay
so many crowns (*écus de banque*) of the value of the
day on which they were issued; and thus they always
represented the same amount of fine silver, whatever
change was made in the coins. So far, indeed, he
simply carried out a system of banking which had been
practised with success in Amsterdam for a century, and
in other places for shorter periods. It was allowed on
all sides that the bank was a great success. " If," says
Thiers, "Law had confined himself to this establishment,
he would be considered one of the benefactors of the
country, and the creator of a superb system of credit."

We are so familiar with banks, and so unfamiliar
with the evils of a fluctuating coinage, that we are apt
to underrate this great improvement effected by Law.
The success of the bank, however, was so great, that
it gradually became in reality a national or royal bank.
The collectors of taxes were ordered to make their
remittances in its notes, and these notes, like those of
Amsterdam, bore a premium. The formal conversion,
however, of Law's private bank into a royal bank took
place in December 1718, and was marked by a change
of vital importance.

The notes issued were now simply promises to pay so many current coins (*livres tournois*), and were thus subject to change in real value with every fluctuation in the coin. At the same time, the first step was taken towards making the notes really inconvertible—for all payments above a certain amount were to be made either in gold or notes, not silver; and as there was very little gold in the country, this practically amounted to a forced circulation of the notes.

Law was so much impressed with the superiority of paper money, that he apparently thought that to compel people to use it by a little pressure was only to promote their own interests against their will; but he overlooked the fact that the essence of all credit is the voluntary action of the contracting parties.

So long as the notes were freely taken as convenient substitutes for metal, they were of advantage to the country; but when they obtained a preference in payments, simply by force of law, the way was open for great abuses.

In the meantime, however, John Law had begun to apply the other leading ideas which he had in vain tried to induce Scotland to put in practice—namely, to promote the national industry by measures of a wide-reaching character.

At that time, in nearly every country in Europe the principal part of the maritime commerce was in the hands of privileged companies. Thus the English East India Company had for more than a century been extending its branches and preparing the way for the ultimate creation of an Indian empire. Holland, also, had a similar company in the same region; and no doubt John Law not only appreciated fully the success already achieved, but anticipated still greater success in the future. The French, too, under Richelieu had started companies for the development of certain portions of America; and their West India Company was intended as the counterpart of the Dutch and English East India Companies. The partial colonisation of Canada by the French took place in this manner. But the French companies seemed to possess no vitality; and when John Law turned his attention to the development of the foreign trade of France, they were all dead or dying.

He did not think the principle wrong, but ascribed the failure to a bad selection of country and bad methods of administration. About the time of Law's birth two Frenchmen, penetrating the wilds from the Canadian possessions of France, had discovered and explored a large part of the basin of the Mississippi, and had in the name of Louis XIV. taken possession of the vast tracts which were afterwards to form some of the most fertile and wealthy of the United States. The whole region had been christened Louisiana, in honour of the king; a few forts had been erected, but beyond this nothing had been done for the development of the country.

It occurred to Law that with sufficient capital and vigorous management on a large scale, this territory might be made to rival or excel the East India of England; and accordingly, in 1717, he promoted the Company of the West—which was the beginning of the famous Mississippi Scheme. The privileges granted

to the new Company were of the most unlimited kind
—and, in fact, it was entrusted with sovereign power
over the whole territory.

It is important to observe that this Mississippi
Scheme was no more a fraudulent projector's bubble
than was the English East India Company; and an
impartial observer at the time might well have thought
that France had a better chance of establishing
magnificent colonies in the fertile and almost unoccupied lands of America, than Britain of bringing under
her sway the millions of India who had already made
great advances in war and civilisation. John Law
was, as events abundantly proved, perfectly right in
supposing that the Mississippi basin was capable of
extraordinary commercial and industrial development;
but he failed to observe that, for success, both a very
large capital and a considerable length of time were
necessary. He was a man of excellent theories, but,
probably owing to his gambling habits, he was apt to
underrate all practical difficulties.

It is true that the capital nominally created was
for the time very large, but the real value obtained
by the Company was far too small. The Company
did not obtain its privileges for nothing—in fact, the
subscriptions for its shares were mainly used for
reducing the national debt and providing for the
immediate extravagance of the Regency. The Company only received the interest—the capital was lent
to the Government. Had John Law been free to act
according to his own judgment—had he not been
compelled to purchase every privilege at an extravagant
price, and to consult a despotic ruler whose natural

abilities had been ruined by excesses, and whose court
was a whirlpool of extravagance,—he might have
relieved France from her burdens and given her new
life by providing freedom for expansion. But the
Regent's insatiable extravagance, and Law's boundless
confidence, from the first made success more than
doubtful, and a new force was soon to come into play
which rendered failure inevitable. This was the most
unbridled frenzy of speculation which the world has
ever witnessed.

It would be hopeless to attempt to condense into
a few sentences the details of the development of
John Law's extensive schemes. Suffice it to say, that
in less than two years from the establishment of the
Company of the West, he had merged it in a new
company, styled the Company of the Indies, the
powers and privileges of which must have surpassed
his most extravagant dreams.

This Company was primarily a commercial company
which absorbed all the old companies, and thus
practically monopolised the whole of the trade of
France with new countries. But step by step it
acquired new privileges and assumed new functions.
Most of the important taxes in France were levied
by a pernicious system of "farming." The privilege
of collection was sold for a lump sum, just as till lately
in this country was the case with the tolls. The
Company of the West had already acquired the
monopoly of tobacco; and the new Company of the
Indies, created in May 1719, had obtained in a few
months the management of all the taxes levied under
the farming system.

9

For this privilege Law undertook a great and novel scheme for the conversion of the whole national debt. He proposed to lend the Government at 3 per cent sufficient money to pay off all the old creditors, which, as the debt was paying 4 per cent, would really relieve the Government of a fourth of the burden. If successful, the operation would thus be a gain to the country as a whole; and, as Law said, although the creditors of the State (*rentiers*) did not like it, the principal part of the State is composed of workmen and merchants in towns, and peasants and labourers in the country, who are the real source of its wealth. At the same time, however, he did not propose to make the conversion compulsory, but to offer sufficient inducement to the owners of *rentes* to accept the capital sum due. This inducement was the privilege of buying shares in the new company; and how great this attraction was will soon be made apparent. Thus in effect the operation consisted in the Company buying up the whole national debt with a great issue of shares. This vast operation was in a fair way of completion before the end of 1719, when John Law attained the height of his power. He had now only to assume the title and office of Comptroller-General to be in name, as in reality, the Prime Minister of France.

A strong light is thrown on the morality of the times by a preliminary step which was necessary.

To start his bank, the foundation of his system, Law had to become a naturalised French citizen; and to become Comptroller-General—to place the last ornament on the summit of the edifice—he was obliged to become a Catholic. The task of conversion was committed to the Abbé Tençin, the peculiar infamy of whose character was sufficient, even in such an age, to arouse popular detestation, and to give an entirely commercial complexion to Law's change of faith. The conversion, such as it was, was rapidly completed, and the Abbé received for payment shares to the nominal value of about £10,000.

The system of Law, during the few months in which it dazzled the world, was a strange mixture of prudence and recklessness, of the soundest finance and the wildest gambling, of favourite theories abandoned and forgotten, and of others carried to impossible extremes.

The good intentions of the system may be noted first, as in the nature of things they have been more readily forgotten than the evil effects.

First of all, then, the burden of taxation was lessened. Under Law's organisation the people paid far less, and yet the State received far more. Not only was the national debt consolidated, and the rate of interest greatly reduced, but a multitude of imposts and monopolies which had strangled commerce were annulled, and legitimate trade began to flourish. He regarded his system simply as providing and ensuring the fundamental principles of industrial organisation as the natural duty of an orderly government; but apart from this, he may be regarded as a thoroughly practical exponent of the principles of Free Trade and natural liberty. He considered the interests of the common people as of primary importance. For example, when the butchers of Paris, for plausible but fictitious reasons, raised the price of meat, Law told them plainly that if they could not distribute meat at a fair price he would soon find others who could. As an experiment, he bought two oxen, and after a careful calculation of all the expenses, and allowing for profits, he found he could sell for nearly half the price charged by the butchers, and thus compelled them to lower their prices.

He did his best to develop the internal commerce of France. His bank advanced to manufacturers immense sums at 2 per cent; a great number of people imprisoned for debt were liberated; money unjustly confiscated by the tribunals was restored; and the artisans who had been driven from France in the time of her distresses were recalled, the State paying their passage. Throughout France many vast improvements were commenced—roads, canals, bridges, and useful and magnificent buildings were the first-fruits of the new system. Under the genius of the Comptroller-General, industrial France vibrated again with new life, like the earth at the approach of spring.

Not content merely with the development of the commerce of the towns, he turned his attention to the country. He relieved the peasants from their most oppressive taxes; he tried to break up the large estates held in mortmain by corporations; he established a sound system of poor relief for the impoverished peasantry; and bought up and extinguished all kinds of unjust and prejudicial monopolies which had sprung up through the sale by Louis XIV. of fragments of his sovereign rights. Unfortunately for France, most of these reforms were nipped in the bud, so that we must judge of their value rather from the intention than the deed. But on the whole, the industrial reforms which John Law attempted in his short term of office and power may be fairly compared with the reforms effected in this country during the present century by a series of great statesmen, who have worked on the same lines in the simplification of taxation, the abolition of monopolies, and the extension of the freedom of industry.

The system of John Law, viewed merely as a system of finance and industrial organisation, was a work of genius ; and had it not been vitiated by the growth of a malignant principle, opposed to its very essence, it would have conferred upon his adopted country inestimable benefits.

But in order to obtain funds for the completion of his schemes, Law had always viewed with favour, and even encouraged, a rise in the value of the shares already issued. He thus called up a spirit of evil which, like the genius of an Eastern tale, placed at his disposal endless wealth, only to make it disappear still more suddenly.

This demon of speculation, at first the slave of John Law's system, soon became its master and destroyer.

Without entering into details, it is easy to see the progress of the enchantment. A trading company was started, with very fair prospects, by a man who had already proved himself an excellent banker, and who had obtained the confidence of the despotic ruler of the country. In spite of its advantages, however, its shares were for nearly two years below par. Gradually other schemes were amalgamated with the original plan (*e.g.* the farm of the tobacco duties), and these schemes found more favour.   But the new shares (*les filles*) were only issued to those who already held old shares (*les mères*), and consequently the demand for the new shares raised the value of the old in a way that is perfectly familiar to the present race of directors and shareholders.   The magnitude which the Company of the Indies attained, on the completion of its privileges, may be judged from the fact that its actual profits were, at the end of 1719, estimated at more than four million pounds sterling per annum.   It is easy to imagine how the gradual issue of shares corresponding to such a vast real revenue would, in the nature of things, encourage speculation. The most ignorant and blind could observe the rapid rise in the value of the old shares, and could see how, merely by the sale of documents, enormous fortunes were made in a few weeks.

Consequently, on a new issue, a rush was made to subscribe, and when the speculation had reached its height, the dividend fixed a few months before was not sufficient to pay $\frac{1}{2}$ per cent on the market value of the shares.

Shares of the nominal value of 500 livres had been issued at 1500, and through speculation had been raised to 12,000 livres in December 1719.   Consequently, the dividend fixed before at 12 per cent on the original share value, would really pay on the 12,000 only $\frac{1}{2}$ per cent.   But every one, in these days, knows that this is a position of extremely unstable equilibrium, and that if the interest does not rise, the value of the shares must fall.

Had Law acted with prudence, instead of with ex-

cessive hopefulness, he would have allowed the shares
to have fallen in the ordinary course of things, and
only have used his influence to prevent the fall being
too rapid. But his system was not yet complete, the
conversion of the debt was only partially accomplished,
and apparently he was afraid that a rapid fall in the
value of the shares would injure the wider prospects
of the Company.

Accordingly he set himself, during the early part
of 1720, to bolster up the shares. He declared that
the Company would pay a dividend of 40 per cent instead of 12. Yet with the shares of 500 livres at
12,000, even this dividend, which was the utmost
that could possibly be paid in the most sanguine estimate, only yielded less than 2 per cent, and a heavy
fall was certain to take place.

In most cases a speculation involving millions
would be checked, owing to the impossibility of finding coin or credit for further extension ; but the Company of the Indies was, from the first, under the same
guidance as the Royal Bank—Law was the moving
spirit of both, and the bank had the power of issuing
unlimited quantities of notes. Then, again, through
its control of the Mint and the coinage, which it had
acquired soon after its foundation, the Company had
the power of giving a preference to the notes by
arbitrary changes in the coins. John Law had truly
remarked that notes were better than a fluctuating
currency ; but it was carrying the doctrine to a
dangerous and immoral extreme, to make the currency
fluctuate in order to stimulate the demand for notes.

Yet in his anxiety to keep up the use and credit

of the notes he resorted to this expedient, and deliberately made rapid changes in the value of the coin, at the same time proclaiming that no change would be made in the nominal value of the notes. By inducing people to believe that gold and silver would be mabe to pass for less than the corresponding notes, in a few days large sums were drawn to the bank.

Imagine what a run there would be for £1 notes if it were announced that after next Monday a sovereign would, in the payment of debts, be considered only as fifteen shillings, whilst before that date the banks would give a note for every sovereign, the note to be always worth, for the payment of debts, the full pound !

Practically, by these measures, notes became the real standard, and very little more was required to make them inconvertible. But Law not only tried to attract specie to the bank by this unworthy device, but he used his political power, no less than his financial authority, and, in contradiction to all his own better principles, absolutely prohibited the use of gold and silver as money, or even the possession of it beyond a certain limited amount. Finally, in the belief that the Company was stronger than the bank under these conditions, he endeavoured to support his notes by joining the two institutions. The creation of notes, in spite of promises to the contrary, went on in alarming quantities. Even at the end of 1719 it was found necessary to simply print the notes without signature by hand, as was at first the case, and the printing-presses were worked day and night.

It was therefore this power of the creation of

money to an unlimited extent which enabled the
speculation to attain a height that would otherwise
have been impossible.   Every one tried to obtain notes
to buy shares, in order simply to sell and pocket the
difference.   No one knew what the real value of the
shares ought to be, and at first even the most prudent
and cautious were enticed by the rapidity of the rise.

Yet even in yielding to these imprudent excesses,
John Law probably acted in good faith, although with
great imprudence.   His confidence in the ultimate
success of his vast schemes was boundless.   The
commercial and financial business of the Company and
the Bank was indeed so enormous, that exaggeration
of the value of the shares was natural, if not pardon-
able.   Again, the constant issues of notes, and the advances made by the bank for all kinds of purposes,
had lessened the rate of interest, and of course every
fall in the rate of interest caused a corresponding rise
in the nominal value of the capital.   There was also
plausibility in the notion that his notes could not be
issued in excess if they simply took the place of the coin,
and if they were issued to meet a corresponding demand.   The national debt was, for example, intended
to be bought up with notes, and the receivers of the
notes were expected to use them to take shares in the
new company; and thus it may be said there was a
demand for the notes.

And in justice to Law, it must be remembered
that he had to make decisions on the spur of the
moment, on questions of credit and finance, which
even now are not thoroughly settled.   The directors of
the Bank of England, during the suspension of cash

payments at the beginning of this century, acted on Law's idea that notes could not be depreciated if they were always issued against a genuine demand. Again, the Government of France, during the great Revolution, based the issues of their *assignats* on a gross exaggeration of the principle which John Law had proposed as the basis of his land bank. Surely no better proof could be given of the plausibility of the banking part of the system than this exaggerated imitation by the very country which professed to hold the author up to detestation as an impostor.

And as regards the wider aspects of the system and its ambitious projects for the development of industry, history has shown that Law discovered, with wonderful foresight, the way in which, in the modern world, credit would become the life-breath of industry.

The great mistake which he made was the attempt to force the growth of generations into months with the vapour and heat of speculation. He admitted as much after his fall, when he wrote: "If I had the work to do again, I would go more slowly but more surely, and I would not expose the State to the dangers which must accompany the derangement of an old-established system."

When we reflect on the unparalleled excitement of those few months—on the sudden elevation of a foreigner and unknown commoner to the highest power and dignity of a great nation—on the opening to an enthusiastic theorist of an unlimited field for the conversion of his ideas into facts—on the gross adulation bestowed by all the aristocracy of Europe on a man already familiar, in a humbler capacity, with the pleasures of fashion and society,—the wonder is, not that John Law made mistakes, but that he kept his reason sufficiently to make any application of his principles. And yet, had it not been for the fierce frenzy of speculation that burst out in Paris, it is not improbable that, in spite of his errors, he would have succeeded in placing his system on a sound basis. Thoroughly to understand the causes of his failure, we must attempt to realise the nature and extent of this national madness.

Milliards and millions, especially when expressed in an unfamiliar currency, only create a vague sense of wonder; and it would be of little use to quote the swollen values of the shares and notes as estimated in French livres. A few concrete facts will probably give a better idea than a mere aggregate of inconceivable figures.

A milliner happened to come to Paris about a lawsuit; she was successful, and invested the proceeds in speculation, and she amassed in a few months a sum which, converted into our currency, represents nearly £5,000,000 sterling. Amongst other millionaires, we have coachmen, cooks, and waiters, as well as representatives of all the nobility of Europe. We are told that, in the closing weeks of 1719, more than 35,000 strangers flocked to Paris to take part in the speculation,—that all the means of transport from the other large cities were exhausted,—and that in Marseilles and other places there was a lively speculation for seats in the coaches. No class of the community escaped the infection. Two of the ablest scholars of France are reported to have deplored the madness of the times at one interview, only to find themselves at their next meeting bidding for shares with the greatest excitement. The scene of operations was a narrow street called Quincampoix, and the demand for accommodation may be judged of from the fact that a house which before yielded about £40 a-year, now brought in more than £800 a-month. A cobbler made about £10 a-day by letting out a few chairs in his stall; and a hunchback, who is celebrated in the prints of the time, acquired in a few days more than £7000 sterling by letting out his hump to the street-brokers as a writing-desk.

In every social circle throughout the city the only conversation was on the rise and fall of *actions* (shares). A doctor is said to have nearly frightened a lady to death by muttering to himself, as he felt her pulse, "Alas! good God! it falls, it falls," alluding, of course, to the price of his stock.

The central figure in these scenes of excitement was John Law, who held levees which were more crowded by distinguished guests than any Court in Europe. Extraordinary devices were resorted to, even to see or hear the famous man. One lady ordered her coachman to upset her carriage on Law's approach, that he might rescue her from the wreckage; whilst another shrieked beneath his window during a dinner-party that the house was on fire.

Nor was the power and influence of Law only celebrated amongst the Parisians. His native city of Edinburgh, proud of having produced so great a man, transmitted to him the freedom thereof, in a gold box of the value of £300 sterling, the diploma being dated 5th August 1719.

But the most remarkable proof of Law's influence is shown by the recall of Lord Stair, the British Ambassador at Paris. This nobleman, apparently with the utmost good faith, had warned his Government that Law was a dangerous enemy; but the only result was that he himself was recalled. He was replaced by Earl Stanhope, and writing to a friend some time after, Lord Stair said: "I shall readily agree with you that if his Lordship (*i.e.* the new ambassador) has gained Mr Law and made him lay aside his ill-will and ill designs against this country, he did very right to make all sorts of advances to him—to promise his son a regiment; to engage to bring Lord Banbury (his brother-in-law) into the House of Lords; and to sacrifice the king's ambassador to him. *If I had thought Mr Law to be gained, I should very readily have advised to do all these things, and a great deal more.*"

We find also from this and other correspondence that Law was regarded as the real Prime Minister of France; and good authorities state that at the time his power was greater than that of the great Richelieu a century before.

A terrible example of his imperious determination is recorded. Robbery, accompanied by violence, and even by murder, had become frequent during this delirium of money-getting. A young Flemish nobleman, Count Horn, who, though only twenty-two years of age, had plunged into the worst excesses, planned and carried out with two associates the murder of a rich stock-jobber. They were taken red-handed. Count Horn was connected with the noblest families in Europe; he was allied to several sovereign houses;

he was even related to the Duke of Orleans himself. The strongest pressure was used to prevent his execution, but John Law was determined to make a striking example ; and according to the letter of the sentence the unfortunate man was broken on the wheel. We ought to blame the cruelty of the law, not of its administrator ; for had the criminal not been a nobleman, not a voice would have been raised against the execution.

Another example of Law's power is worth quoting, because it shows that he made every effort to render his Mississippi Scheme a commercial success. He scattered press-gangs through France, with instructions to seize and ship to America all who could not prove they were earning an honest living. The intention was no doubt good, for France was crowded with paupers, and the new colony only needed hands. But in the end the refuse of the streets and prisons was exported, to the disgust of the earliest colonists ; whilst a shock of horror passed through France on the discovery that several young men and women of good family and honourable life had been seized for the plantations, that the abductors might get their reward.

But in both respects Law's agents alone were to blame. He himself arranged, in the most careful manner, although, of course, the worst side of French raillery was stirred by it, for the emigration of some young women brought up in charitable institutions ; and many of them in the sequel were honourably married, and became the founders of some of the best families in New Orleans, which was one of the few tangible remnants of the system.

But Law's power, great as it undoubtedly was, was destined to be short-lived, and the catastrophe was in keeping with the rest of the drama. The dangers of the outrageous speculation, and of the excessive issues of notes, had already been foreseen by the more prudent speculators in the early part of 1720, and cautiously and silently they began to convert their paper into gold and silver or other forms of real wealth. At first Law tried to counteract these sinister influences, but he soon became convinced that a heavy fall was inevitable, and that his whole system was threatened. The great mass of people, however, had no more idea of the collapse of the system than the inhabitants of Pompeii of the eruption of Vesuvius. Thus the edict of the 21st of May 1720 caused sudden and universal consternation. Its professed object was to reduce the nominal value of the shares and notes to what was supposed to be their fair commercial value, but the result was—not to restore reason, but to hopelessly shatter confidence.

The essence of the edict was, that by gradual stages, but in a very short time, both shares and notes were to be reduced to about half the nominal value at which they stood when the decree was issued. The natural question people asked was—If the paper is forced down one half by the edict of to-day, how much will it be worth after the edict of to-morrow ? Thus a panic ensued, from which the system never recovered. " On the day following the edict," says Sir James Steuart, " any one might have starved with 100 millions of paper in his pocket. "

There can be no reasonable doubt that John Law himself was responsible for this fatal edict, although attempts have been made to ascribe it to his enemies. It has been said that he would have foreseen the result, and would never have consented willingly to the ruin of his plans. But the most striking characteristic of his genius was the bold way in which, regardless of time, place, or circumstance, he applied his theories to practice. And some time before he had certainly become fully aware of the necessity of reducing the inflation. Early in March he had caused a decree to be issued to suppress speculative bargains; and a little later the street where the gamblers were wont to congregate was closed, and all dealings in paper prohibited except directly with the Bank or the Company. But laws and decrees were powerless over the popular delirium, and the speculation went on as keenly as ever in new quarters.

Again he had made vain attempts to reduce the issues of notes, and place them on a more sure foundation. This, indeed, was the primary object of the union of the Bank with the Company. The excessive issues had in the natural course of things caused a general rise of prices, the poor began to suffer severely, and some remedy was urgently needed. In some parts of France the notes had already been refused.

Thus the decree of the 21st of May was a desperate attempt to avert the threatened catastrophe when milder measures had failed. And nothing is more natural than that John Law should have seen that his magnificent system was endangered by the fury of speculation, and that, in the height of his power, he should have relied on his own strength to govern the fall, as he had apparently governed the rise. The best proof, however, that he really suggested the decree is, that in spite of the immediately disastrous consequences, he strenuously opposed its withdrawal; and the actual circumstances of its promulgation, as well as the peculiar style of the preamble, confirm this view. In a few days, however, the edict was annulled; but it had already done its work, and notes and shares fell of their own accord more rapidly than had been ordained by compulsion.

There is a popular impression that the whole system collapsed immediately after this official recognition of the necessity of checking the inflation; and Sir James Steuart even writes as if John Law was at once banished from France.

As a matter of fact, however, he remained in Paris more than six months, striving with the utmost coolness and pertinacity to regain the field, or at least to convert the rout into an orderly retreat. He tried every expedient to restore the credit of the Bank, and to promote the commercial prosperity of the Company. However much we may condemn the man for his criminal imprudence in leading astray a whole people, it is impossible not to admire the courageous honesty with which he laboured, under the most depressing circumstances, to restore the really sound part of his system, by getting rid of the abuses.

Unfortunately, just at the time when firm resolute guidance was necessary to avert the worst consequences of the crisis, his authority was broken. A few days after the fatal decree, he was deprived of his office of Comptroller-General, and for two days he was actually placed under arrest.

The influence, however, of his friends restored the

original confidence of the Regent in his ability, and he was allowed to devise new schemes. "These ingenious combinations," says Levasseur, "prove that in the midst of his peril Law preserved all his presence of mind, and that his genius, fruitful in resources, was not yet exhausted."

The interest of the drama, however, at this point consists not in following the stages of the hopeless retreat, but in observing the consequences of the collapse on the French people, and the character of John Law when struggling with adversity.

As regards the effects on the nation, they were such as almost to alienate all sympathy from the man. If the blow had only fallen on the Mississippians, and had taken away their ill-gotten gains, the people at large might even have rejoiced, for large as was the number of speculators, they did not embrace the great mass of the real workers of the country.

But the actual currency of the country consisted entirely of these discredited notes, and thus the discredit, like a pestilence, affected the good and evil alike. The bank had very little real reserve; but to relieve the popular distress, attempts were made to redeem the smaller notes.

A few weeks before, the streets were crowded with throngs of people eager to obtain new issues of shares and indulge in the wildest speculation. Money was abundant, and the consumption of wealth most extravagant.

Now the approaches to the bank were packed with people driven by hunger and misery to try to exchange their bits of paper, often the reward of hard work, for money with which they might obtain the means of life. Day after day, and night after night, for months, they waited for the chance of making the exchange, and were only kept in order by military force. When the doors of the bank were opened, the pressure was often so great that men and women were crushed to death.

On one occasion, on a hot dark night in July, about 15,000 people were wedged in the narrow streets about the bank, trying to get to the front, like drowning men to the shore, and filling the air with tumultuous cries and savage imprecations. When day broke, it was found that fifteen persons had been crushed to death and trampled upon. As the news spread, the crowd was silenced with horror; then, after hasty indignant consultations, some rushed to the palace of the Regent, whilst a large body carried the corpse of a woman to place before the windows of the young king, and urged him, with furious threats, to hang both Law and the Regent.

This scene, dreadful as it is, perhaps hardly strikes the imagination with such horror as the discovery, in the middle of December, of a house in which the husband had killed his wife and children and hanged himself through destitution, whilst in the very room was found, with two or three halfpence, 200,000 livres of bank-notes, which at one time would have been worth £10,000 sterling.

Yet in the midst of these appalling scenes the courage of John Law no more faltered than that of

Napoleon on the retreat from Moscow. The miserable besotted Regent, when the crowd tried to burst open his palace gates on that famous July morning, at first implored his servants to say that he was not there; and when the military had been smuggled in in disguise, he appeared, white as a sheet, and " did not know what he asked for."

Very different was the conduct of John Law. As soon as he heard of the tumult, he hurried to the palace: he was recognised, his carriage was surrounded, and he was at once assailed with fierce threats. A woman shook her fist at him and cried: " If there were only two or three more like me, you would be torn to pieces."

It seems marvellous, when we remember what a Parisian mob is capable of, that Law escaped, and he certainly did so only by his courage. He leaped through the door of his carriage, and in a tone of contempt thundered, " Vous êtes des canailles!" and the mob, always respectful to audacity, allowed the carriage to pass.

It is worth recording that when it came out, and the coachman tried to use his master's authority, the carriage was at once smashed, and the man only escaped with his life.

Again, on the 15th December 1720, when Law knew that the Regent had been pressed to assent to his arrest, and that his very life was in danger, he calmly went to the opera, affected the utmost security, and treated with contemptuous silence the hisses and threats of the people. And during all these months, from June to December, in spite of the machinations of his

enemies, the vacillating imbecility of the Regent, and
the hatred of the people, he laboured night and day to
restore confidence and prosperity.

If the educated mind is now growing too peaceful
to profess to admire personal courage, there is another
side of Law's character shining out with pleasing lustre
at the close of his romantic career, which can hardly
fail to command respect. "Virtue!" said Dirk
Hatteraick, when upbraided by the sheriff,—"Donner !
I was always faithful to my ship-owners—always
accounted for cargo to the last stiver." And those
who most condemn John Law must allow him a large
share of this kind of virtue. In the midst of his power
he accumulated far less wealth than hundreds of
ordinary speculators, and he did not invest one farthing
of it beyond the frontiers of France. He entered Paris
with £100,000 sterling, and he left the whole of it
there. He refused even to accept money on retiring
from France.

Whatever his faults and failings, he believed in
his system, and staked his whole life and fortune
upon it; and as in ability so also in virtue, he would
serve as an example to many directors of the present
day.

He did not long survive his fall. He obtained his
full pardon from the English Government for the
technical crime for which he had first fled the country,
and an interesting debate took place in the House of
Lords because an admiral had taken upon himself to
bring over the celebrated financier in a man-of-war, as
if he were still a person of great importance.

The last we hear of him is from Montesquieu, who

found him at Venice, shortly before his death, still involved in all kinds of schemes and projects,—the same man as of old.

His remains rest in the Church of St. Moses, where they were placed in 1808 by the dutiful affection of a descendant, who was a celebrated soldier and a marshal of France.

As the judgment, implied rather than expressed, in my account of John Law, may seem to some too favourable, I will quote, in conclusion, the opinion of Levasseur, who has exhausted research for material, and has shown in the treatment of his subject the utmost impartiality, and who is besides a native of that country which Law is supposed to have ruined for his own purposes.

" If John Law," he writes, as the closing sentence of his work, " was too absolute in his ideas, and too violent in his means, he was at any rate animated by the desire of doing good, steadfast in the principles which he believed to be true, and honest in his conduct : his system rested on a false principle, which was, however, only the exaggeration of a truth. By cleaving to this principle Law perished, but he made valuable contributions to economic theory, and would have rendered great services to commerce if a more prudent reserve had kept him within more narrow limits. "

I shall not attempt to add to this judgment, nor to point the many morals which spring up from all parts of the narrative. I shall be well satisfied if I have brushed away some of the dust of oblivion and the mire of calumny from the name of a man who, in power and determination and sheer ability, was one of the strongest men Scotland has produced, and who crowded into two or three years of his life a series of events which find no parallel out of the tales of Eastern imagination.

ONE-POUND NOTES

*READ BEFORE THE BRITISH ASSOCIATION AT
BIRMINGHAM, SEPTEMBER 1886*

To discuss profitably within the limits assigned to this
paper the advantages and disadvantages of a system of
£1 notes, it is absolutely necessary to make the question
as definite and precise as possible. For there is
scarcely any argument usually advanced on either side
which, if examined critically in all its aspects, may
not lead to disputes on the fundamental principles of
banking, credit, currency, and even the proper functions
of government. It is, however, much more easy to
point out in general terms the necessity of limiting the
field of inquiry than to put a ring-fence round a
definite space; and in attempting this operation I am
quite aware, from the difficulty I have experienced
myself, that the limitation I have assigned as best may
not appear reasonable to others interested in the
question. The temptation is certainly great to take
up, first of all, the general principles of the regulation
of a convertible paper currency, and to apply these
principles to the special case of £1 notes; but in this
way I am afraid that the sermon would be so long

that we should never arrive at the practical application.

It is, however, primarily as a practical problem in our England of to-day that I would consider the subject, and in currency, as in other matters, for a long time to come, we must recognise that the actual will fall short of the ideal, and the less revolutionary any change proposed, the more likelihood there is of its being carried. We can only take thought for the morrow in so far as to choose, of possible paths, that which seems to lead in the direction of our ideal, or at any rate does not lead us backwards.

Briefly stated, then, the problem which I wish to attack is this : What would be the effect of introducing, with as little disturbance as possible, into our present system of currency £1 notes ?

It follows at once, from this limitation of the inquiry, that many topics often discussed under the title of this paper must be excluded. For example, the wisdom of the principles and the benefits derived from the operation of the Bank Act of 1844 have been questioned, and the repeal of the Act, or at least great reforms in the direction of freedom of issues, have been advocated, and, *inter alia*, it has been proposed that the issue of £1 notes should be left entirely to the discretion of individual competing banks.

For the present, however, these large reforms must be left on one side, and the attention must be confined to the effects which might be expected to follow if that Act were amended in the comparatively small particular of the alteration of the minimum denomination of bank-notes issued under the Act, from £5 to £1. A change of this nature would leave the general principles of the Act unaffected. Briefly stated, the principal provisions are as follows :—

A certain amount of notes, at present about £16,000,000, may be issued by the Bank of England against Government securities, and for any issues beyond that amount there must be gold (for the possible use of a certain amount of silver may be left out of consideration) in the issue department. The issue department is thus practically purely automatic. The banking department cannot, within the terms of the Act, even in the case of a foreign drain which threatens to exhaust its resources, make use of this gold except so far as it can offer in exchange notes to that amount held by it as a banking reserve. The reserve stored to secure the convertibility of the notes issued is absolutely independent. Accordingly, when we take into account the fact that the profits on the issues of the greater part of the £16,000,000 of notes not issued against gold are appropriated by Government, whilst the profits on the remainder are supposed to be equivalent to the expenses of management, it will be seen that as a banking institution, compared with other banks which do not issue notes, the Bank of England has no peculiar advantages. The country banks which had the right of issue at the time of the passing of the Act, retained that right only in so far that the maximum of their issues was, for the future, never to exceed the average of a certain time before the passing of the Act. They did not acquire the right, which was in the corresponding Act of 1845 for Scotland, of increasing their issues beyond this amount.

even against gold held by them. Accordingly, the issue of bank-notes in England, beyond a certain amount absolutely fixed, depends entirely on the amount of gold brought to the issue department to be exchanged against notes.

It follows, then, according to the main principle of the Act, with the exception noted, that in England bank-notes are not regarded as a form of banker's credit, but simply and solely as a convenient kind of currency. Any one who prefers it can carry about with him, instead of five or fifty sovereigns, a £5 or £50 note, and these notes will be equally legal tender. But, on the other hand, a person who prefers a £1 note to a sovereign, or four such notes to four sovereigns, whilst he would have the option in Ireland and Scotland, has no choice in England.

It may, I think, be fairly argued, from the experience of Scotland, that if the present banks of issue in England were entitled to issue £1 notes, these notes would very soon, to a considerable extent, replace sovereigns in the currency.

It must be remembered that the use of notes, which are really convertible, in preference to gold, must depend entirely on the convenience and inclinations of those who have the option ; and the people of Scotland being proverbially cautious and far-sighted in money matters, would certainly not make a general use of £1 notes unless in their opinion the advantages and conveniences were considerable.

I wish to avoid carefully any appearance of resting too much on the experience of Scotland, and I am quite willing to admit that the use of these small notes is partly due to the way in which, for a long period, they have been intimately connected with the credit system of the country, and to the interest of the banks in putting them into circulation. But, under present circumstances, the interest of the banks in increasing the circulation is by no means either of the degree or the precise kind that is imagined in England.

According to the Act of 1845, the banks are obliged to have gold against all notes in circulation above the authorised amount. This is about £2,750,000, whilst the actual issues are about £6,000,000, of which £4,000,000 are in £1 notes. On this excessive issue, then, there is no direct gain, but, considering the expense involved, a certain loss.

The gain to the bank consists, first and principally, in the power of over-issue, if necessary, which enables them to keep notes as till-money; and secondly, there is often some advantage owing to the fact that the gold held must be against the average monthly circulation; and in some cases notes may remain out but a very short time—*e.g.* on term-days notes may be issued in excess, but returned the same day. The power of over-issue (against gold) has certainly enabled the Scotch banks to establish branches when otherwise they could not have done so; but still the general proposition I have stated remains true—neither directly nor indirectly can the banks force their issue on the public. The conclusion, then, seems inevitable, that the use of these notes in preference to sovereigns is founded on real and solid advantages, and that if their use were permitted in England, they would in time, to a large extent, replace sovereigns. It must, however, be admitted that, in matters affecting currency, the maxim *quieta non movere* is always held to apply with much force. English people are familiar with sovereigns, and the bulk of the population, consisting of wage-earners, have never, unfortunately, use for notes of such a large amount as five pounds, and accordingly know nothing practically of bank-notes. At first, then, there might be a prejudice against £1 notes, and it is possible that, even if they were put into circulation, an unreasonable panic might occur which would cause indirectly, by the disturbance created, some loss. So that many authorities, as, for example, the late Mr. Bagehot, although acknowledging the advantages theoretically of £1 notes, speak doubtfully of the expediency of their practical adoption, and in effect they say we should leave well alone. Unfortunately, however, for this argument, the present state of the gold currency is far from well, and one of the strongest practical arguments in favour of £1 notes is the facilities their adoption would afford for the rehabilitation and maintenance of the gold currency.

There can be no doubt that something must be done to restore the gold coinage to its nominal value. No one disputed the urgency of the proposed reforms of Mr. Childers,—the only doubt expressed was on the method he advocated,—and there is no need to waste time in proving that matters cannot be allowed to go on as at present. The inevitable result would be that at no distant date the gold coins would cease to circulate at their nominal value, and we should be thrown back on all the uncertainties and inconveniences of a rudimentary currency by weight.

The principal difficulty to be overcome, if the present system is to continue, is one of expense, and although it is plausible to argue that the advantages of a sound currency are so great that the expense of restoration ought never to be considered by a wealthy country, that is not the way in which it strikes the Chancellor of the Exchequer. As the law stands at present, the person technically responsible for a light-weight gold coin is the holder of it, and in many cases the holders are large and wealthy banks, but in others they are people of the poorer sort, and both classes would appeal to the sense of justice.

The banks, by breaking the letter of the law, have spared the public, and no one would dream of practically taxing the poorer classes for the benefit of the community. If the sum necessary is to be raised from general taxation, the Chancellor of the Exchequer has to face additional expenditure with, it is to be feared, a declining revenue. He must also devise some method of a more efficient character than that adopted in the Coinage Act, which is at present supposed to be in force to secure the coinage for the future. It is not unnatural that in Scotland, at any rate, the plan which seems most plausible is the adoption by England of £1 notes. It would certainly be unfair to tax Scotland for the wear and tear of coins which it does not use, and Ireland has of late had a good deal of practice in formulating grievances, and would no doubt object to pay for restoring coins mainly worn down by England. If £1 notes become as popular in England as in the sister countries, for the future the wear and tear of coins would be greatly lessened, and there would be far greater facilities for withdrawing them when necessary from circulation. As regards the immediate expense of restoration, the adoption of £1 notes, with a slight alteration in the provisions of the Bank Act, would meet what was required, in a way which seems unobjectionable. Without going into details, a scheme on the following lines may be suggested.

In the first place, let the Government call in all the gold coins, and issue in their place notes promising to give gold in exchange on demand after a certain date, a sufficient time being allowed for the collection and restoration. At the same time it must be made clear that those who refuse to give up their gold will be made liable for any defect—in fact, that the existing, or some more efficient, law will be put in force.

This ought to be a sufficient inducement to make the calling in of the coins effective.

On the date fixed, those who wished could obtain gold for their £1 notes, and unless it were also thought advisable to keep in circulation the notes of ten shillings, they would be gradually cancelled. It is hardly conceivable that all the £1 notes would be offered for gold, and it might be assumed that from the beginning a considerable number would be retained in circulation. The Government could then quite fairly, and with full confidence, reckon on making up the expenses of the restoration from the gold corresponding to the notes which would remain permanently in circulation. The only change necessary in the Bank Act would be that the Bank of England would be allowed to issue notes to the value (suppose) of £20,000,000 instead of £16,200,000 as at present, without having corresponding gold in its vaults. It would be absurd to suppose that the convertibility of the note would not be absolutely secured. If it was safe in 1844 to assume that £15,000,000 of Bank of England notes would, in any case, remain in circulation, surely there can be no doubt, with the great increase in wealth, population, and security since that date, that a somewhat higher limit could now be reckoned on. And if the reasoning advanced above in reference to Scotland is sound, we may assume that every year a larger amount of £1 notes would be issued, and consequently the danger of a drain of gold become continually less and less. At present about £18,000,000 of Bank of England notes are issued against gold, and there is no reasonable doubt that that amount of gold would support, with perfect safety, a larger circulation of notes.

According to the scheme suggested, the whole of the gold obtained from circulation would be retained on security against the new notes ; but the gold would be reckoned as equivalent to its real and not to its nominal value, and besides this the expense of the restoration would have to be met.

There is no suggestion to make a financial gain to the Treasury. All that the proposal amounts to is the restoration of the currency to its full value by substituting notes for a part of it.

An alternative plan on practically the same lines would be for Government to issue £1 notes to the extent of the estimated loss of restoration, and call in the worn coins and substitute others directly. The advantage of the first scheme is that the mass of the people would become familiar, for a limited time, with the note issues.

It is necessary to notice, in conclusion, some of the principal arguments advanced against the adoption by England of £1 notes, even on the basis of the Bank Act of 1844 amended as proposed.

1. It is said that if the substitution of £1 notes for sovereigns were as thorough in England as it has been in Scotland, at least £50,000,000, and possibly more than £80,000,000, of gold, in addition to that already held, would be locked up in the issue department. This would offer, it is urged, an irresistible temptation to the Government at a time of expenditure and increasing burdens. If year after year such a mass of gold remains untouched, the feeling will arise that much less would answer the purpose quite as effectively. Then, the process of abstraction once begun, the reserve will soon pass from an absurdly large to a dangerously small amount. As a consequence, the money market will become extremely sensitive and trade will suffer. There would, under these circumstances, even be a possibility, it may be said, of a foreign drain, perhaps instituted for speculative purposes, exhausting gold at such a rate that the notes will become temporarily depreciated, or at any rate really inconvertible and liable to depreciation. And in support of this view it may be plausibly argued that Governments have generally shown themselves ready to take advantage of sinking funds and other reserves without much pressure; and that to borrow money with millions lying not only idle, but apparently useless, would at some time or other appear to some strong-minded Chancellor of the Exchequer the most puerile conservatism. It must be remembered also, in reference to the danger of a small reserve

11

and the chance of a foreign drain, that convertibility of notes is a very different thing from solvency of the issues. A strictly convertible note is convertible on demand—it is not a promise to pay, even with full interest on a liberal scale, at some future date. Every commercial crisis shows us the ruin of concerns which can ultimately pay twenty shillings in the pound, and in international payments the importance of bullion may become paramount.

I have tried to put the objections of this class as strongly as possible, because, strong as they are, I do not think they are insuperable. The practical question is : Should we, under the scheme proposed, be worse off in the matter of security than we are at present ? It is no doubt quite true that, so long as the people of England use gold as actual circulating medium, there is in appearance a great gold national reserve ; but under the existing law it is so in appearance only.

There is no method by which, if the banking department of the Bank of England were threatened by a foreign drain, it could obtain supplies from this source. On the contrary, a time of panic would be a time in which all history shows there would be a tendency to hoard gold.

I do not mean to assert that it is at all probable that gold would be hoarded in this country to any great extent. My point is this—that, under our present system, the ultimate banking reserve is the gold and notes (mainly notes) in the banking department : these notes can be exchanged for gold in the issue department, but the rest of the gold in the issue department, and *a fortiori* the gold in the hands of the public, are absolutely, so long as the Bank Act holds, unavailable for banking purposes. If in an emergency the Bank Act is suspended, that only enables the bank to issue more notes against its existing stock of gold; and if there were a persistent foreign drain, as soon as that stock was exhausted the notes would be inconvertible, and gold would rise to a premium. The bank could not obtain the gold from the actual circulation. Now, under the system proposed, if effectively carried out, the gold in the issue department would be increased by a large amount, and then a suspension of the Act would make the gold available in case of need. The whole strength of the opposing case rests on the assumption that the Bank Act would be broken without cause, and that insufficient reserves would be held against the note issues. But assuming that no further changes are made in the law than are suggested in this paper, and that the law is never suspended, except in extreme cases as formerly, the position of the Bank of England would be strengthened.

2. An objection may also be raised from the possibility of an internal drain arising at the same time as a foreign drain. But, in the first place, the experience of Scotland lends very small probability to this supposition. £1 notes are not of such a low denomination as to be held in large quantities by the mass of the people, who are quite unfamiliar with credit, and who might be liable to a sudden panic. And, secondly, if there were a corresponding reserve in the issue department, the convertibility of the notes would never be in danger. The foreign drain could only operate through the notes.

3. As regards the danger of forgery, it is a curious fact that in Scotland spurious sovereigns are more frequently met with than forged £1 notes, and the art of engraving notes has made much progress since England had £1 notes in circulation * (1826).

The limits of this paper will not allow me to notice the wider aspects of the question. I have supposed throughout, the minimum of change in our currency regulations. I will only say in conclusion that the change suggested is, in my opinion, so far a step towards a system more in harmony with the requirements of the country.

These more fundamental questions, however, it would be useless merely to mention cursorily at the conclusion of a paper written from a much lower standpoint.

I will repeat, that the question to which I think the discussion, if it is to be practical, must be at present confined is this : What would be the effect of the introduction of £1 notes without contravening the principles of the Act of 1844, which has since that date formed the basis of our currency ?

* It may be said that in Scotland the notes come back more rapidly to the bank issuing them than would be the case in England under the plan proposed ; but, on the other hand, the notes would be uniform, and this would assist the general public. Reissues of notes must be permitted on the ground of expense.

THE EFFECTS OF GREAT DISCOVERIES
OF THE PRECIOUS METALS

READ BEFORE THE
CHARTERED ACCOUNTANTS STUDENTS' SOCIETY
OF EDINBURGH, DECEMBER 1, 1886

MANY circumstances combine at the present time to
direct public attention to the subject on which I have
to address you this evening.   In the first place, there
is an idea generally prevalent that we are on the eve
of an enormous increase in the production of gold.
As to the soundness of this belief I am quite unable to
give an opinion, but I may perhaps remind you that,
just as a very small amount of gold in the vaults of
the Bank of England supports a gigantic system of
banking and credit, so a very tiny amount of gold
discovered in some new region seems able to support a
most extraordinary amount of speculation, hopefulness,
and credulity.   But of the interest aroused by these
reported new discoveries there can be no doubt, and I
hope some share of this interest may be directed to
the more general aspects of the question.

In the meantime, however, we are feeling the
effects of a contraction in the supply of gold relatively

to the demand made upon it, and one of the best
methods of obtaining an accurate view of these effects
is to study carefully the converse case. The key to
the present controversy on the connection between the
currency and the fall in prices is found in the dependence of prices on the quantity of standard metallic
money. Those who experience a difficulty in tracing
this great and general fall largely to currency causes,
may find that difficulty much lessened by considering
the way in which, at previous times, a rise in prices
has undoubtedly been connected with an increase in
the supplies from the mines.

But, apart from this fundamental difficulty, there is
a difficulty of a more special character, connected with
the fact that there are two precious metals used as
standard money in the currencies of the world. The
principal point that arises in the controversy as to the
possibility of bi-metallism, is the effect on the relative
values of gold and silver of variations in the production of either of them, and it will be instructive to
notice the changes which have occurred in previous
times.

I shall then, in the first part of this essay, examine
the effects of great discoveries of the precious metals,
with special reference to the influence on prices of an
increase in standard metallic money; and, in the
second part, I shall consider the changes which have
occurred in their relative values, when great changes
in production have taken place.

It will be most convenient to give in outline the
general theory applicable in the first case, and afterwards to bring in the special historical illustrations.

Suppose, then, that in some distant country there are suddenly made great discoveries of gold, and assume that gold is the standard money of the country in question, which implies that any amount of the metal can be taken to the mint and converted into coins.

Before the discoveries are announced, we may suppose that the labour and capital of the country were devoted to a variety of industries, and that all of these industries were in an average condition, furnishing steady supplies to regular demands. We may suppose further, that, owing to the *comparative* difficulty of producing some things, and the comparative ease of producing others, a foreign trade existed, in which the former class of commodities was imported, and the latter exported.

In any new country, for example, labour and capital devoted to the production of raw materials would obtain, through their exportation, a larger amount of manufactures than if they were directly devoted to this form of production. It is this comparative advantage in one form of industry, and relative disadvantage in others, which is the primary cause of all foreign trade.

It is, however, in terms of prices that movements of trade are generally expressed; and as we are concerned mainly with prices, this theory of comparative cost may be put in that form.

Let us assume, then, that in the country taken as our example there is a certain general rate of wages, reckoned in money, differing in different employments according to well-known causes of difference, such as the skill required, the hardships involved, etc.; and further, let us make the same assumptions as regards profits.

If, then, at these money rates, the cost of producing any article is greater than the price at which it could be imported, it will naturally be imported; and, similarly, an article which can be produced more cheaply (including carriage) will be exported. All this, no doubt, seems simple and obvious enough, but the difficulty really arises at an earlier stage.

What is it that determines the general level of prices in the country? The only answer is, that it must depend on the quantity of money in circulation, including, of course, that part which is held as the basis of the credit system. For suppose that, compared with other countries, the general level of prices is very high, what would happen? Obviously, imports would be stimulated—every foreigner would wish to sell in such a favourable market; and, similarly, there would be a corresponding check on purchases. As a consequence, the aggregate value of the imports would exceed that of the exports, and it would be necessary to export gold; and, apart from the influence of debts, or other monetary obligations, this export of gold would go on until, at the average level of prices, the exports just balanced the imports. But this is really the same thing as saying that prices would fall through the diminution of the quantity of money in circulation. And, in fact, we cannot proceed a single step in any argument on general prices without assuming their dependence on the quantity of money.

We must then assume in the country which we have taken as the example that, when the gold dis-

coveries are made, prices are at such a level (owing
to the quantity of money) that the balance of trade
is even.   Observe now what will naturally happen on
the discoveries.   Labour and capital will be drawn
from other industries to be devoted to mining, and
the consequent shortness of supply will tend to raise
prices, including, of course, the price of labour and the
rate of profit.   This change in the level of prices
would of itself tend to check exports and increase
imports, and unless gold is furnished from the mines,
the consequent exportation of the metal would again
reduce prices, the only real difference being (unless
foreign capital is imported) that the country, owing to
the diversion of part of its labour and capital to
unproductive mining, has a less amount of wealth to
consume.

Suppose, however, that the mines are successful,
then it is quite possible for the high level of prices
to be maintained, or to rise still higher.   The more
abundant the supplies from the mines, so much more
will labour and capital be attracted from other industries to mining ; and so much higher can the level
of prices rise, because the new gold being exported,
corrects of itself what otherwise would be an adverse
balance of trade.   So far, then, as the gold-producing
country is concerned, what we should naturally expect,
first of all, is a great rise in prices, accompanied by a
corresponding increase in imports, a check to exports
except gold, and a falling off in the production of everything except gold.   Such would be the immediate
results ; but we must advance a step further.

Another circumstance must be taken into account,

still considering the effects in the gold-producing
country—namely, the influx of foreign capital and
labour which is certain to take place. This may be,
and probably will be, more than sufficient to replace
the withdrawal to the mines; and if only sufficient
supplies are forthcoming of gold, in spite of the increase in production through foreign importations of
the means of production, the high level of prices will
be unimpaired, and the development of the country
will go on at an enormous rate, always accompanied
by great importations. In fact, the very operation of
sending capital from abroad to the mining country
will, as is well known, increase the importations—
any loan at the time it is made rendering the adverse
balance due to a falling off in exports so much less.
Such, in brief outline, is the theory of the effects
of great discoveries of gold on the gold-producing
country.

Now let us take a practical illustration, and for
the present purpose the gold discoveries in Victoria in
1851 is a good example. I quote a few sentences
from a shrewd observer who wrote in 1855. " When,"
he says, " the gold fever set in, towards the end of
1851 to the middle of 1852, every necessary except
beef and mutton, and every luxury except the precious
metal itself, had to be imported for the sustenta-
tion and convenience of the teeming myriads who
poured into the colony. As a natural consequence of
the demand being greater than the supply, the prices
of all commodities rose immensely."

Perhaps, however, we see the stimulus given to
importation even better from the statement by the

same writer, that at one time there were lying at the docks in Melbourne a three-legged iron pot and a camp stove for every man, woman, and child in the colony—the importation under the stimulus of high prices having naturally been overdone.   I may quote also a few prices of articles of consumption in Melbourne.   Eggs, which in January 1851 had been 1s. the dozen, rose to 6s. in 1853, and to 10s. in July 1854.   A pair of ducks, which in 1851 sold for 5s., in 1854 cost £1 : 4s.; and cabbages rose from 2d. to 5s.   These articles might of course be considered luxuries, so that it is worth noticing that between the same dates the price of flour was doubled, and the 4 lb. loaf in 1854 sold at 1s. 9d.   It is also noteworthy that amongst the imports we find large quantities of butter, timber, and other articles which would in the ordinary course of things be produced in the colony, or even exported.   Timber abounded in all parts of the colony, but the price for cutting it was more than the expense of bringing it from America or Norway, whilst Ireland, Scotland, and America supplied most of the butter and cheese, although dairy produce could be easily raised in Victoria.   As regards exports, with the exception of wool, and, of course, gold, they became almost nominal in amount.   The rise in wages may be judged of from an extract from the *Argus* newspaper, October 28, 1854: "The state of the labour market may be ascertained from the following *Wanteds* which have appeared within these few days in the local papers—500 pick and shovel men at 10s. to 12s. per day, tents, tools, wood, and water being provided; 500 stone-breakers at 6s. to 10s. per yard, it being possible for any tolerable workman to break from two to three yards a-day." When the least skilled and most simple kinds of labour were paid at these high rates, it is easy to understand how joiners and masons earned from £6 to £7 : 10s. per week.

The growth of population is shown by the fact that it had risen from about 33,000 in 1846, and 77,000 in 1851, to 236,000 in 1854; whilst, as regards the wealth of the colony, we are told that the sudden and unexampled rise and prosperity of the city of Melbourne had, in a few years, produced effects which it takes centuries to accomplish in the settled countries of Europe. The writer from whom I have already quoted says (observe it is only three or four years after the gold discoveries): "If I could tell a tenth part of the wonders of Australian wealth, the statement would appear so exaggerated that few at home would believe my statements. Men with incomes of £5000 to £50,000 per annum are as common in Victoria as bakers' boys in London—you meet them in every street." Thus we find every point in the theory practically illustrated in the experience of Victoria—a great rise in prices, a stimulus to importation, large exports of gold, and a rapid development of all kinds of commercial prosperity. The gold obtained from the mines was partly used to support the enormous increase of transactions within the colony at a higher level of prices, and partly exported to pay for the imports which, in spite of the flow of capital to the country, were still so great as to leave an adverse balance.

It is time now to examine the effects of large

exportations of gold from the gold-producing countries
on the rest of the world, and for this purpose it will
be necessary to extend our view; but before turning
to practical illustrations, some attention must again be
given to the theory of the subject.

For the sake of simplicity, and in order to lay
bare what is always the fundamental principle, however much it may be concealed, it is best to assume,
first of all, that there is little or no credit; and
accordingly, that the new supplies of the precious
metals can only raise prices in any particular country,
or industrial area, or city, or town, or village, by
actually getting into circulation.   If the gold or
silver is obtained in exchange for commodities, these
commodities will naturally rise in price—in fact, such
a rise is necessary to attract them to the mining
country; then the money wages and profits of the
producers or traders in these articles being raised,
they in turn can demand more of other articles, and in
this way the rise in prices will be transmitted from
one industry to another.   According to this view,
then, the great trading centres, and the great highways
of commerce, will be the first to feel the influence
of the new treasure; and out-of-the-way places and
regions, with little commerce, will only gradually and
slowly be affected.   Even if the treasure is obtained
in the first place by plunder, as was generally the
case in the sixteenth century, the effects will be
similar as soon as the precious metals begin to be
dispersed; and a tyrannical Government, with piratical
subordinates, is generally a very rapid distributer of
money.   Such is the general principle of the distribu-

tion of additions to the world's stock of precious metals, and we find apposite illustrations in commercial history.

In the sixteenth century the new supplies of the precious metals were obtained by Spain, through her discoveries and military successes in America, and were largely squandered in ambitious political schemes in Europe; but, in the natural course of things, they soon found their way into the great channels of trade.

At that time the Netherlands held the commercial supremacy of the world, and Antwerp was the Queen of the Netherlands. It was almost entirely by trade that the Dutch amassed their wealth. The celebrated description of Holland, written about the middle of the seventeenth century, is equally true of the sixteenth. "Never any country traded so much and consumed so little; they buy infinitely, but it is to sell again. . . . In short, they furnish infinite luxury which they never practise, and traffic in pleasures which they never taste." It was, then, through the great cities of the Netherlands, with their wide-spreading trade connections, that the treasure of Mexico and Peru was diffused over the world, and no one is surprised to hear that Antwerp was the dearest city in Europe.

It would, however, be a great mistake to suppose that, even in the sixteenth century, when credit was comparatively, and, according to our notions, quite undeveloped, this distribution of the new supplies of the precious metals took place, without any other noticeable result than a general rise in prices, accompanied by a natural increase in production. It is easy to speak of a general rise in prices, and of the gradual extension of this rise, but when we descend to details and concrete facts, there is no more difficult problem than to measure such a general rise, and to account for the failure to respond in particular localities and particular commodities. General prices are made up of particular prices, and the relative prices of particular commodities are influenced by a variety of causes which operate on the demand and supply.

In the sixteenth century we find, at the very time when England was beginning to feel the effects of the new treasure, that all the commodities of Greece, Syria, Egypt, and India, were obtained much cheaper than formerly—presumably owing to the fact that, by a direct trade through Turkey, the charges of the Venetian carrier were dispensed with.

At the same time, too, if we refer to contemporary writers on the social state of England, and to the statutes passed by paternal Governments to remedy disorders by frantic endeavours to suppress the symptoms, we find, side by side, complaints of the decay of certain places and industries, and dismay at what seems the unnatural and dangerous growth of others.

We find that careful and prudent monarch, Queen Elizabeth, aided by still more careful and prudent counsellors, issuing regulations, on the one hand, to check the growth of London by actually prohibiting new buildings, and, on the other hand, by granting privileges and monopolies to other towns, to restore their former prosperity. As with places and commodities, so it is with classes—some are prosperous beyond measure, others suffer severely. In the famous dialogue of William Stafford, the knight asks of the doctor: "What sorte is that which yee said should have greater losse hereby, than these men had profit?" and the reply shows for the time a singular grasp of economic principles. "It is all noblemen, gentlemen, or others, that live either by a stinted rent or stypend. . . . Therefore gentlemen doe study so much the increase of their lands and enhaunsing of their rents, and to take fearmes and partners to their own use, as yee see they doe; and all to seeke to maintain their countenances as their predecessors did, and yet they came shorte therein. . . . The other sort be even serving men and men of warre, that having but their olde stinted wages, cannot finde therewith as they might aforetime without rauin or spoile."

It was peculiarly difficult for the people of that time to estimate the force of discoveries of the precious metals; for, apart from currency causes, influences were at work which were effecting great changes in relative prices, and consequently in production. Even before the mines of Potosi were discovered, English wool had begun to rise in value, owing to foreign demands; and, as a consequence, great sheep-walks were taking the place of tillage, and the outcry against sheep was as loud and bitter as in the present century in Scotland.

No doubt, however, wool, being very easily carried compared with other forms of agricultural produce, felt the influence of the new money most quickly and most effectively. But apart from these and similar causes of variations in value, a general rise in nominal prices had occurred, owing to the debasement of the coinage by Henry VIII. and his son. The effects of this debasement were too obvious to be overlooked, and it was natural for people to expect that, as the abuse was remedied, as it speedily was, by Queen Elizabeth, prices would be restored to their former level. As it happened, however, the new supplies of silver reached this country in effective amounts just as the coinage was reformed, and consequently prices did not fall.

Before passing from the sixteenth century, let me resume in a few words the general effects of the discoveries.

By a curious coincidence, they were made just at the time when the civilised world was breaking through its mediæval fetters. The discovery of the New World had given a great stimulus to venturous trading, and the maritime nations were vying with one another in their zeal for appropriating new lands and new treasure; the Church of Rome, which had weighed down individual freedom, not merely in matters of speculative theology or astronomy, but equally in what we are accustomed to consider matters of practical business, which taught that everything in the form of speculative trade partook of the nature of the deadly sin of usury, and which, with its swarms of dependent paupers, was the most gigantic embodiment of the unproductive consumer the world has ever seen, was compelled to relax its hold. The old industrial guilds, which had threatened to entail the trade of the nation, as the nobility had entailed the land, in a few families, and had become, in the words of Bacon, fraternities in evil, found, on the one hand, that the craftsmen were fleeing into the country,

and to the towns not oppressed with guild regulations,
and on the other that the Government, in the interests
of the general public, was determined to curtail their
privileges, and, in its own interest, to confiscate their
wealth.   The guilds, like the Church, were discovering
that they must yield to industrial freedom and competition; even Queen Elizabeth, in spite of her strong
will, had at last to give way in the matter of
monopolies.   In the country, no less than in the
towns, good old customs, which had long since begun
to corrupt the world, such as slovenly cultivation in
common of old crops and old weeds by old methods,
were beginning to yield to individual enterprise,
involving, it is true, much hardship and social
discomfort, but preparing the way for giving Britain
the lead in agriculture; in short, from whatever
point it is regarded, the sixteenth century showed
signs of the breaking up of an old system which
rested on law, custom, and superstition, and the
appearance, in its place, of the beginning of our
modern world, with its freedom of contracts and
freedom of competition.   The mediæval edifice was
full of cracks and seams, and the new treasure may
be compared to villainous saltpetre, which, finding its
way into these cracks, regardless of all respect to
antiquity, tumbled down huge fragments, and made
the whole structure totter.   I trust you will not
think this metaphor exaggerated; but we are so much
accustomed to hear money spoken of as so many
counters—so many units of measurement—that it
seems desirable sometimes to point out that money
governs prices, and that great movements in prices

operate in a convulsive, partial, spasmodic manner
on the interests of various classes, and the stability
of various social institutions; that all the production,
distribution, and exchange of wealth rests on prices
—the price of land, the price of capital, the price of
labour; that, whether we like it or not, the great
mass of the nation is most intensely interested in the
acquisition and consumption of wealth; and accordingly, when any great revolution occurs in prices, we
are likely to find the most appropriate illustrations of
the effects of money, not in children's games of cards,
or in the abstractions of the pure mathematician, but
in the great forces of nature or art—in earthquakes,
tidal waves, or gunpowder. Not that I mean to
imply that the effects of the discoveries in the
sixteenth century were disastrous. On the contrary,
there seems to me no reasonable doubt that if the stock
of the precious metals had not been increased, simultaneously with the opening up of new routes to the
East and the West, and the growth of individual
enterprise, the progress which took place would have
been impossible. The metaphors I suggested were
intended only to convey an idea of the enormous
power of monetary changes; and that in this case the
disturbance was beneficial, we have the authority of
the *History of Prices*, by Tooke and Newmarch—the
most laborious and judicial work on the historical
side of Political Economy ever written. It is there
asserted that " we have the fullest warrant for concluding that any partial inconvenience that might
arise from the effect of the American supplies of the
sixteenth century in raising prices was compensated

and repaid a hundredfold by the activity, the
expansion, and vigour which they impressed for more
than one generation upon every enterprise, and every
act which dignifies human life or increases human
happiness."

Coming now to the discoveries of the present
century—in California in 1848, and Australia in
1851—it is interesting to observe that, just as was
the case three centuries before, this was a period of
great industrial and social changes, and I cannot do
better than again quote from the authors of the
History of Prices some weighty remarks on the period
between 1848-1856 :—

"The rapid increase in railways in every part of the
world; the improvements in the navigation and speed
of ships; the rapid spread of population into new and
fertile regions; the quick succession of important discoveries in practical science; and the ceaseless activity
with which they are applied to increase the efficiency
of all mechanical appliances; and perhaps, more
powerful than all, the setting free of the enterprise, the
industry, and the ingenuity of some of the leading commercial states, by the adoption, more or less completely,
of principles of Free Trade, are all causes which, singly
and conjointly, have assisted to accelerate the rate of
progress; [but with all this,] the influence of the *new
supplies of gold*, year by year, has probably been that
particular cause, or train of causes, which has modified
in the most powerful degree the economical and commercial history of the last nine years." The principle
of the influence is precisely the same as in the earlier
period, but the initial stages are different.

In the sixteenth century silver was obtained by the Spaniards through plundering and slaughtering the unfortunate natives, whose lands they had occupied with the ostensible purpose of spreading the truths of Christianity; it was spread over Europe first of all in payment of further ambitious projects, and it was not till in the course of trade it reached the Dutch, that its full effects on commerce began to be noticed.

In the nineteenth century, on the other hand, from the outset commercial influences alone determined the acquisition and distribution of the precious metals. The whole of the complicated processes by which the new gold was distributed over the world may be explained by one simple principle. The distribution took place in the precise proportion in which the extended demand for commodities, which originally proceeded from the labourers who picked up the gold, set in motion increased numbers of labourers and increased amounts of capital to supply, first, the wants of the gold countries, and, secondly, the wants of those who traded with these countries.

Time will not permit me to point out in detail the way in which the great development which had taken place in banking and credit generally, increased both the rapidity and the degree of the influence of the new gold; it is enough to insist on the main result, and that is—*not* that the game of commerce was now played for higher nominal stakes—for more yellow tokens—but that the whole industry of the civilised world was quickened with new life, and that the production and the consumption of all kinds of real wealth were stimulated. A rise in prices certainly occurred, but the rise was not in many cases in proportion to the increase in the quantity of the precious metals, and it did not merely mean the profit of debtors at the expense of creditors. The new gold was used *not* simply to circulate the same amount of wealth at higher figures, and play the game of trade with more counters, but to circulate more wealth—at higher prices, it is true, but, for all that, a greater quantity of real wealth.

And now I may perhaps introduce, in an appropriate manner, the practical application to our own times of these historical illustrations.

For some years past, since 1874, there has been a diminution in the supply of gold, and an increased demand for it, especially for purposes formerly performed by silver. We have, in fact, the direct converse of what happened thirty years before. Then the supplies of gold were increased, and they were converted at once into standard money; wages of every grade—the incomes of all engaged in production— were increased both nominally and really, and there were all the signs of exuberant prosperity. I would ask those who seek to connect the depression of the last twelve years with improved communication and over-production, to remember the improvements and the enormous expansion of trade in the gold era, and to explain how it is that the same causes can produce such opposite effects. Surely it is simpler to apply what logicians call the method of concomitant variations, and when you find advancing prosperity with increasing gold supplies, and diminished prosperity with diminishing supplies, to argue that there is a causal connection between the two phenomena. And observe, it is not simply as if the gold supplies had fallen off a little—the fact is of equal importance, that the work of gold has been enormously increased.

I must now notice very briefly the *second* subject of inquiry suggested by the title of this address— namely, the effects of great discoveries of the precious metals on their relative values. I have hitherto, with the object of confining the attention to one point at a time, carefully refrained from mentioning the striking fact that, in the sixteenth century, the discoveries were mainly of silver, whilst in the nineteenth they were mainly of gold.

According to the statistics usually quoted,* the facts of the case in the sixteenth century are broadly stated as follows :—

At the commencement of the sixteenth century, the relative production of silver compared to gold was about 34·3 silver to 65·7 gold, and the relative values of the two metals were in a ratio of nearly 11 to 1— the highest computation for the value of silver being 10½ to 1—that is, 10½ to 11 oz. of silver were worth 1 oz. of gold.

In the course of the century the proportion of the production of silver to gold rose to 78·6, as compared with 21·4 of gold, and the ratio of the relative values became only by gradual stages 12 to 1.

It may be interesting to quote the absolute amounts reckoned in pounds sterling. At the commencement of the sixteenth century the yearly production of silver was in value about £425,000, and that of gold

* Compare Soetbeer's *Materialen*, etc.

£800,000 ; whilst at the end the yearly production of
silver was more than £3,750,000, and that of gold
only £1,000,000. Surely it is very remarkable that
in spite of these great changes in the relative production of the two metals, the ratio of their values should
only have moved from 11 to 1 to 12 to 1.

The limits of my subject compel me to pass over
the interesting period embraced in the next two centuries, and to come at once to the great gold discoveries
of our own century. At the beginning of the century
(1801-1810), the relative rates of production of silver
and gold were 76·4 silver to 23·6 gold; whilst at
the culmination of the gold era in 1856-1860, the
proportions of yearly production were 22·1 silver to
77·9 gold—that is to say, just as in the sixteenth
century the relative proportions of the production of
silver and gold had changed, silver becoming just as
much more abundant as gold was before, so in the
nineteenth century the converse took place ; and whilst
at the beginning the proportions were about $\frac{3}{4}$ of
silver to $\frac{1}{4}$ of gold, they became by 1855 less than $\frac{1}{4}$
of silver to more than $\frac{3}{4}$ of gold.

And yet, in spite of these changes, the change in
the ratio of the relative values was such that in 1801-
1810 the ratio was 15·61 to 1—that is to say, 15·61
oz. of silver was exchanged for 1 oz. of gold ; whilst
in 1856-1860 the ratio was 15·30 to 1—that is to
say, the value of silver, in spite of the enormous
increase in the relative production of gold, had risen
little more than 1d. per oz. And observe that this
steadiness in the price of silver was maintained in
spite of the very general belief that its value, com-

pared with gold, must rise, owing to the enormous
supplies of gold, so that all the speculative tendencies
of a speculative period were in favour of a general rise.

Now let us look for a moment at the variations
since 1874 in the relative values of gold and silver
inter se.

It is quite true that from 1871-1875 the relative
rates of production were 57·3 gold to 42·7 silver,
and that since that time they have gradually changed
to about 43·5 gold to 56·9 silver; but in the meantime the relative values of the precious metals have
changed from $15\frac{1}{2}$ to 1 to 20 to 1 ; and not only
has the ratio changed on the whole in this manner,
but it has been subject to violent fluctuations.

Thus, while the changes in relative production have
been very moderate compared with the tremendous
changes we have noticed before, the changes in the
ratio of the metals, or their relative values, have been
unprecedented.

The conclusion seems to me, then, inevitable, putting
all these facts together, that variations in the relative
values of gold and silver are to be attributed almost
entirely to changes in the demand; and the changes
in demand again are mainly due to the coinage regulations of various Governments.

For the first seventy years of this century, notwithstanding unparalleled changes in the production and
distribution of all kinds of wealth, an enormous increase
in the population of new countries, gigantic wars and
violent political revolutions, a wonderful development
of banking and credit, with periodical crises,—notwithstanding such vast economical and social movements

that the old order of things seems to have completely changed, and in spite of the striking variations in the relative production of gold and silver,—the relative values of the two metals remained practically steady. All kinds of food and clothing, the staple necessaries of life, and the infinite variety of luxuries, fluctuated in their values during the same period; whilst the relative values of gold and silver alone remained undisturbed, until, in an evil moment, Germany, flushed by military and political success, imagined that by adopting one of the accidents of Great Britain's commercial supremacy—namely, the gold standard—she would gain the lead as effectively in commerce as in war and politics.   A uniform system of coinage, especially with effective regulations for the prevention of deterioration, is undoubtedly an important factor in commercial prosperity, and it is the recognised duty of every civilised power to provide such a coinage; but for Germany to imagine that, by imitating the coinage of England, she would achieve her commercial success, is as absurd as for France to suppose she would be a match for Germany in war by clothing her soldiers in German uniforms.

The value of the precious metals compared with commodities—in other words, general movements in prices—and the relative values of gold and silver, which largely determine the course of trade between gold- and silver- using countries, are now more than ever they were beyond the power of any single nation to control.   Monetary independence, in its most essential features, has become less and less possible with the growth of international commerce, and in fact no

longer exists. If, for example, the United States were
to repeal the Bland Act, and to throw her silver on
the market, the consequences would be a further fall in
gold prices, and a further depression in trade, not in
that country alone, but in every gold-using country.
Every great commercial nation has, it is true, still
enormous power by acting in isolation in monetary
policy; but it is only a power for evil,—any power for
good can only be exercised by co-operation.

A moment's reflection will show that this is only
one example of the principle which pervades all
civilisation. A few fraudulent directors in one great
bank may shake the credit system of a whole country;
an unprincipled statesman may plunge Europe into
war; but the stability of credit and the blessings of
peace can only be attained by forbearance. The lines
so often quoted in regard to individuals—

> 'Tis excellent to have a giant's strength,
> But tyrannous to use it like a giant,—

are as true of nations, and as true of their monetary
as of their military policy. I must not, however,
detain you with general reflections. In conclusion, let
me try to sum up the bearing of these historical illustrations on some of the prominent points in the present
controversy on the Currency.

In the *first* place, we have seen how the new supplies in the one case of silver, in the other of gold,
gave a real and generous stimulus to the industrial
activity of the world. The rise in prices which occurred was not, as we are too often told, merely
equivalent to a nominal change of values and a benefit

to debtors at the expense of creditors; for as soon as prices began to move in response to the new money, enterprise was quickened, employment extended, and production increased. If in the sixteenth century the trading nations had been afraid of the depreciation of the new silver, and had refused to use it as standard money in unlimited payments, the mediæval system might have retained its immobility for many generations, whilst the only gain to the world would have been a profusion of cheap silver ornaments; and in the nineteenth century, if the nations had listened to the alarmists who urged them to take time by the very tip of the forelock and demonetise their gold before it became worthless through depreciation, Australia and California would have been left to sheep and cattle, the enormous expansion of trade which took place over the whole world would have been impossible, and the only gain would have been an addition to the stock of the gold plate of those who held mortgages in one shape or another over the old industries of the world.

But if an increase in the supplies of the precious metals when freely coined has the effect which history reveals, surely it does not require much reason or much imagination to discover that, with diminishing supplies of gold, and a refusal to use silver, the contrary effects—in a word, a dragging depression of trade—might be expected. Surely this explanation is more reasonable than to allege that only wars can raise prices, and that the natural effects of peace are over-production, loss of profit, and depression. It is true that in some cases war may raise prices by directly diminishing supplies, by increasing the diffi-

culties of communication, and by withdrawing labour
and capital from production; and so also may pestilence
and famine and earthquake. But political economy
would be indeed the most dismal of sciences if it taught
that to ensure a period of prosperity we must submit
to a period of horror, and that a long continuance of
peace is the sure precursor of depression. Political
economy, however, teaches no such thing; on the
contrary, it shows that, in the long-run, destruction
is not good for trade, and that what we call general
over-production is, in reality, simply bad organisation.

There are two other lessons to be learned from the
history we have examined to-night, which also bear on
the present controversy. It is said that for the civilised nations to agree to coin silver freely—to use it as
standard money—would no doubt be a good thing for
the silver-producing countries, and presumably for no
others. Remember, then, that in the sixteenth century
it was Spain—the most tyrannical despotism of the
day, the home of the Inquisition—which first obtained
by plunder and slaughter the new treasure, and tried
by every device of monopoly to keep it to herself, and
yet in a few years it was diffused over the trading
world, and the freest nations, Holland and England,
became the greatest gainers. And *finally*, as regards
the possible variations in the values of the two metals,
history shows that great revolutions have occurred
in the relative production of gold and silver with comparatively slight changes in their relative values, and
gives us good ground for believing that if the civilised
world adopted a conventional ratio, there would be
little danger to its stability on the score of supply.

BI-METALLISM BOTH ADVANTAGEOUS AND PRACTICABLE

ADDRESS AT THE MANCHESTER ATHENÆUM,
MARCH 31, 1887

THERE has been a great and rapid change in public opinion on the subject of bi-metallism since the International Conference held in Paris in August 1878. At that time Mr Goschen described the American proposal for a universal double standard as a veritable Utopia, and stated that the English delegates were instructed to say that no change of the gold standard by the United Kingdom would be entertained. But it has never been the habit of the Government of this country to appoint a Royal Commission composed of eminent politicians and practical men simply to inquire into the theoretical advantages of any Utopia; and the appointment of the Royal Commission on Currency last autumn shows clearly enough that bi-metallism has passed into the sphere of practical politics. Accordingly the advocates of bi-metallism at the present time have to show, not that their plan might be theoretically advantageous, but that the practical advantages would outweigh the trouble and expense involved

in the actual change of currency; and to show not
simply that the plan is theoretically possible under
certain assumed conditions, but that it is really
practicable under actual conditions.

I do not intend to imply that there is now no need
to appeal to principles, and that we have simply to
collect a mass of facts, for any array of facts and
figures without guiding principles would be as im-
penetrable as a jungle without paths. All I mean is
that the principles must be applied, not to imaginary
examples but to the real facts of the case.

In the *first* place, then, I shall endeavour to balance
the principal advantages and disadvantages of the
scheme; and, *secondly*, to examine the practicability of
its adoption, and its stability once adopted.

The advantages of international bi-metallism, with
a fixed ratio agreed to by the great commercial countries, are best disclosed by considering the disadvantages of the present system, for bi-metallism is proposed
as a remedy for the evils resulting from mono-
metallism. These evils are conveniently grouped in
two great classes, the first embracing the consequences
of a sudden and rapid appreciation of gold, the second
the consequences of a sudden and fluctuating depreciation of silver.

Now although, since Mr. Goschen first made the
phrase popular, a great deal has been written and
spoken about the appreciation of gold and its consequences, it is doubtful whether popular ideas on the
subject have yet become very clear and distinct; and
perhaps it may be useful, in spite of the able address
on this subject recently given to you by Mr. Smith,

if I say a few words on the general aspects of the question. The price of every particular commodity, from a landed estate or a great ship down to a pound of cotton or a tin tack, depends upon two distinct sets of causes—first, on causes affecting peculiarly the article in question; and, secondly, on causes affecting the general level of prices. The first set of causes is familiar to every one. Every one knows, for example, that a great improvement in any manufacture will lower its price compared with other things.

But the causes affecting the general level of prices are by no means so simple and obvious. In fact, in all the transactions of business and ordinary life, what people practically assume is that the only causes which they need consider are these peculiar influences: they assume, in fact, that the standard of value remains as invariable as the standard of length or the standard of weight,—that on the average in the long-run general prices will remain the same. But this assumption may in some cases be quite false, and may lead to most unpleasant consequences. If the standard pound weight were defined as the weight of a pennyworth of standard bread, or the standard yard as the length of a pennyworth of standard tape, then the standard yard and the standard pound weight would be on a level as measures of length and weight with the sovereign as a measure of value. The sovereign is simply a certain weight of standard gold; it does not mean a certain value of any one thing or any number of things. If the price of bread and tape were fixed and invariable, a yard or a pound of the imaginary kind described would be invariable, and so also if general prices were quite steady the sovereign would be an invariable standard of value.   But as a matter of fact the general level of prices does not remain steady and fixed; and if it becomes lower, that is an appreciation of gold.

No one will deny that the more steady the standard remains, so much the better it is for the whole community.   Now for any short period the general level of prices may be considered steady.   A prudent and far-sighted trader will discount beforehand any change in relative prices—the successful trader, indeed, is the man who can calculate a day or two, or it may be an hour or two, in advance of his competitors in buying and selling.   But in any contract for any length of time a change in the general level of prices may become serious, and may upset all calculations.   If the change is very slow and gradual, bargains will be adjusted without any difficulty, especially when we take into account the fact that relative prices are always changing; but if the change is sudden and severe, there will be a great disturbance of interests. For such changes in the general level of prices do not operate uniformly and simultaneously, as is too often supposed.   Every farmer will tell you that the prices of his various outlays have not fallen in proportion to the fall in his produce, and I imagine most manufacturers have found since 1874 that prices have fallen more than expenses.

Now, if the fall in prices is due to special causes —e.g. over-production of some things—in process of time a revival may be expected.   Production, in the case supposed, will be checked, and prices will rise. But the important point to observe is that if the fall

in prices is general, and due to general causes—if the
fall, for instance, in agricultural produce is due not to
the over-supply of commodities but to the contraction
of the currency, then there is no such tendency for a
reaction to set in. The years 1872 to 1874 were
undoubtedly too fat, and it was quite natural that
they should be followed by lean years; but if the
depression had been due simply to the after-effects of
overtrading, it ought, on the analogy of the commercial
history of a century, to have disappeared in six or
seven years. Before this time another inflation should
have come and gone.

Well, then, the first charge the bi-metallists have
to bring against the demonetisation of silver, or its
general degradation in the West to a token currency,
is that it has caused a sudden and serious appreciation
of gold. As a consequence, agriculturists especially,
and all who had made contracts for long periods, have
suffered severely. Producers of all kinds have also
experienced a loss of profit, because it has been
impossible to readjust money wages, and labour has
suffered through irregularity of employment. Probably the only class which has gained much has been
that of middlemen, for it is notorious that retail prices
have not fallen to the same degree as wholesale prices.
It is usual to say that those with fixed incomes have
gained; but I apprehend it would be nearer the truth
to say they ought to have gained, for the middleman
has most effectively broken the fall in prices so far as
the consumer is concerned.

Attempts have been made recently to minimise the
effects of the depression which set in after 1874, and

even in the Report of the recent Royal Commission
the general prosperity of the country was considered a
subject for congratulation.   But I venture to think
that, under the circumstances, a much greater amount
of prosperity ought to have been experienced but for
some exceptional oppressive influence.   Since 1874
there has been a period of profound repose, marked by
great progress in the arts of production and the means
of communication.   There have been neither great
wars nor unsound speculations on a large scale.   The
efficiency of labour and capital has increased, the
effects of general education have begun to tell on the
habits of the people, crime has been lessened, and
thrift has been growing.   Now, surely depression of
any kind is a very strange result to spring from this
general peacefulness and this marked improvement in
the *morale* and *physique* and intelligence of the people.
Political economy has often been called a dismal
science ; but it never gave rise to a belief so dismal as
that the causes of a general depression in industry
should be looked for in vast improvements in production and better organisation of commerce.   Yet that
is what we are invited to believe by those who refuse
to consider the natural consequences of the great
monetary disturbance.   They say, in effect, that the
causes of the depression have been railways, telegraphs,
steamers, and the opening up of new countries.   The
Suez Canal has done its share in the work of mischief,
and the increase in the wealth and population of our
neighbours has contributed to the evil.   This is,
indeed, reading backwards the truths which made the
political economy of Adam Smith and his great

successors honoured and respected of all who took the
trouble to understand it.

Take a rapid survey over the growth of the industrial progress of this country since the end of last
century, and you cannot doubt that the principal
causes of that marvellous expansion have been precisely those forces which are now said to be the fore-
runners of depression—the infinite variety of mechanical
appliances, both in production and distribution, and
the breaking down of international barriers. If I am
asked to describe in one phrase, in one word, the real
character of this marvellous progress, I should say it
is due to constant over-production. Every decade has
produced far more than its preceding decade could
have produced and consumed. No doubt partial inconvenience may arise from a temporary glut of some
commodities; but every increase in productive power,
and every extension of the arms of trade, and everything which tends to what may seem like over-
production, is, when you look beneath the surface,
the mainspring of material wellbeing.

Even then, if the most favourable view possible be
taken of the trade and industry during the past twelve
years, it is much less favourable than might have been
anticipated; but I think the facts of the case do not
warrant this complacent survey of the past and this
hopeful regard of the future. As regards the past,
look at the condition of our colonies, which ought to
be advancing by leaps and bounds. In every case
their public debts have increased much faster than
their population, and it is to be feared that mortgages
on land have increased still more rapidly. Consider,

again, the condition of the landed interest in this
country. It is well known that arrears are accumulating, that tenants cannot be found for farms even at
great reductions, and that the burden of old contracts
is becoming intolerable. But agriculture is still by
far the most important industry of the country, and
no one is bold enough to deny that it has suffered most
severely. Sanguine people point to the gross returns
made to the income-tax assessments, and say triumph-
antly that the gross profits of the country continue to
increase. But, in the first place, it is well known that
with a declining revenue the fiscal net is thrown farther,
and the mesh is made finer; and yet, in spite of all,
the rate of increase, allowance being made for population, has dropped from more than 30 per cent in the
ten years preceding to less than 3 per cent in the ten
years following 1875.

And, again, when we look into the details of these
gross profits, we find some surprising official calculations. We see, for example, that from 1875 to 1880
the gross rental of the United Kingdom from lands
actually rose, and that down to 1885 the decrease was
only about 3 per cent; whilst in Ireland, of all places
in the world, the gross rental in the latter year exceeds
that of the former, and yet Sir James Caird has made
a moderate estimate that the real rental of the country
has lost 30 per cent; and I am afraid there is reason
to suppose that in other cases the returns have been
made on a basis that is no longer sound. It is signifi-
cant that the only very considerable increase has
been in houses, the gross rental having steadily risen
30 per cent since 1875, whilst population has only

increased 11 per cent. It would be very remarkable if
such a rate of increase were to continue, and there are
clear signs that a depreciation of house property has
occurred, and will continue.

Now, if this depression, or, to put it more mildly,
this absence of prosperity, is to be mainly attributed
to the demonetisation of silver and the consequent
pressure on gold, the natural remedy would appear to
be the restoration of silver to its former level ; and, it
must be observed, it is not as if the effects of the
appreciation had been definitely worked out and everything had been readjusted to the new level of prices.
In that case there would be some excuse for crying
out against another disturbance. We have no evidence
that the readjustment is complete ; on the contrary, we
have every reason to believe that a further appreciation
will occur. For with every increase in the volume of
trade and the numbers of people, with every expansion
of commerce into new regions, with every displacement
of old customs by competition and contract, a greater
demand is made on gold for currency. But the amount
of gold produced is diminishing, and the amount absorbed by manufacturers and by the East is increasing.

Thus there is every reason to anticipate a diminution
in supply, with an increase in demand ; and as the
inevitable result, a further fall in prices and a further
increase in the burden of old debts, and a further dislocation of contracts and agreements. I wish to discuss
the subject in its practical aspects, and to put the case
in a moderate, reasonable form, and without any exaggeration. Accordingly, I shall not ask you to believe
that even with bi-metallism you are certain to escape

altogether from a gradual appreciation of the standard when you come to compare a long term of years. But what I do maintain is, that with the two metals in full use, the general level of prices will be much more steady, and any appreciation of the double standard will be much more gradual than in the opposite case. This appears to me evident, whether we regard supply or demand.

Under present conditions, there is no doubt that the abundance of silver would compensate the scarcity of gold. In this matter our task is very easy, for we can leave our case to be established simply by allowing our most distinguished opponents to destroy their own case by contradictory arguments. You will find that at one time we are threatened with a perfect flood of silver, which is to drive all the gold from the banks, and the circulation of the West to the secret hoards and goldsmiths' workshops in the East; and at another time we are told that all rich countries naturally prefer gold to silver, that the silver will be boycotted, that gold will rise to a premium, and that there will be no effect on general prices.

The truth is often found between two untenable extremes. The flood of silver is a myth which has no real evidence in its favour: the only scientific evidence worth considering is against it, for the geologist supports in this instance the assertion of Scripture that there is surely a vein for silver, with the addition that veins of silver, embedded in hard and deep rock, are not easily made to pour out in a flood. Again, as regards the opposite extreme, that the silver will make no substantial addition to the world's currency, the argument is a pure conjecture—a piece of guess-work opposed to all experience. In the most advanced communities gold itself is becoming rather the basis of the circulation than a mere medium of exchange. The adoption of bi-metallism will not destroy the banking systems of the civilised world and the payment by cheques of all large sums. Probably one of the first effects, indeed, of bi-metallism would be to extend banking facilities. All civilised nations are familiar with silver for small payments, and the tendency is for all other payments to be effected through the agency of the banks.

But this objection may be met on even more general grounds. For any slight inconvenience (assuming there was any) which might be felt, through the use of silver, would be as nothing compared with the use of inconvertible paper notes issued in variable and excessive quantities. Yet no one will deny that any Government in the world, simply by making its payments and receiving its taxes in that form, and by making such notes legal tender, can force these notes into circulation, and keep them in circulation. This is no mere theory; it has been an accomplished fact at one time or another in all the great countries in the world, and it is only quite recently that America and Italy have reverted to cash payments. Well, then, if highly civilised nations have been induced to accept as their standard money the worst possible form of currency, is there any reason to believe that if silver were raised from the position of a token, a merely limited representative of the sovereign, a cumbrous form of an inconvertible

metallic note—for that is the real position of our
half-crowns and florins—if silver were raised from
this position to that of a standard metal, at a fixed
ratio to the other metal, is there any reason to believe
that it would cease to circulate, and that new supplies
could not be put into circulation ?

The question, put in its simplest form, becomes
practically this : If about sixpence worth more silver
were put into our florins, and a double florin were
made, of about the size of the old silver crown, would
the people of the country refuse to circulate these coins ?

The general conclusion on this part of the argument, putting aside the imaginary cases of ingenious
theorists, seems to be, that with bi-metallism we
should at first have a movement of general prices
towards the old level, though in all probability not
to the high level of 1872-74, which was under the
influence of exceptional causes, and for the future the
level of prices would remain much more steady.   We
should have, as before, credit cycles and periods of
comparative inflation and depression, but we should
have, on the whole, much greater stability ; and it is
agreed on all sides that the more stable the general
level, so much the better for the public good.

But it is time to observe that bi-metallism is
proposed as a remedy not only for the appreciation of
gold but for the depreciation of silver.   The inconvenience which arises from a fluctuating and uncertain
exchange with silver-using countries, must be too
obvious to those who export largely to such countries
to require any discussion at my hands, and on this
simple aspect of the question I shall confine myself

to one remark.   It is sometimes said that all inconvenience may be avoided by making bargains either
on a gold basis or by forward exchange contracts.
In precisely the same manner, also, you may avoid
the inconvenience of the loss, or partial loss, of your
cargoes at sea by the simple device of insurance; but
I have never heard it said that you could effect an
insurance for nothing.   And the fluctuations of exchange due to the uncertainty in the price of silver
are on the same footing.   It is a matter of risk,
and you can either insure against the risk through
banks willing to undertake it, or through throwing
the burden on native dealers; but neither Indian
banks nor native dealers are likely to do insurance
business without premiums, and in some form or other
the export trade will be made to feel the burden.

This, however, although the most simple and
obvious of the effects of the depreciation of silver, is
not the only one nor the most important.   There are
other consequences, more difficult to detect and much
more difficult to remedy.   For purposes of illustration,
the case of India may be taken, and the consequences
to which I allude may be described by saying that
the depreciation of silver acts like a bounty given on
exports from India, and like a protective duty imposed
on imports to India.   Now, in order to prove this
assertion, the first step in the argument is to show
how the general level of prices in India is determined.
There is a very popular delusion that with every fall
in the value of silver compared with gold, the general
level of Indian prices, being measured in silver, ought
to rise.   The case is thought to be the same as that

of a country with inconvertible notes—the United States, for example, with greenbacks. It is well known that after a time every addition to the premium on gold marked a further rise—a corresponding rise in the general level of prices measured on paper. If the premium on gold was 150, general prices were 150 per cent above their former level. Now it is imagined that precisely the same thing ought to happen with Indian prices in silver—that is, if silver becomes depreciated, there should be not only the premium on gold which is shown by this depreciation, but a corresponding rise in other commodities. But the two cases are not parallel; theory shows they are not, and experience confirms the theory. In the United States the actual medium of exchange was greenbacks, and the only meaning people attached to these greenbacks was that they represented so much gold. Accordingly merchants really made their bargains on a gold basis, and translated them afterwards into notes—at least, that is what they did if they were wise, and the choice was open to them. And it was only so far as this method was pursued that the fluctuating premium on gold caused corresponding fluctuations in general prices.

But at first, as is well known, such was not the case: a premium on gold arose through special demands for it for war or export before general prices were affected, and for some time it continued at a higher level. That is to say, at first the notes became depreciated as regards gold but not as regards commodities, and then not so much as regards commodities.

Now, apply this illustration to India. Silver is there both the actual currency and the standard of value: it is in silver that the people are accustomed to think of values, and they look on gold simply as a commodity, like pearls or tiger-skins. There is from the Indian point of view no more reason why a fall in the value of silver compared with gold, or, what is the same thing, a rise in the price of gold, should raise general prices, than a rise in the price of pearls or tiger-skins, or any other luxury. To the great mass of mild Hindoos the depreciation of silver means simply a rise in the price of gold; it means that they will have to give more than before for ornaments made of that metal, or for little ingots to put away in their hoards. But the depreciation of silver has in itself no more effect on the general level of prices in India, than a fall in the price of the finer classes of note-paper would have had on the value of greenbacks in America.

This illustration is, no doubt, an extreme one, and that is indeed the principal distinction between an illustration and an argument—the purpose of an illustration is to magnify as with a lens the truth of an argument. And the truth I am trying to enforce is this: unless you throw masses of silver actually into circulation in India (and India is only an example of silver-using countries), you cannot raise general prices. The depreciation of silver compared with gold will, as I said, no more raise general prices than a fall in the price of the paper of which bank-notes are made.

And now I may make use of that part of the

American illustration which is really applicable—the failure at first of general prices to rise, in spite of the premium on gold. So long as the notes were used by the mass of the people both as currency and as the standard, prices could only rise by an enormous increase of issues; and in precisely the same way, general prices in India will rise only through enormous importations of silver. This, then, is the first position, and it is borne out by the well-known fact that general prices in India have not moved, or if they have moved at all, it has been downwards.

The next step in the argument is that the gold price of silver is practically determined by the demand and supply of the metal in the London market. And here we get precisely the reverse of what happens in India. A large quantity of silver might be added to the currency of that country, and dispersed through its vast population, without having any appreciable effect on general prices; but a comparatively slight increase in the supply in London, or a falling off in the demand, at once operates on the price. Thus silver has fallen 30 per cent in London without any response being made by general prices in India. These, then, are the two steps by which we attain to the position that the depreciation of silver is a bounty on exports from India and a protective duty on imports into India. For since general prices have not moved upwards, the same amount of silver as before will give the Indian producer his usual or expected profit; but this is the same thing as saying that Indian produce can be sold for less gold than before

in Western markets, and the effect is similar to a
bounty on Indian exports.

We know from other cases how a bounty operates :
it increases the quantities exported, lessens their price
in the foreign country, and cripples foreign competitors.

In exactly the same manner it may be shown that
prices in India remaining about the same, depreciation
of silver acts like a protective duty on imports ; and
I was not surprised to read in Mr. Ellison's valuable
and interesting work on the cotton trade, that Lancashire has more to fear from India than from Europe
and America in competition.

The fall in Eastern produce may have a depressing
effect on other markets and other produce, and the
general fall in Western prices is probably due partly
to the indirect effects of the depreciation of silver as
well as to the direct effect of the pressure on gold.
If, for example, the fall in the price of silver has
encouraged the export of wheat from India, and has
caused a fall in its price, it is easy to see that a
sympathetic fall will take place in other grain- and
food-stuffs ; and then if all the gold-using countries
try to improve their position by raising sheep and
cattle, the increase in quantity will tend to lower the
price of beef and mutton, and of wool and hides, and
thus the depreciation of silver, though it strikes most
severely at the producers of wheat, indirectly affects
the whole farming class.*

---

* It is not maintained that *in all respects* the depreciation of silver
acts precisely like a bounty in one case and a protective duty in the
other. It is sometimes said that there is no bounty on Eastern exports, *because* their gold price has fallen. But it was shown by Adam

Let me resume in a sentence the principal points in the argument. I have been labouring to prove that bi-metallism would be a remedy for certain evils which have arisen from the demonetisation of silver, and the consequent depreciation of that metal and the appreciation of gold. Now it may seem that the last disadvantage which I have just mentioned must be an unmitigated blessing, and that every member of the general public ought to pray for a still further depreciation of silver. And if all the consumers of this country were in receipt of fixed money incomes, and the middlemen were simply brokers with a fixed and modest charge per cent, undoubtedly every fall in prices would mean an increased power of consumption; but just as this point requires neither introduction nor illustration, neither also does the position that the mass of the community are not in receipt of fixed money incomes, even if we grant for the sake of argument that the middleman never receives more than the minimum rate of profits.

Smith, and the recent experience of the sugar bounties furnishes a good illustration, that the principal effect of a bounty is a reduction in price to the foreign consumer. A bounty cannot, except at first, give *exceptional* profits. But growers and exporters of Indian wheat will do a profitable business so long as they obtain the same silver as before, and thus the production can be extended, whilst English farmers cannot grow the wheat profitably for the same silver (because it means less gold) until all other prices have been adjusted. Thus the general effect of the depreciation is so far analogous to a bounty.

In the same way, a protective duty is a convenient analogy for showing that, if silver prices remain the same, and the price of silver falls, exports to India are only possible if a lower gold price is accepted —just as in exports to protective countries in general, the prices actually obtained are less than they otherwise would be. For the full theory, see p. 302 *et seq.*

The three great classes of income in every great country—wages, profits, and rent—all depend on prices, and the remaining class of those who receive fixed interest on former investments is comparatively small. Any disturbance of the general level of prices must in time affect the nominal amount of incomes. Profits and rents have already felt the reduction, and if regard were paid to the regularity of employment, wages have already suffered, and will probably suffer still more. The question is one of comparison—we must compare actual receipts with actual expenditure, and not possible nominal receipts at high figures with actual expenses at very low figures. It is possible that hitherto wages, or the real consuming power of labour, has suffered least—that nominal wages have not fallen so much as real expenses. But it is contrary to all principles and to all experience to suppose that the labouring classes can derive more than temporary benefit by a disturbance of the currency, even if that disturbance leads to lower prices. The price of labour cannot be an exception to the general fall in prices. If profits fall, enterprise is contracted; and if enterprise is contracted, wages must fall, and employment become irregular.

It is sometimes said that the fall in the price of agricultural produce has simply had the effect of diverting the rents of great landowners—who have long loved to reap where they have not sown—into the pockets of the people. But I think you will find with a very little examination that no such simple redistribution has happened or was possible. The blow could only reach the landowner through the

tenant-farmer, and it is that class which has suffered
most severely. Again, it must be remembered that
a large part of the rental of this country is simply
profits, and very low profits, on capital sunk in the
soil, and that this capital can only be renewed from
year to year through agricultural profits, and so far
it would be just as reasonable to look at the failure
of the railways to pay dividends as a cause for congratulation. During the agitation for the repeal of
the Corn Laws, nine out of ten educated people had
mastered that elementary proposition in political
economy which shows that the rent paid for natural
superiority of fertility or situation cannot enter into
the price of the produce; and since that time the
truth may have been forgotten, but it certainly has
not been disproved.

I must not, however, make any further digression
on this interesting topic, and I will only add that the
cheapness which springs from improvements in the
efficiency of labour and capital, and from the extension
of foreign commerce on the basis of a world-wide division of labour, is in its causes and in its consequences
altogether different from the cheapness which springs
from a disturbance of the currency. In the former
case there is a common gain by all parties concerned;
in the latter the gain of one class is only possible
through the still more serious loss of another.

There could be no greater delusion than to suppose
that cheapness which is caused by the scarcity of gold,
and which must in a short time make labour also
cheap, is a benefit in the same sense as cheapness
caused by the bounty of nature or by the ingenuity

14

of men.   If it were so—if artificial cheapness of this kind were desirable—you have only to make your sovereign of greater and greater weight whilst retaining the same nominal value, and the consumers will be filled with plenty.   Make your pound sterling into a pound-weight of gold, and you will find by an easy calculation how wonderfully cheap the quartern-loaf will become.   At present an ounce of gold makes nearly four sovereigns, and twelve ounces, as we know, make a troy pound.   So that the new sovereign would contain as much gold as forty-eight of the old sovereigns, and everything would fall to one-forty-eighth of its former price, and the quartern-loaf, instead of being 5d. or 6d., would become less than half a farthing. The mono-metallists accuse us of wishing to give a semblance of prosperity to commerce by raising prices ; we may fairly retort that they wish to give a semblance of cheapness to consumers by lowering prices.   The truth, however, is that what bi-metallists contend for is steadiness of prices and a cessation of the irregular, spasmodic actions of independent Governments.   They wish to restore on a rational basis the monetary equilibrium which was upset by the ill-considered action of Germany when glutted with the ransom of France.

I have addressed myself mainly to the advantages of bi-metallism, because that is the best mode of showing the practicability of the proposed reform.   As matters stand at present, there can be no reasonable doubt that if this country were to make a proposal for a fixed-ratio bi-metallism to the other great commercial nations, such a proposal would be readily and gratefully adopted.   It would have been adopted in 1878, and every year since then the reasons for its adoption have gained strength. The only obstacle to general bi-metallism is the public opinion of this country, and public opinion is rapidly turning in its favour, simply because the merits of the proposal are every day becoming more widely known and appreciated. The traders with silver-using countries have begun to see the evils of the depreciation of silver and the un-accountable fluctuations in its value. The agricultural interests here, as in Germany, are beginning to open their eyes to the evils of the appreciation of gold; and the greatest class of all, the taxpayers, are becoming aware of a want of elasticity in the revenue, and the increase in the real weight of public burdens. It seems, then, that we have only to give our proposals plenty of light and air, to put them before the public in the plainest manner possible, and the details of the method of action will soon be decided. In the world of prac-tical politics it is the advantageous which is the practicable. Every important reform has been branded as impracticable until its advantages have been shown to be unquestionable, and then party has vied with party and leader with leader for the honour of practical achievement.

At the same time, it may perhaps be desirable to make a few specific observations on the practicability of international bi-metallism, and to answer some objections commonly urged on that ground. We may, I think, take it for granted that if the great commercial nations agreed to a fixed ratio and kept to their agree-ment, the ratio adopted would remain steady. I assume this not simply because it has been demonstrated over

and over again by bi-metallists, but because a strong
advocate of mono-metallism, Mr. Giffen, has taken pains
to show that even without any convention, if only the
countries of the world would avoid changing their
standards, the ratio would remain practically steady.
His object was to show, not that a convention could
not preserve the stability of the ratio, but that there
was no need for a convention, as natural causes were
sufficient. Bi-metallists do not think Mr. Giffen is
right in this belief; but they have no need to fight for
a position which is already more than granted.

But if the stability of the ratio is admitted, provided the great nations make an agreement and keep
to it, the only practical difficulties to overcome are—
first, to show that such a convention is possible; and,
secondly, that if entered into it would be observed.
As regards the possibility of the convention, it might
be sufficient to repeat the opinion that England alone
bars the way; but with many people the mere mention of a general international agreement makes them
quite deaf with their own volubility. In the first
place, they say, we can never get all the nations of
the world to agree. The answer is, that the four
great commercial nations would be more than enough.
Countries such as Turkey or Greece or Portugal, or
even Russia, might join the convention or not join it,
and it would make no more difference than two or
three old ladies moving to the side of a great steamer
would capsize it : such countries, if they happened to
have any metal to coin, would probably find it convenient to keep within the rules of the convention,
just as the old ladies would find it convenient to

keep within the steamer, though it would make no
difference to the steamer if they fell overboard.   Then,
when the word general or universal is seen to be intended in a practical and not a metaphysical sense,
an attempt is made to magnify the initial difficulties
—to show that any agreement on such a mysterious
subject as coinage is impossible.   The way to make
a molehill appear like a mountain is to cover it with
a thick fog, and the way to make a moderate difficulty
appear insuperable is to clothe it with vague and
mysterious language.

Now, what is in reality the essence of this agreement which appears to be so formidable ?   It is simply
this—that on and after a certain date the countries
which are parties to the convention will coin all the
silver and gold brought to them at a fixed ratio.
Each country will please itself as to the names and
weights of its coins.   One thing is enough at a time,
and for the present nothing need be said of the
ultimate possibility of an international coinage.   The
essence of international bi-metallism is simply that
both gold and silver shall be freely coined and shall
be unlimited legal tender on a fixed ratio, and all
that this country need do would be to make the
florin or half-crown of full weight at the ratio agreed
to.   As before, small coins might, if it were thought
desirable, remain token-money.   So long as both gold
and silver are coined freely at the fixed ratio, it
makes no difference how many or how few different
sorts of coins are used.   One of each metal is quite
enough.   Now, as regards this country, the half-
sovereign seems to be slowly dying of consumption,

and our currency would certainly be brought to a much better state if this emaciated half-sovereign were replaced by five robust and full-weighted florins. Surely such a revolution in England is not beyond the genius of the present Chancellor of the Exchequer, and in France, America, and Germany the actual disturbance would be still less.

Then the difficulty is raised, What is the ratio to be? Between the old ratio of 15½ to 1 and the market ratio, which occasionally happens to prevail, of 20 to 1, there are, as every mathematician knows, actually an infinite number of possible ratios to choose from ; and to choose precisely that ratio which, having regard to all past and present and future interests, would cause the very least possible disturbance —that, I admit at once, is impossible. But it is only impossible in the same way as every other realisation of perfect justice is impossible. And in all probability the difficulty would be solved in reality before the commissioners appointed to decide it had elected their president. For there can be no doubt that what most people would expect to be adopted is the old ratio of 15½ to 1, and any general belief of this kind would gradually cause the market price to move up towards that ratio, and on the day the decision was announced in all probability the market ratio would have reached the old ratio. No one would sell silver to-day at 59d. per ounce if to-morrow he expected the price would be 60d.

And now only one other practical difficulty remains. It is often said, How can you expect the nations to keep to their agreement? and again the language of

mystery and foreboding is employed to obscure a very
simple set of facts.   Suppose that the great commercial
nations have respectively adjusted their coinage on the
basis of bi-metallism at a fixed ratio, the question is
asked, How can you be sure that each nation will
observe the compact,—that none will break away,
regardless of the others, simply for its own convenience?
The answer to this question reminds me forcibly of the
answers to the most foolish and irritating of all
riddles—those answers which are overlooked because
of their extreme and obvious simplicity.   The question
is, Why will any nation not recede from its engagement?
And the answer is, that by doing so it will cause
more injury to its own subjects than to any one else.
We cannot allow the mono-metallists to oppose us
with contradictory arguments.   They must make their
choice.   Well, then, if they say—and certainly they
very often do say—that it is next to impossible to get
any nation to change its currency, then they must
admit that if once any country adopted bi-metallism
at a fixed ratio, it would be next to impossible to
induce it to change.

But I do not wish to rely on the inconsistencies
of opponents, for of course one opponent may say
one thing and another a different thing.   Let us
assume, then, that the great commercial nations have
adopted bi-metallism at the fixed ratio, which, so long
as the compact is observed, will remain perfectly
stable, and try to imagine the circumstances under
which one or more of these nations might recede from
the agreement, and the consequence of doing so.   The
case which is apparently most dreaded is that silver

will come to the mints in excessive quantities and choke the channels of circulation, and that a desire for a single gold standard will arise. Let us suppose that in England the robust florin of which I spoke has largely replaced the sovereign, and that in an unreasoning panic a weak Government wishes to restore the gold. How is this to be done? Now there is only one answer, and I recommend it to the careful attention of our opponents, who are never tired of quoting Gresham's Law—that the worst metal always drives the better from circulation. The only way to get rid of this silver, unless the Government buys it up at a loss, would be to debase the gold standard—to make the gold in a sovereign equal to nine florins and still call it equal to ten. Recall the conditions of the case. The country is full of silver, and the reserves of the banks are in silver, and this silver is supposed to be either actually depreciated or in danger of depreciation—that is, the gold in the sovereign is considered to be worth more than ten florins. Well, then, to drive this silver from the country and bring back gold, you must not only declare that the legal-tender sovereign is worth less than ten florins, but you must actually make it worth less than ten florins— you must diminish its weight. But this really amounts to saying that you begin your reform by compelling the banks to sell their stores of silver under the market value, and you debase the standard you wish to adopt.

I will not weary you with further imaginary cases —we are not bound to provide our opponents with objections; it is enough to answer the objections they raise themselves, and no one yet has shown even an imaginary case in which a nation might gain by breaking its engagement. In the meantime we may rest assured that if the great nations agreed to remodel their coinage on the same plan, and entered into an agreement for the purpose, there would be very obvious and forcible reasons why they should keep that engagement. There is the importance of public credit, there is the probability that the country which broke faith would cause more inconvenience to its own subjects than to any one else, and there is the danger of provoking retaliation.

We must remember that in the convention proposed, every nation in reality enters into an engagement with its own subjects in the first place : it declares that it is about to remodel its currency on a bi-metallic basis, one reason being that other nations have agreed to do the same. Every nation enters into the agreement for its own interest and keeps it for its own interest, and surely that is such a simple kind of international convention that even Russia might see the advantages of observing it. It is just as if the nations agreed to adopt the same weights and measures —the only difficulty is in making the change. Once the change was effected, no nation would give itself the trouble of making another change.

This, then, is the only real practical difficulty, and that difficulty would be solved if the great English statesman who is now Chancellor of the Exchequer were to set himself to the task. Fortune has thrown in his way a splendid opportunity of doing a great service to his country and to the world, and at the same time of converting a reputation founded largely on criticism into a reputation founded on a great practical reform. Something more is expected of Mr Goschen than the recitation of a humdrum Budget and an ingenious display of the anomalies of taxation and the difficulty of making any change. Mr Goschen ought to abandon the microscope for the field-glass. He stated the other day that too roseate a view had been taken of the elasticity of the revenue, and of the revival in trade; and the man who first directed the attention of the general public to the appreciation of gold knows very well that neither the revenue nor trade can expand when fettered by a contracting currency. He is perfectly familiar with all the arguments and all the facts of the case, and he has had ample time to strike a balance, and he ought in this matter to lead and not follow public opinion. If to one who is always swayed by the nicest ideas of justice, an appeal may be made through personal ambition, I would venture to say that if, in attempting to make this practical reform, by any accident of fortune he made a mistake—and there was never a practical proposal in which the chance of a mistake was less—such a mistake would gain for him the regard and sympathy of the public. It is only the critic who never runs the risk of making mistakes. In ancient Greece there was a celebrated conservative statesman named Aristides, and surnamed "The Just." He was ostracised and driven into honourable banishment for ten years, and the reason given by one of the voters has become historical. "I was tired," said he, "of hearing him called The Just." Let Mr Goschen beware of the fate of Aristides. He could wish for no

better opportunity of passing from criticism to perform-
ance than by taking the lead in a great reform which
would restore prosperity to industry and commerce, and
remove one more barrier from the friendly intercourse
of nations.

THE MORALITY OF BI-METALLISM

ADDRESS TO THE GLASGOW PHILOSOPHICAL SOCIETY,
ECONOMIC SECTION, MAY 16, 1887

THE advocates of bi-metallism have to defend a position which is open to attack on many sides. In the first place, they are told that the system is theoretically impossible and contradictory, and the heavy artillery of distinguished authority is dragged out from ancient arsenals. But it often happens in currency as in war, and many other interesting matters, that a position which is proved to be untenable according to all the recognised rules, is, as a matter of fact, impregnable.

Then when it is reluctantly admitted that the bi-metallic theory is possible, the practical man delivers an assault, and the artillery has to stop fire for fear of injuring its own side. The practical man rushes to close quarters and lays about him with hard facts drawn from his own particular calling ; but owing to the divergence of interests in this world, there are in most controversies practical men on both sides. Thus the debtor hammers the creditor, and the exporter the importer ; the consumer raises his battle-cry of cheap-

ness, the producer answers him with profit, and the
working man drowns both with a cry for regularity of
employment.

When the battle of the standards has thus reached
a condition of most admired disorder, and both sides
think they are getting the victory, a peacemaker in the
garb of a moralist appears on the scene.   He shows in
the usual way that there is much to be said on both
sides, that mono-metallism inflicts some hardships, and
that bi-metallism might confer some benefits.   But a
peacemaker is generally a person of strong opinions,
and the conclusion of the sermon is the sanctity of
contracts and the horrors of disturbance.   Thus, in
the end, bi-metallism is declared to be not only
theoretically absurd and practically impossible, but
morally most wicked in general and dishonest in
particular.

It is to this last aspect of the question alone that I
wish to direct your attention, and, accordingly, I must
ask you to grant, for the sake of argument, some large
admissions.   I shall assume that bi-metallism at a fixed
ratio would be quite possible if the great commercial
nations entered into an agreement, and not only that
it is theoretically possible, but that it is actually
practicable, and that after the necessary stages of
agitation, Royal Commission, Parliament, diplomacy,
conference, convention, and ratification, it becomes an
accomplished fact.   Having thus cleared the ground, I
invite you to take up the position of the future historian
of British civilisation, and to declare whether this
monetary revolution was or was not justified.

The first charge brought by the moralist against bi-metallism is, that it is an interference with contracts ; and it is gratifying to find, in spite of the large inroads made by Governments on the field of contract, that this objection is still considered perfectly valid if it can be established.   The contention is, at any rate so far as this country is concerned, that there is an almost infinite number of contracts which have been expressed in terms of the pound sterling, and that the pound sterling means a certain weight of standard gold.

If bi-metallism is adopted, it is urged that all debtors will have the option of paying in silver instead of gold, and that in consequence creditors will be defrauded.   Now it must be admitted at once that this difficulty cannot be evaded by providing that the option of paying silver shall be confined to contracts made after the change in the standard has been adopted. For, to take only one example, it would follow from such a provision, that whilst the Government received its taxes in silver, it might have to pay the interest on its debt and all fixed charges in gold, and the confusion introduced into banking would be extreme.   Apart from this, the mere insertion of such a clause in the new Coinage Act would of itself tend to discredit silver, and to render it liable to depreciation, and thus defeat the primary object of the change.

Accordingly, in dealing with this objection, I shall suppose that the new interpretation of the pound sterling is made to apply to all contracts drawn up in terms of money, and that the pound sterling will mean in the option of every debtor either a golden sovereign

or five double florins, if we may assume the double
florin to be the standard silver coin.   Well, then, the
charge made is essentially that a vast multitude of
persons who had covenanted to pay so much standard
gold, are to be allowed to pay instead fifteen times and
a half as much silver—supposing that is the ratio
adopted.

Now at first sight this appears a terrible interference with contracts, and I will try to make it appear
as heinous as possible by illustrations.   Suppose that
a man had ordered a golden spoon or a golden candle-
stick, and, owing to the interference of Government,
the goldsmith sent him instead fifteen or sixteen silver
spoons or silver candlesticks, he would certainly have
serious cause for complaint; and similarly a manufacturer of teeth, who absolutely needed gold in his
trade, would do well to be angry if he received some
fine morning a mass of silver instead of the more
precious metal.   And even if we come a little nearer
to the essence of the proposed change, it may be
admitted that an ounce of gold is much more easy to
carry about than a pound-weight of silver, and that
two pockets full of silver would be much more inconvenient than a little purse of sovereigns.

But this objection, formidable as it may seem when
thus stated, only gains the appearance of strength by
neglecting the principal elements in the case.   A
pound sterling may be defined as consisting of so much
gold at present, just as in early times it meant really
a pound-weight of standard silver, and to dealers in
bullion and to exchange-brokers the metallic meaning
of the pound sterling is of real importance; but to say

that contracts expressed in terms of pounds sterling
are to be fulfilled by the actual transfer of gold, is to
overlook the most striking distinction between the trade
of civilised nations and the rudimentary barter of
savages. At a low computation 97 per cent of wholesale transactions are settled without the use of gold,
and so long as the ratio of gold to silver remains
constant, silver would answer equally well the purpose
of reserve in the vaults of the Bank of England, which
is the ultimate reserve of the United Kingdom. With
the ratio fixed and stable, the bank would adjust the
proportions of the two metals held as reserve, so as to
meet the convenience of its customers, and it would
not make the smallest difference to the trading community whether the £18,000,000 or £20,000,000 of
bullion usually held against the issue of notes, and
lying dead in the issue department, consisted of gold
or silver. And it is worth while pointing out that
according to the Bank Charter Act of 1844, the Bank
of England is actually entitled at this moment to hold
against its issues an amount of silver equal to one-
fourth of its gold reserve.

Thus, so far as large payments are concerned, the
adoption of bi-metallism would possibly affect the
nature of the reserve held against notes. We may
test the truth of this argument in a very simple manner.
I am contending that contracts expressed in terms of
pounds sterling do not mean in the minds of the parties
concerned certain weights of gold of a certain fineness;
and in support of the contention, I venture to say that
not one merchant in a thousand could tell you the
weight of a sovereign, or the proportion of alloy to fine

gold of which it is made. All that the ordinary merchant knows or cares about the pound sterling is, that it is the unit in which his banking account is kept, and he need have no more fear of being invited to carry on his back a ton of silver than a sack of coal or a bale of cotton. A dealer in cotton goods examines his samples with a lens, to such a pitch of carefulness has competition pushed him, and a wool-broker will divide wool into dozens of different qualities, but the money with which they are paid is practically "bank" money, and if the banks were called on to furnish immediately the gold which this money represents, they could not pay sixpence in the pound. The argument may be summed up in a sentence by saying that the great mass of wholesale transactions are settled not in bullion but in money, and that any large use of metallic money is, like bi-metallism, according to its opponents, inconceivable in theory, and quite impossible in practice; and if a large use of metallic money in wholesale transactions were conceivable and possible, it would, at any rate, be a most intolerable nuisance. I will conclude these remarks on the hardship inflicted on the creditor by taking from him the right to receive gold, with the observation that at present he may be compelled to take Bank of England notes, and that a cheque duly honoured by a bank by a transfer in its books is the usual form of giving the creditor his gold.

Turning for a moment to the question of small payments and retail transactions—to the expenditure of the creditor on consumable commodities in which metallic money is more generally used—it is only necessary to remark that to a great extent silver is already used, and silver which is by law merely token-money, and that even in retail transactions bank money plays an important part, especially in Scotland, where most people have the sense to prefer £1 notes to sovereigns.

The argument which I am advancing may be supported by an interesting reference to the champion of gold mono-metallism, Lord Liverpool. In his celebrated letter to the king on the coinage, he has to meet the objection that hitherto contracts had been based on silver as much as gold, and he rejoins that, as a matter of fact, owing to well-known causes, gold had become the principal medium of exchange. Well, we may say at present that "bank" money has replaced gold. And even when Lord Liverpool wrote, in comparing the relative market values of gold and silver, for that was before the price to be paid by the Bank of England was fixed by law, he found it most convenient to express the values in terms of Bank of England notes. Thus, even at the beginning of the century, when England was on the point of adopting gold mono-metallism in place of the historical bi-metallism, we find as a matter of fact that the principal medium of exchange was bank money resting on both gold and silver.

Thus an examination of the facts of the modern industrial world shows that the adoption of bi-metallism would directly, and in the strictest sense, imply no real interference with the vast majority of contracts; but the real difficulty lies in the indirect effects attributed to the system.

From this point of view two accusations may be

brought—first, the alleged injury to trade with, and in,
silver-using countries; and, secondly, the alleged inflation of prices in gold, and the consequences of such an
inflation in the relative distribution of wealth.   The
first of these accusations need not detain us long, so
far as trade proper is concerned, for there can be no
doubt that fluctuations in the relative values of gold
and silver, in the sovereign and rupee for example,
introduce an element of uncertainty, which, like all
other risks, must on the whole operate injuriously.   It
is of course possible that, just as insurance companies
make a profit on shipwrecks and fires, accidents and
diseases, and all kinds of evils by land and sea, certain
banks and brokers may make a profit out of the fluctuations in the gold price of the rupee.   But, as regards
the great mass of commercial transactions, the flow of
capital to the places in which it is required, the fulfilment of prior obligations, and the provision for enterprise in the future, these fluctuations in the ratio of
gold to silver must be the reverse of beneficial.   The
advantages of a stable ratio, provided the difficulty of
adjustment has been surmounted, will not, I think, be
seriously disputed by any one.   It is, however, on the
ground of the immediate consequence of the actual
readjustment that the moral accusation is based.

It is said in the first place, that if the price of silver
were suddenly raised by 20 to 30 per cent, a great
dislocation of trade must ensue.   But in the matter of
reform, Royal Commissions are slow, diplomacy is more
slow, and the Parliament of Great Britain and Ireland
is most slow, and we may be tolerably certain that the
rise in the price of silver towards the conventional

ratio would not be characterised by a few leaps and bounds. It is of course very gratifying to bi-metallists to find the power of international legislation so fully recognised; but in this case, at any rate, they are content to have the pure theory tempered with facts. They argue that an international convention could fix the ratio and keep it stable; but if there appeared to be any danger of excessive haste, they would be quite willing in the interests of morality to press for a little delay. For my own part, however, I think the danger is all the other way, and that the moralist should set himself to hasten the readjustment. For, in the meantime, a great disturbance of industrial relations is in progress. India, for example, is receiving in some departments of production a purely artificial stimulus compared with Western nations.

In the natural course of things, after a painful and tardy process, we may expect the reaction to occur.

It is generally agreed that every fall in the value of silver acts at the time as a stimulus to Indian exports, and as a check on imports into India. Taking into account merely the fall in exchange, that must be the effect, and the actual statistics of large imports into India only show that in some way this check has been neutralised.

I will take the effect on the imports into India first.

The Lancashire manufacturer, in order to cope with the fall in exchange, has had to reduce profits to a minimum, and to strive to the utmost in every way to economise production. To some extent he has been able to throw the loss on the raw material; but the general result is that, owing to the difficulty of forcing up prices in India, some kinds of manufacture cannot be sent at all now, and other kinds are subject to most severe competition. And when you look beneath the surface of things, that means that, purely owing to monetary changes, the Indian manufacturer is for the time being protected.

Well now, suppose silver begins to rise again, or that prices in the East begin to move upwards, then suddenly this protective duty is repealed by the high court of nature which we are invited to treat with such respect, and the Indian manufacturer has to compete with Lancashire, educated to a high pitch by years of constant effort.

India would then feel the burden which Lancashire feels now.

Now consider the export trade of India, with wheat for the example. Every fall in silver acts like a bounty on the production of wheat in India, and the area under cultivation is rapidly extending.

But again, suppose that silver ceases to fall, and that silver prices begin to move upwards.

The Indian producer, in this case, will require more gold than the Western producer: he wants not only the same number of rupees, but more, and then he can only afford to sell for more gold. But if gold prices rise, the west of America and the Lothians of Scotland may again find it profitable to grow wheat, and the Indian producer may suffer.*

It is only with the morality of bi-metallism that I

* On this subject compare p. 309 et seq.

am concerned at present, and the objection I am
trying to meet is, that the present condition of things
gives a benefit to India, and that it would be unjust
to India to return to the fixed ratio.   Unjust it would
be, certainly, if we were, simply in the interests of
England, to propose a monetary change to the detri-
ment of India.

But nothing of the kind is contemplated.

The proposal is simply to neutralise a stimulus
which cannot be permanent, and to put Indian trade
on the firm basis of natural advantages; to balance
the interests of the future against the gain of the
moment—for in the life of a nation a few years is
but as a moment; and, in a word, to reduce money
as far as possible to its proper position as the medium
of exchange, and not to allow it to assume the guidance
of production.

For the moment, India might lose, but even the
momentary loss would be subject to compensation.
The capital of the West would again be advanced for
the development of her resources, and the reduction
of usury by her money-lenders, and the burden of
taxation and the interest on debt, would be proportionately lessened.

I pass on to consider an objection which rests on
a wider basis, and which concerns this country more
directly.*

It is said that bi-metallism would lead to a great
inflation of prices, that all creditors would be pre-

* For a full discussion of the nature of the stimulus in different
cases, see p. 309 *et seq.*

judiced at any rate, and that probably a wild out-
burst of speculation would ensue.   It is mainly on
the ground of this prospective inflation that the
argument as to the interference with contracts rests,
for, as we have seen, the feature of money which is
of importance is not the material of which coins are
made, but the command of money, in whatever shape,
over things in general.

Now it seems to me it is impossible to deal with
this objection unless we can roughly estimate the
degree in which prices will be affected.   Over and
over again various nations have suffered from excessive
issues of inconvertible paper, and from a debasement
of the coinage.   It is thus quite possible, theoretically,
that an inflation of prices may be injurious, and it
is quite conceivable that if silver were made into
standard money such an inflation might ensue.   It is
quite conceivable, and the morality of the operation
will depend on the way in which it works.   But it
must also be observed, on the other hand, that the
world as a whole, and also particular countries, have
also suffered at times severely from an *insufficiency*
of currency and a consequent fall in prices.   There
can be little doubt that throughout the Middle Ages
commerce was hampered and restrained by the deficiency of the precious metals, and the large discoveries of silver in the sixteenth century gave a
generous, and perfectly healthy, stimulus to trade.   In
the modern world an elaborate system of credit has
economised the use of the precious metals in a
wonderful degree, and we have an abundance of what
is practically representative money.   The evils which

spring from any contraction of credit, which is, so to speak, the raw material of this representative money, have been made familiar in every commercial crisis. A commercial crisis does not merely burst the bubbles of speculation, but it puts a drag on the course of legitimate trade, and it does so mainly by causing a fall in prices.   The suspension on these occasions of the Bank Charter Act of 1844, with the express object of increasing if necessary the note circulation and of rendering advances possible, has been the recognition on the part of the Government of this country, that it may be its duty to endeavour to check the fall in prices, or the consequences of such a fall.

For the sake of argument, and in order to put the objection in its strongest form, let us assume that the ratio to be adopted is the well-known ratio of $15\frac{1}{2} : 1$, which would involve a rise in the gold price of silver of from 25 to 30 per cent.   The question then is — What would be the effect on general prices?

Well, in the first place, the advocates of bi-metallism would argue that the adoption of this ratio would be simply a return to the monetary position which was upset by the action of Germany.   For seventy years this ratio had been practically main-tained, and its stability was really taken for granted. For example, in Tooke's *History of Prices* (vol. iii. p. 213), issued in 1840, I find it stated in an argu-ment against the adoption of bi-metallism by this country: "There is always a market for silver in this country for any quantity, and the utmost variation in

the market price is very trifling, rarely so much as 1
per cent; but for this variation, trifling as it is, the
merchant shipping it obtains an abatement in the
price."

The ratio remained practically steady for seventy
years, and was disturbed, not through the super-
abundance of silver, as was demonstrated in the
report of Mr Goschen's Committee, but simply by
the legislative action of Germany and other nations.
Accordingly, it may be fairly argued that, so far as
the general level of prices was affected, if bi-metallism
were adopted on what is essentially the old basis, it
could not be raised higher than it would have been
in the natural course of things, but for this ill-
considered action of foreign States.

But we may go much further than this in answer
to this supposed inflation of prices. For there can
be little doubt that even under the old conditions,
when silver did part of the work which is now done
by gold, even then there was really a tendency towards
a general fall in prices. Many people at the time
believed that the great gold discoveries about 1850
would cause such an inflation of prices as to produce
a commercial catastrophe; but, as a matter of fact,
this enormous increase in the supply of gold was no
more than sufficient to meet the growing demands of
the commercial world, and before the speculative
inflation of 1872 to 1874, the old level had again
been reached. It is of course difficult to estimate
the general level of prices, but that is the result,
taking the one hundred important articles of the
Hamburg list; and by other methods of calculation,

the level seems to have become really lower in less than twenty years after the great discoveries. An elaborate essay would be required for the full investigation of this intricate problem; but I have no hesitation in saying, as the result of a careful inquiry, that, quite apart from the monetary disturbance about 1874, general prices could not be maintained by the existing supplies of the precious metals.   But since that time a very great increase has taken place in the trade and commerce of the world, so that if the old monetary position were restored, we should expect, so far as the metallic supplies are concerned, that we should still fall short of the old level of prices.   In fact, instead of any great inflation from the adoption of bi-metallism, we ought, perhaps, only to anticipate a check to the downward movement, and thus bi-metallism would be rather a preventive of further disorder than a simple restoration of the old order.

There is, it seems to me, only one possible answer to this argument, and that is the assumption of a tremendous increase in the supplies of silver.   Recently calculations have been placed before the public tending to show that silver can be produced in abundance at 1s. 6d. an ounce, or even lower figures.   I think it is only necessary to say in reference to these calculations, that with the present low price of silver this would be a minimum profit of 150 per cent, and if that is not enough to bring out a flow of silver, the owners of the mines must be hard to please, and the promoters of mining companies must be in a lethargic condition; or else the investing public must, for this time only

in the annals of speculation, be more distrustful of
mining than it ought to be, for a profit of 150 per
cent translated into the language of the money pro-
spectus would be, on all analogy, about 3000 per
cent. I will only add, that if under present conditions
silver is likely to fall rapidly to 1s. 6d. an ounce, the
world will be compelled to choose between international bi-metallism and a practical silver currency,
or mono-metallism on a gold basis, involving, so far
as prices are concerned, a choice between a tropical
sun of inflation and a polar night of depression.

But when we are discussing a question of morality,
it seems proper to consider rather the facts of to-day
than the chances of to-morrow; and taking the facts
as we find them, there is no reason to expect that
gold and silver together would more than suffice to
check the natural tendency of prices to fall with the
enormous expansion of population and trade.

Well, then, if this position is granted, it follows
that under bi-metallism the standard of value would
be much more steady, and thus the real meaning of
contracts expressed in terms of money would be less
variable under the proposed than under the present
system. Thus the charge of inflation falls to the
ground, and those who wish to reap where they have
not sown are not the advocates of bi-metallism and
debtors of all kinds, but the approvers of the recent
revolution, and the creditors who want their pound of
gold to grow year by year more valuable.

An illustration on a large scale may be drawn
from this year's Budget. The foundation of Mr.
Goschen's financial proposals rests on the fact that,

in spite of a great growth in the consuming power
of the people, the revenue has lost its elasticity;
that the income-tax in particular, in spite of the
greater strictness of collection, is not expanding—in
a word, that the value of the national wealth is not
increasing in proportion to its volume, and accordingly,
that the burden of the old debt must be lightened.
The point is, that every million of taxes is heavier
than it was, and the national debt is only a large
example of similar burdens carried by municipalities
and corporations, by companies and by individuals.
Thus if, in the matter of contracts expressed in terms
of money, the moralist says we must beware of lightening the burden of just debts, the obvious retort is, we
must beware also of increasing their burden.

There is another charge brought against bi-metallism closely allied to that just noticed, and depending in the same way on the supposed results of this
supposed inflation.   It has been observed in the
recent depression of trade that rent and profits have
suffered more than wages, and some people go so far
as to maintain that wages have not fallen so much as
the prices of commodities consumed by labour, and
therefore that the so-called depression has actually
benefited labour, and that any check to the fall in
prices, and still more, any reversal of the fall, would
really be injurious to the masses of the community.
Now this is a very plausible argument, because it is
founded on a principle which, under certain conditions,
is quite true, and which has been illustrated in
the practical experience of nations.   It is generally
admitted, for example, that a rise in prices due to

excessive issues of inconvertible paper has given profits
a relative advantage over wages, because wages do not
rise so quickly as the prices of wholesale commodities;
and when, owing to particular influences, a great rise
has taken place in some commodity, *e.g.* coal, it is
generally allowed that, in the first place at any rate,
capital has gained more than labour. In the converse
case of a fall in prices, it is quite possible that profits
may vanish before any attempt is made to reduce
wages; and if the prices of food and other necessaries
fall, and employment remains regular, it is clear on
arithmetical grounds that the wage-earners must gain.
The truth of this general theory, and the validity of
these particular illustrations, I am quite prepared to
admit; but that a continuous fall in prices, with a
consequent shrinkage of profits, is, on the whole, a
good thing for labour, I strenuously deny.

The whole position rests on the exploded doctrine,
which used to make political economy seem so dismal
and immoral, that profits can only rise at the expense
of wages, and wages at the expense of profits, — a
doctrine which contains just enough superficial truth
to make it plausible. For if we take the industrial
world as it is actually constituted at the present time,
we find that the whole of industry depends for its
stimulus upon profit, and if profits fall to a minimum
or vanish, enterprise is at once contracted, and there
is less scope for employment. If an employer cannot
reduce wages, he will at any rate try to economise
labour; and if he cannot transfer his loss through a
fall in prices to other capitalists in the chain of producers, in the end that loss must fall on labour.

Capital may for a certain time be employed without profit, and machinery and plant may be kept up out of previous accumulations, but that is only possible for a limited time, and when the limit is reached, wages must suffer.   I have been told on excellent authority that in some parts of England agricultural wages have recently fallen 30 per cent, and every one knows how much the wages of miners have fallen with the fall in the price of coal.   In fact, the modern doctrine of the relation of wages and profits rests on the basis that both wages and profits are paid out of the price of the product, though wages may in some cases be advanced out of capital.   Accordingly, what we ought to expect in the natural course of things is that wages and profits will rise together and fall together.   It is of course quite true, if the proceeds of a sale are divided into two shares—the share of labour and the share of capital—that the larger the one the smaller the other: every one pays sufficient respect to arithmetic to admit that, and if prices were fixed and unalterable, wages could only rise at the expense of profits.   But with falling prices both wages and profits will fall; and though profits may fall first, we may be sure that wages will follow.

If we look beneath the surface, what are the real changes produced in the distribution of wealth by a rapid appreciation in the standard or a general fall in prices?   In the first place, incomes of all kinds which depend on prices — and they are by far the greater number—are paid at the lower level, whilst all prior obligations must be honoured in terms of the letter of the bond. Consider, for example, the case of agriculture. The farmer's surplus will depend over a term of years on the run of prices. Well, suppose prices fall, and for the time being he cannot or does not reduce wages. Not only may he have to pay his rent out of capital except for the indulgence of his landlord, but he may have to trench on his funds to pay these high wages, and to keep up his stock and implements. Well, the farmer may suffer first, and the landlord may suffer next, but in the third place the labourer will suffer. And the labourer will suffer not merely by having his wages reduced to the level of the articles of his usual consumption, but he will probably find that after a time less capital will be available for agriculture, land will be idle, and the hands of labour will be idle too.

These are elementary truths, and I should apologise for bringing them under your notice, were it not for the fact that many who profess to be the friends of labour are endeavouring to show that what is to the capitalist dulness and depression must, by a kind of see-saw, be for the labourer a time of joyfulness and elation. Bi-metallists are charged with a desire to rob labour of the gifts of fortune, and to check the beneficial and natural tendency of profits to a minimum. In truth, all that they propose is to minimise, as far as possible, fluctuations in the standard of prices, and their moral position is that all fluctuations are of themselves injurious, and that fluctuations with a downward tendency are far more injurious than in the converse case. To tell the working classes that an appreciation of the standard is a good thing for them, though a bad thing for their masters, is not only misleading in fact, but rests on the most immoral and degrading of all economic sophisms—namely, that any gain by one class is only possible through the loss of another; that the only way to elevate labour is to depress capital; and that industry is not becoming more and more a highly organised system, the life-blood of which is good faith, confidence, and fidelity to the real meaning of contracts, but that it is a state of war and hatred, of deceit and mistrust, of tyranny and slavery.

I must pass on, however, to another species of immorality of which bi-metallists are accused, and for which it is difficult to find a name, but which may be described negatively as a culpable want of common-sense, of patriotism, and of foresight. This charge arises from the fact that bi-metallists advocate the adoption of an international convention as regards the coinage of gold and silver. It is argued that this country already possesses an excellent monetary standard, known all over the world, and that we have no right to sacrifice our interests to the interests of other nations; that the silver-using countries may be left to take care of themselves, and that, in any case, a convention would be probably impossible, and if possible, would not last. To be possessed of too little prudence and too much credulity and enthusiasm, is not perhaps on a level in respect of immorality with the deadly sin of depriving the poor of their wages; but so perverse is human nature that many people would rather be accounted positively wicked than simply foolish, especially in money matters.

In the first place, as regards the supposed monetary independence of this country, and the assertion that we may well leave silver to the silver-using countries, I should rejoin that in all essentials monetary independence would be only possible with commercial isolation. The most important characteristic of a good monetary standard is, that it should preserve comparative stability of value. The principal reason why, of the multitude of commodities that have been used for the material of money at different times, gold and silver have survived as the fittest, is because their great durability renders the total stock always extremely large compared with the annual supply, and thus eliminates one element of instability of value. But when we speak of stability of value, we can only refer to prices ; for, as every schoolboy ought to know, if political economy had its proper place in education, the value of money is the same thing as the level of prices. Now the fact which has been forced upon the attention of the least observant with increasing emphasis is, that foreign competition and foreign influences determine to a very great extent the level of prices in this country—that, in a word, prices are more and more determined by international and not by purely national causes. The very land on which a nation is located, and all the necessaries and luxuries which it consumes, may rise or fall in value by influences which spread from India or America, and it would hardly be possible to name an article the value of which does not directly or indirectly depend upon foreign competition. But if every item in the endless series of purchasable commodities is thus influenced,

how is it possible for the series as a whole to escape ?
If every particular price is affected, the sum-total of
prices must be affected, and the sum-total of prices is
the real meaning in this country of the value of gold.
This seems to me one of those facts which, like the
standing up of the egg by Columbus, requires only to
be mentioned to be understood.   Every nation can of
course make its coins exactly as it chooses, but as
regards the real value of its coins, it has no such power.

Under present conditions, some nations use gold
and some silver as their standard, and, owing to the
monetary disturbance, the relative values of these
standards are constantly changing.   Again, all the
Western nations have practically adopted a gold
standard ; for although several of them hold large
masses of silver which is still legal tender, they do
not coin it freely.   As a natural consequence, there is
a pressure on gold which must make prices fall.   All
that the bi-metallists do is to invite the nations to
recognise the very palpable fact that they are mutually
dependent, and once for all to destroy these purely
artificial causes of instability of value.

Now, if it be granted that an international convention on the lines proposed would benefit every party
to the convention, and if it be further granted that,
whether they like it or not, the value of money
depends actually on the resultant action of many
nations, surely it does not savour of very extreme
enthusiasm or credulity, or of a want of patriotic
independence, to urge that this cosmopolitan character
of money should, in the interests of each, receive the

recognition of all. When, for example, every one
knows that, for the Government of India, the most
important financial fact is whether the Bland Act will
or will not be repealed by the United States, and that
Germany, by forcing sales of silver, can dislocate our
trade with the East; when the mutual dependence of
nations in their monetary policy is forced on the
attention every day,—surely the immorality of imprudence must be charged, not against bi-metallists, but
against those who wilfully blind themselves to obvious
facts. The choice lies between joint action on a
reasoned and settled basis, and a conflict of interests
in which all must suffer—between the benefits of a
real and recognised combination, and the dangers of
actual and unrecognised dependence.

Now, in conclusion, I should like to touch for a
moment on a very general aspect of the question. It
is said that the adoption of a fixed ratio would be an
interference with nature, artificial protection to silver,
and a contravention of the principles of free trade. I
suppose I shall be told that in this city opposition to
free trade is at present rather a merit than otherwise.
I cannot enter into any general discussion of the
question, but from a moral point of view I do not
suppose there is one person in a thousand of those
who advocate protection who does not profess to
desire universal free trade. The strength of the
opposition to free trade lies in the idea that other
nations are doing their best to injure us, whilst we
do nothing but heap coals of fire upon their heads
without burning them; and the weakness of free trade
lies in the exaggerated dogmatism of its supporters.

I shall try to say one word to lessen the opposition to free trade, and one word to strengthen the defence.

It seems to me that every impartial reader of the recent report of the Royal Commission who takes the trouble to weigh the evidence as a whole, must allow that the principal feature in the depression is the continuous fall in prices and the consequent loss of profit. Now, if this fall in prices is mainly due to currency causes, the natural remedy to apply is not protection but bi-metallism; and there can be no comparison, on moral, political, and economic grounds alike, of the superiority of the latter remedy. The essence of protection is selfishness; at the best it is retaliation,—the hopeless attempt to secure love and peace by a preliminary trial of hatred and war.

The old objection urged by Adam Smith, when he laid the foundations of the *Wealth of Nations* in lectures in the University of Glasgow, is as true now as it was then. The adjustment of interests under a system of protection is a task which is too difficult for any council or senate whatever, and certainly for any Parliament with three mountains on its back.

On the other hand, international bi-metallism is one more step towards the federation of nations, one more advance in the path by which civilisation has progressed. Let protectionists remember that we were free-traders during the leaps and bounds of trade fourteen years ago, and let us see what the restoration of the old monetary position will do before we turn our backs on the teaching of Adam Smith and the work of Cobden and Peel, and try to re-establish the fiscal position which they destroyed.

And let our fervid friends, the dogmatic free-traders, who have in some cases converted free trade from a generous belief into a narrow superstition, refer for edification to the Authorised Version. They will find that freedom and liberty are not identical with anarchy and lawlessness; but that everything that increases the mutual dependence of nations is a guarantee for peace and an extension of the sphere of freedom of contract. A monetary convention of the simple character proposed would, under present conditions, do more to further real freedom of trade than the most adroit and unpleasant retaliation on foreign nations, or the closest practicable union of our colonies and dependencies in a nominal federation. Do not let us, through fear of protecting silver, encourage the gold-using nations to protect themselves against every export from silver-using countries, and, through a narrow observance of the letter, break the spirit of our orthodoxy.*

* It ought to be remembered that bi-metallism did not become a question of practical politics in this country until long after the battle of free trade had been fought. So far as I know, Cobden has given no opinion on the question, and even if he has done so it must have been under widely different conditions, since his death occurred in 1865. There is, however, ample evidence in his speeches and writings that he did not regard international conventions as an infringement of the true liberty of nations, or as useless and unstable in their nature. When, for example, he was arguing in favour of reforms in maritime law, in the interest of neutrals in time of war, he said (*Speeches*, p. 459): "With the general spread of free-trade principles —by which I mean nothing but the principle of the division of labour carried over the whole world—one part of the earth must become more and more dependent upon another for the supply of its material and its food. Instead of, as formerly, one country sending its produce to another country, or one nation sending its raw material

to another nation, we shall be in the way of having whole continents engaged in raising the raw material required for the manufacturing communities of another hemisphere. It is our interest to prevent, as far as possible, the sudden interruption of such a state of dependence." . . . The argument is, as stated above, in favour of certain international agreements as to contraband, but it applies equally well *mutatis mutandis* to an international monetary convention, and so also does the reply to objections with which he proceeds : "To what I am urging, it may be said, 'But you won't get people to observe their international obligations even if they are entered into.' That remark was made in the House of Commons by a Minister who, I think, ought not to have uttered such a prediction. Why are any international obligations undertaken unless they are to be observed ? We have this guarantee that the international rules I am now advocating will be respected, that they are not contemplated to be merely an article in a treaty between any two Powers, but to be fundamental laws, regulating the intercourse of nations, and having the assent of the majority of, if not all, the maritime Powers in the world. Let us suppose two countries to be at war, and that one of them has entered into an engagement not to stop the exportation of grain. Well, we will assume the temptation to be so great that, thinking it can starve its opponent, it would wish to stop this exportation in spite of the treaty. Why, that would bring down on them instantly the animosity, indeed the hostility, of all the other Powers who were parties to the system. The nation which has been a party to a general system of international law, becomes an outlaw to all nations if it breaks its engagement towards any one." To this argument, as applied to a monetary convention, it need only be added that every nation has learned the value of keeping its word in financial more than in any other obligations.

STABILITY OF THE FIXED RATIO BETWEEN GOLD AND SILVER UNDER INTERNA-TIONAL BI-METALLISM

"SCOTSMAN," DECEMBER 7, 1886

IT has often been asserted by bi-metallists that if a fixed ratio between gold and silver were adopted by an International Convention, it would be theoretically impossible, except under very exceptional circumstances, that the market rate should vary from the conventional rate, or that gold should to any large extent be demonetised. But, so far as I am aware, no attempt has been made to show in detail the practical application of the general argument to present circumstances. There is no doubt, however, that practical men to a great extent distrust theoretical reasonings, even when they appear of the most convincing kind: they have too lively a recollection of the failure of theories in their practical application in many economic questions, to believe that on such a mysterious subject as currency the theory is sure to be right because it is expressed with emphasis and a great appearance of wisdom. What they know for

an undoubted fact is, that since 1874 silver has fluctuated in value, compared with gold, more than 30
per cent; and, besides this, they have a general distrust in the power of Governments to interfere with
market price of any kind.   Accordingly, they will
not believe that any Government can do any good
in the matter, and they refuse to admit that a union
of many Governments would be better than one—
probably, indeed, they think it would be worse—and
it is impossible to convince them by any theory of
compensatory action, and still less by any simile,
such as that a stool may stand on three or more legs,
though not on one.

The working out of the theory in actual figures is,
however, so startling in its results that it seems to me
opposition to bi - metallism on this ground must be
abandoned by all who take the trouble to follow out
the investigation.   The statistics in this paper, when
no special reference is made, are taken from Mr. Palgrave's Appendix (B) to the Third Report of the Royal
Commission on Trade, and refer to 1884, the last year
given.*

The estimated stock of gold in money and
hoarded in the civilised nations was, in 1884, about
£654,000,000, and of silver, £437,000,000.   The
total production of gold for 1884 is estimated at
about £19,500,000, and that of silver at less than
£26,000,000.

The net consumption of gold in the arts and manufactures is 90,000 kilogrammes, equal (at £139 : 10s.
per kilogramme) in value to about £12,500,000 ; and

* Mr. Palgrave relies mainly on Soetbeer.

the flow to the East (deducting imports thence) is, for the four years 1881-84, 120,000 kilogrammes—say, for 1884, 30,000 kilogrammes of the value of £4,000,000. Thus the total consumption of gold for other purposes than monetary is £16,500,000, which leaves £3,000,000 of new gold available for maintaining or increasing the coinage, or hoarding.

The net consumption of silver for the arts and manufactures is 515,000 kilogrammes, equivalent to (at £9 per kilogramme) about £4,500,000; whilst the net flow to the East is 1,603,000 kilogrammes, equivalent to about £14,500,000. Thus the total consumption of silver for non-monetary purposes is about £19,000,000, leaving a balance of about £7,000,000 for coinage purposes and hoarding.

These being the facts of the case, suppose that the civilised nations adopt bi-metallism at a ratio of $15\frac{1}{2}$ to 1, which is the ratio on which in these figures the value of silver has been reckoned. The adoption of bi-metallism will involve free mintage of both metals to any extent, and unlimited legal tender of either metal at the option of the payer.

Assume, if it is possible, that the market ratio of gold and silver diverges from the conventional ratio, and observe what will happen. It must be premised, in the first place, that operations in bullion are conducted by special dealers at a small rate of profit per transaction, and that there is very keen competition. Under the assumption made of a possible divergence in the market rate, gold as bullion will exchange for more silver than gold coins will obtain of silver coins at the legal ratio. Accordingly, so long as the divergence exists, no gold will be taken to the mints, either new or old, and gold coins will be melted. It is, however, clear that these gold coins which are to be melted must be obtained by a substitution of silver coins for them, either in the banks or in the circulation. Where, then, are these silver coins to come from? Plate is protected by being in a manufactured form, and it is quite opposed to the law of demand that, because silver is comparatively cheap, people should demand less of it for general purposes. Besides, how are the dealers in bullion to buy the plate? There can, then, be no doubt that the silver which is to take the place of the gold coins must come from the new silver available for coinage. It may, perhaps, be thought it would come from hoards. But, apart from the fact that in the civilised world hoarding is becoming less common, it is quite clear that any one who hoarded would only exchange his hoard of silver for a hoard of gold; so that the deficiency in the gold coinage caused by melting coins must be met by the new silver. But, according to the present rates of consumption of silver in the civilised countries for non-monetary purposes and for transmission to the East, there are, at the present rate of production of silver, only £7,000,000 available for monetary purposes.

Since, however, no new gold is sent to the mints, owing to the assumed disturbance of the ratio, the £3,000,000 of new gold formerly available for coinage must be replaced by silver, and this will reduce the amount of new silver available for driving the

£654,000,000 of gold from circulation to the sum of £4,000,000.

The question must also be regarded from the point of view of gold. The amount of gold available for non-monetary purposes will now be increased by the £3,000,000 of new gold formerly minted, and by the £4,000,000 of coins driven out by the silver—that is, by £7,000,000. Thus there will be available for the non-monetary purposes of the civilised nations £23,500,000 of gold per annum in place of £16,500,000 ; but such a sudden increase in the demand for gold for non-monetary purposes is palpably incredible, especially when we assume that a similar demand for silver is stationary.

Another step in the argument may now be taken. Suppose that, owing to the rise in its value (though, be it observed, we are assuming it is still to some extent depreciated), the use of silver for the arts is diminished, and also its use for exportation to the East; and suppose that in this way £20,000,000 are available for driving out gold. Then £20,000,000 of "driven-out" gold and £3,000,000 formerly used for coinage must be added to the £16,500,000 at present used for non-monetary purposes. But where in the world—in the East or the West—are the consumers of this amount of gold to be found ? Is it conceivable that, the range of prices remaining the same (for no absolute addition to the currency has been assumed), and the general distribution of wealth being unaffected—is it conceivable that 140 per cent more gold could be consumed ? Now, suppose that the amount of silver produced is largely increased owing to the nominal rise in its value; suppose it is more than doubled, and that £50,000,000 are available yearly for "driving out" gold, so much the more difficult will it be to find a non - monetary consumption for the gold. For so long as gold continues to be driven out, the silver will simply take its place in the currencies of the world, so that there will be no general rise in prices and no fall in the value of gold. Thus the supposition of any deviation from the fixed ratio on an international basis leads to glaring absurdities, and those who speak of international bi-metallism ending in silver mono-metallism cannot have realised the amount of the present stock of gold, and the limited extent of the demand for other than coinage purposes. They make absolutely contradictory suppositions, without any discoverable reason, concerning the production and concerning the demand for the two metals. They assume that, as regards production, gold will steadily diminish, and silver enormously increase; whilst, as regards consumption for non - monetary purposes, they assume that the use of gold will be enormously increased, whilst that of silver will remain stationary or decline. It is, of course, impossible to foretell the relative rates of production of the two metals, but it is quite certain that if, owing to excessive production, silver became of less than the ratio value, it would drive out gold, and this gold must be added to the stock available for non-monetary purposes. Accordingly, the more silver there is produced, the more gold (if the ratio is disturbed) will be turned from monetary to non-monetary purposes. But if the world suddenly becomes so rich, or distributes its wealth in such a manner that the demand for gold plate is doubled, trebled, or multiplied in proportion to the increased production of silver, can we suppose, with any show of consistency, that the demand for silver plate, in spite of silver being assumed to be relatively cheaper, will not increase equally? Can we suppose that the world and his wife will be in a position to demand an indefinitely larger quantity of gold ornaments, and yet that there will be no corresponding demand for silver? But the silver cannot be used both for the arts and for driving out gold.

It follows, if the foregoing reasoning is sound, that the stability of the fixed ratio, if generally adopted, could only be disturbed and lead to silver mono-metallism under hypotheses which are opposed to all experience—namely, coincidently with an enormous increase in the production of silver there must be an effective demand to the same amount for the gold which is to be displaced for non-monetary purposes, and yet at the same time there must be no corresponding increase in the demand for silver for such purposes. Increased production of silver alone will not disturb the ratio; there must be an equally increased demand for gold, and no corresponding demand for silver, for non-monetary purposes.

What we ought reasonably to expect, if the rate of $15\frac{1}{2}$ to 1 were adopted, is something very common-place and unromantic in comparison with these wild hypotheses. (1) The production of silver would be to some extent increased. But since silver is at present produced at very different rates of cost, the increase would only be effected by opening or reopening less fertile mines or working more difficult veins. (2) Any silver not required for the arts or for the East would be added to the coinage of the civilised nations. (3) There would be just as much gold used as before, unless the demand for the arts and the East increased so much as to absorb more than the annual production. In this case, the deficiency must be made up from the existing coinages; but if any such increase in the non-monetary demand for gold is probable, the sooner gold-using countries make use of silver as standard money, the better for their commerce. The mere adoption of universal bi-metallism would not cause such an increase in the demand for gold for the arts, which can only arise from the growth of wealth and population, or some change in the distribution of wealth that would increase the relative power of gold consumers. It is, however, possible that the more equal diffusion of wealth will cause a greater relative demand for silver, and at any rate there must be an increased demand for silver to some extent. There is, again, no reason why the adoption of bi-metallism should increase the flow of gold to the East, or diminish the flow of silver. The East requires silver for coinage, and imports gold as a luxury; and so long as this is the case, the value of the former is likely to exceed greatly that of the latter. At any rate, taking the facts of the case as they are at present, any disturbance of the ratio once generally adopted, and any extensive substitution of silver for gold as coinage, are plainly impossible. In former times it was simply the want of agreement between the nations which rendered it possible for dealers in bullion to make a profit by altering the local distribution of the metals; and it should never be forgotten that, whilst in the sixteenth century the production of the precious metals was at the commencement about 2 of gold to 1 of silver, and became at the end more than 3 of silver to 1 of gold, the ratio only moved from 11 to 1 to 12 to 1; and in the nineteenth century, whilst the production of silver to gold was at the beginning about 3 to 1, and in 1860 about 1 to 3, the ratio was practically stable, and continued stable until the *de facto* agreement of the Governments was broken.

THE MEASUREMENT OF VARIATIONS IN THE VALUE OF THE MONETARY STANDARD

READ BEFORE THE ROYAL SOCIETY OF EDINBURGH, MARCH 21, 1887 *

It may seem at first sight almost contradictory to speak of variations in the value of the monetary standard. How, it may be asked, can the standard, which is the measure of values, itself vary in value? At present in this country the sovereign is apparently the standard measure of value, just as the yard is the standard measure of length, and it would certainly seem odd to most people to speak even hypothetically of variations in the measuring power of the standard yard. It may be useful for purposes of comparison and contrast to quote the definitions of the standard yard and of the sovereign or pound sterling. By Act of Parliament, 30th July 1855, it was enacted, "That the straight line or distance between the centres of the transverse lines in the two gold plugs in the bronze bar deposited in the office of the Exchequer

* Published in the Journal of the London Statistical Society, March 1887.

shall be the genuine standard yard at 62° F., and if lost shall be replaced by means of its copies." According to the Coinage Act, renewed in 1870, "the sovereign is defined as consisting of 123·27447 grains of English standard gold, composed of eleven parts of fine gold and one part of alloy, chiefly copper."

When we compare the two definitions, we see that whilst the former refers definitely to the distance between two points or to length, the latter refers only to the weight of a particular substance, and says nothing of value.

In the definition of a standard yard, a definite place and a definite temperature are mentioned (and other precautions are implied), which render the standard for practical purposes invariable. In the definition of the sovereign, also, similarly precise elements are found, but they refer only to weight and chemical composition, not to value. Strictly speaking, then, it is only by accident that the sovereign can ever be a standard of value at different times and places in the same way as the yard is the standard of length. "At the same time and place," says Adam Smith, "money is the exact measure of the real exchangeable value of all commodities. It is so, however, at the same time and place only."

I will try to show how a standard yard might be constructed which would correspond logically to the sovereign as the standard unit of value, and under what conditions the sovereign would really correspond to the standard yard actually adopted. There are, of course, an infinite number of ways in which a thoroughly bad standard may be chosen. The one I

have chosen is this : a standard yard might be defined
as the length of a shilling's worth of standard mercury
enclosed in a standard tube placed on a standard sun-
dial in every market-place at noon-day by Greenwich
time. Now in the standard yard as thus defined, there
would be no dispute as to the meaning of the term at
any given time and place—at least in any market at
noon-day. Any merchant who had agreed to sell a
yard of cloth need only repair to the market-place at
noon-day to find out how much or how little he must
cut off the roll. The contract would be capable of
a certain interpretation. If standard mercury were
cheap, and the sun hot, the buyer would gain and the
seller would lose, if the contract had been made beforehand. At the same moment, and in the same market,
however, all traders in all kinds of goods sold by the
yard would be able to conduct their business in a
perfectly accurate manner.

This will perhaps seem an extreme illustration of
the nature of the standard unit of value, and I admit
that in degree the sovereign is not quite so bad as the
standard yard I have just described, if the standard
tube were a very sensitive thermometer and the price
of mercury were very variable. But in one celebrated
case in history this illustration, even in its most exaggerated form, would have been really inadequate. The
assignats issued by the Government in the great French
Revolution in about four years sunk to $\frac{1}{30,000}$th part
of their nominal value. The *assignat* was, it is true,
an inconvertible note, but it was for a time the standard
unit of value, and in different times and places the
value was much more uncertain than the length of a

standard yard of the kind just described. We could, however, easily imagine a standard yard of this kind being quite stable under certain conditions. Suppose, for example, that the price of mercury were fixed by law, the climate of the country uniform, and the tube of a particular kind, it would be possible for the new standard yard to be as accurate as the old.

Under certain conditions, also, the sovereign might be as good a measure of value as at present our standard yard is of length. Such, for example, would be the case if prices, whether by law, or custom, or accident, were always the same. If the price of everything bought and sold were fixed, the sovereign, as defined by the Coinage Act, would be a perfect measure of value, but with every movement in prices the purchasing power of the sovereign varies—that is to say, so far the sovereign fails in its primary function as a standard measure of value. It is not a standard in the same sense as the other standards of the country. The use of a standard of value, as distinct from a mere medium of exchange, is to measure values at different times and places, and it is only so far as the sovereign of specified weight and fineness happens to preserve the same purchasing power that it can be considered even sufficiently accurate for practical purposes. The difference between the standard of value and other standards is shown in the case of an agricultural lease. Acres, bushels, tons, have a precise meaning as regards extension, capacity, and weight, but the pound sterling has no precise meaning as regards value. So many pounds' weight of ten thousand different articles of a certain quality would, so long as the Act defining the pound weight remains in force, mean precisely the same thing—a definite amount of commodities; but so many pounds' worth of ten thousand articles would, in all probability, vary in meaning every day, although the Act defining the pound sterling were observed most religiously.

Against some kinds of uncertainty in the interpretation of contracts, the legal definition of the sovereign is ample guarantee. Illogical as it may seem, as now defined, the sovereign as a standard of value would be much worse if, according to the needs of a tyrannical Government, its weight and fineness were constantly changing.

A contract for a certain amount of standard gold is certainly to be preferred to a contract for an uncertain amount, and after repeated warnings from history, civilised nations have recognised the foolishness of making petty gains by debasing their standard.

Still, a certain weight of standard gold is a very different thing from a certain amount of purchasing power; and the inquiry into the variations in the value of the monetary standard is probably by far the most important problem or group of problems in the wide field of economic science. For, in other words, such an inquiry is an attempt to give precision to the vague expression, general movements in prices. A general movement in prices is, however, the resultant of a number of particular movements; and in these particular movements, again, we find the proximate causes of the distribution of the industrial forces of the world, and of the wealth which these forces create. "Every science," * says Clerk-Maxwell, "has some instrument of precision which may be taken as the material type of that science which it has advanced, by enabling observers to express their results as measured quantities. In astronomy we have the divided circle, in chemistry the balance, in heat the thermometer; while the whole system of civilised life may be fitly symbolised by a foot-rule, a set of weights, and clock." To these symbols of civilised life I would add a piece of standard money; and in illustration of the general observation, I would point out that the principal quantities with which the economist has to deal are prices.

In discussing variations in the value of the monetary standard, two kinds of inquiries of a very different nature are usually blended together, which it would be much better to keep distinct. In the *first* place, we have a purely statistical problem—namely, the observation and classification of prices, and the measurement of the rise or fall observed in particular groups, in combinations of these groups, and, finally, in the whole mass of exchangeable commodities. Further, the record of prices may refer to different places at the same time—a comparison may be made between different industrial areas in the same nation, or between different nations.

But there is a *second* kind of inquiry implied in the general expression, which is still more difficult and complex. The primary object of all scientific classification is the discovery of causes; and, even for practical purposes, the mere observation of variations,

* *Theory of Heat,* p. 75.

without any further inquiry into the causes, would be
incomplete. It is only when the causes have been
estimated that any idea can be formed as to whether
the variations are likely to be temporary or pro-
longed, or whether, by any action of Government or
individuals, they may be reversed or modified.

There ought to be no difficulty in seeing that these
two inquiries are quite distinct, and that it is one
thing to measure variations in the purchasing power of
the sovereign, and quite another to give a scientific
explanation of the variations.

I propose, then, for the present to postpone altogether the second inquiry as to the causes of variations
in the value of the monetary standard, and to discuss
in the first place the methods by which such variations
may be measured. The principal difficulty arises
from the fact that relative prices vary, whether we
consider times or places. Between two dates, for
example, bread may fall and meat may rise—or,
taking a wider illustration, all kinds of manufactures
may fall, whilst all kinds of agricultural produce rise
in price; and similar differences may be observed
when comparing different industrial areas. Even if
there is a rise or a fall in every particular commodity,
or a variation in the same direction, still there is
almost certain to be a difference in the degree of the
rise or fall in different articles. Take, for example,
the comparatively simple case of the purchasing power
of the nominal or money wages of unskilled labour.
Suppose that, in comparing two points of time, it is
found that every other article of the labourer's usual
consumption has fallen in price, but that bread has

risen. If the rule of one commodity one vote is adopted, the result would be that the purchasing power of wages had risen, whilst in reality the labourer was compelled greatly to curtail his consumption. A similar difficulty arises when comparing the purchasing power of wages at different places.

It would be easy to give a number of particular examples of temporary and local variations in the value of the standard. The same nominal rent for land may mean at different times very different things, both to the landlord who receives and to the farmer who pays, and the purchasing power of the sovereign compared with various groups of articles in London and in the rural districts would vary very much. It would be easy both as regards rent and wages to construct a better standard than is given by the pound sterling, and practically such standards have been resorted to in produce-rents and sliding-scale wages.

But it is important to observe that in every one of these cases we should assume that the particular movements in prices between different times are caused partly by special causes—e.g. improved processes of production, etc.—and partly by causes of a general and wide-reaching character. In other words, every particular price depends partly on the relative value of the commodity compared with others, and partly on the relative value of money compared with things in general. In some cases this distinction is quite obvious, as for instance when there is a sudden and general rise in prices owing to large issues of inconvertible paper. But usually the cause of any general

change will for a long time remain unobserved.
Often the change is gradual, and can only be detected
after a long interval, and in any case it does not
affect all commodities simultaneously in the same degree—that is to say, a disturbance of relative values
is caused by the process of a readjustment. The object
of the present paper is to show how any general
change between two points may be measured, it being
assumed that such general changes are possible. I say
nothing for the present either of the causes or the consequences of such variations. The present inquiry is
simply a problem in the method of statistics, with a
few examples which must be considered rather as illustrations than deductions.

In the first place, what are we to understand by
the purchasing power of the standard over things in
general?

At any date taken as the basis of comparison, the
aggregate of purchasable commodities in the widest
sense in any country may be expressed thus :—$\pounds_1 m_1 =$
$(q_1 \cdot p_1 + q_2 \cdot p_2 \cdots + q_n \cdot p_n)$, where q represents the
total quantity of any item in the national inventory
and p the price per unit. Strictly speaking, every item
should be stated separately which, through quality
or locality, has a special price, and the series would be
practically infinite. Suppose, for example, that in
1870 the total mass of purchasable "things" was
£8,000,000,000, then the purchasing pound of the
pound sterling would be strictly $\frac{1}{8,000,000,000}$ part of
each item (q_1, q_2, etc.) in the series.

Such a conception of purchasing power, or of the
value of money, would be of no practical use except

for clearing up the obscure phrase, " the value of money in terms of things in general." The series, however, might be simplified (1) by various devices of grouping. Thus, instead of various prices of land of all qualities, and in all situations, we may take only a few classes, and finally only two—agricultural and building. So again of houses, we may take a few classes, or even group all together. By proceeding in this manner we might reduce the series to a limited number of terms. (2) This number might be further diminished by neglecting all below a certain value, and the idea formed of the purchasing power of the standard would be adequate, according to the proportion of the total rejected to the aggregate. In proportion, however, as the series was simplified and abbreviated, the conception of purchasing power would become illusory, for it would lead to something of this kind: the purchasing power of the sovereign would be represented as $\frac{1}{8,000,000,000}$ part of the land of the country, of the houses, of the furniture, of the railways, and of the services of labour; or dividing out the quantities, we should say that a sovereign would purchase $\frac{1}{100}$th part of an acre of cultivated ground, plus $\frac{1}{1000}$th part of a house, plus $\frac{1}{1000}$th part of the furniture of a house and the labour of a British working man for a quarter of an hour. Thus the whole meaning of the expression has been squeezed out in the process of condensation.

But although the unit of purchasing power has been thus reduced to an imaginary or impossible quantity, it is quite possible, as in many mathematical problems, that it may for some purposes be used and not appear in the final result. Such might be the case if we measure the appreciation or depreciation of the standard or the change in its purchasing power between two points of time.

The national inventory at the second date would consist of the old inventory, plus or minus any difference in the old items and plus the new items. This might be expressed symbolically by saying that $£_2w_2 = £_2w_1 + d\,(£_2w_1) + £_2N$. Now if there has been only a relatively small addition to the national wealth, either by an increase in the old or an addition of new elements—if, for example, the population has remained nearly stationary, no great changes in the production of wealth have occurred, or in its distribution, or in the material wants of the community—then the two last terms may be neglected, and the change in the purchasing power of the £ is equal to the fraction $\frac{w_1}{w_2}$.

I propose to call this fraction the coefficient of appreciation.

Thus, if the total value of the old inventory at the new prices be doubled, that means that the purchasing power of the £ is one-half of what it was.

The simplest case would occur when the two last terms vanish, and the movement in prices has been perfectly uniform, for then $\frac{w_1}{w_2}$ would measure exactly the change in purchasing power. Such a case would occur theoretically on excessive issues of inconvertible paper as soon as equilibrium is restored.

In the series given, in every case p has become $n\,p$.

Again, if the increase in the quantities of the national wealth has been uniform, and relative prices have remained the same, q in every case becoming mq, and p in every case pn, then, $£_2 w_2 = £_2 . w_1 . mn$, and $n = \dfrac{w_2}{w_1 . m}$, and the new purchasing power of the standard is $\dfrac{w_1}{w_2} . m$ of the old ; that is, $\dfrac{w_1}{w_2} . m$ is the co-efficient of appreciation.

The case might, however, be reduced to the former under the conditions assumed, for the purchasing power of the standard will obviously be the same for the old inventory, and for every uniform addition to it. Thus the change in the standard may be measured by the old inventory at the old prices, divided by the old inventory at the new prices.

Suppose in any interval the nominal wealth of the country has increased : this may be due either to an increase in quantities or to a rise in nominal prices (or depreciation of the standard), or to both causes. Now if the increase in both q's and p's has been uniform, the change due to the standard may be found, and the change in quantity deduced. We first find n and then m.

It may be objected that if we assume relative prices remain the same, we might calculate the change in the standard by the change in the price of any single article. The objection is quite valid, but it does not destroy the value of the method proposed. For the use of the method is as the basis of an approximate calculation. As a matter of fact, relative prices are constantly changing, by peculiar changes affecting the demand and supply of particular commodities. No one would dream of saying: the price of potatoes has fallen one-half, and therefore all prices have fallen one-half; and similarly of every particular commodity.

Next, suppose then that the old inventory has remained the same as regards items and their quantities, but that relative prices have changed. The purchasing power of the unit at the first date would, as was shown, consist strictly of an nth part of every item where $n =$ the quantity of the national wealth measured by the standard. Similarly of the second date. If relative prices have changed, the two series cannot be compared, but the sum totals of the series may; and the only meaning of change in the purchasing power of the unit is (quantities remaining the same) $\dfrac{w_1}{w_2}$, when w_1 is the total at old prices, and w_2 the total at the new.

But hitherto it has been assumed either that the national inventory remained the same, or else that the articles increased uniformly; but relative quantities change no less than relative prices, and in fact both changes are constantly going on. As a rule, e.g. a fall in relative prices due to the improvements in manufactures leads to increased production, and a fall due to the lessened demand leads to a decrease in production, and vice versâ. There are, besides, changes due to a variety of special causes.

In this case the only plan seems to be, in the first place, to estimate generally the change in quantity. This can only be done strictly by reducing to some common measure, and that measure must be the standard of value. Let the total value of the new inventory (consisting of different quantities of the old items), reckoned at the old prices, be v_1, and the total value of the old inventory, also at old prices, be w_1, then $\frac{v_1}{w_1}$ is the measure of the increase in the quantity of wealth, or the m of the formula for appreciation.

But if the quantities had increased uniformly m, then, as was shown above, $\frac{w_1}{w_2} . m$ would give the measure of the new purchasing power compared with the old. Substituting for m its value $\frac{v_1}{w_1}$, the expression becomes $\frac{v_1}{w_2}$. That is to say, the change in the purchasing power of the standard is found by dividing the value of the new inventory at the old prices by its value at the new.

Only one other difficulty remains. It may happen —and in progressive societies is sure to happen— that at the second date the national inventory consists partly of new articles, and partly of different qualities of old articles. In this case we cannot adopt the method last described, so far as these articles are concerned, for the old prices of undiscovered articles cannot be obtained directly.

Let N be the total value of this part. We may then either neglect it, and obtain the coefficient of appreciation by considering only that part of the new inventory for which corresponding prices may be obtained; or the only other resource seems to be to estimate the prices which would probably have been obtained at the former date, if the articles had been in existence.

If N is left out of consideration, and is small in amount, relatively, the coefficient thus obtained will be approximately correct. If, however, N is relatively too large to be neglected, the coefficient obtained by neglecting it will only be correct on the assumption that the articles considered are fairly representative of the whole group N included.

If the interval between the two dates is small, N will also be small; but if it is very great, and the society progressive, N will be relatively very large. N might be neglected comparing 1880 with 1881; and probably, comparing 1830 with 1880, N, though large, might be considered as represented by the other articles.

But if we compare 1880 with 1280, N would be very large, and that part of the modern national inventory which corresponds to the mediæval would not (it may be thought *primâ facie*) fairly represent the whole.

Nor does the second plan suggested—viz. that of probable estimated cost of N at the earlier period—seem even theoretically possible, when we consider the different methods of production, the cost of raw material, etc. It may however be pointed out that if between very remote periods the coefficient of appreciation cannot be found, the fact is not of much consequence, for in general, at very long intervals, we only wish to compare the purchasing powers of particular kinds of income, so as to discover the relative material prosperity of various classes.

Before passing on to consider the practical uses of the formula in a simplified form, it may be convenient to restate the general principles involved in this method of coefficients. The leading idea is this: Between any two points of time a change occurs in the aggregate value of the national wealth. This change will be due either to an increase or decrease in quantity, or to an increase or decrease in nominal value in the general level of prices—*i.e.* the appreciation or depreciation of the standard — or to a combination of both causes. Now if we can find the increase in quantity, we can deduce the change in value. The theoretical method gives a plan by which, with sufficient statistics, the change in quantity might be computed with comparative precision. At present, however, even as regards the present century, and even in the last twenty years, sufficient statistics are not forthcoming for the application of the formula in the strict sense. It may be of use, however, as the basis of a practical method of approximation, and as leading to qualifications in the use of existing methods.

Such a method is given by taking $\dfrac{w_1}{w_2} . m$ as the formula, when $w_1 =$ the aggregate wealth at the first date, and w_2 at the second, whilst m is the increase in quantity, m being estimated from various independent considerations. For example, other things remaining the same, m should be proportioned to the increase in the population and to the increase in the efficiency of the labour and capital. It will be observed that we assume in this formula that N may be considered as fairly represented by the average of the articles in the old inventory: taking this method, I have worked out roughly some examples.

From calculations made in Porter's *Progress of the Nation*, the total personal property of Great Britain was in 1821 about £1,400,000,000. In 1841 the total had risen to £2,000,000,000; thus $\frac{w_1}{w_2} = \frac{1400}{2000} = \frac{7}{10}$. Now to find m, the increase in quantity, we observe first that population increased from 14·3 to 18·7. The period also was marked by great improvements in the efficiency of labour and capital. Even in agriculture, the productive capacity of the soil had been nearly doubled, with a very small increase in the rural population. Porter calculates that 10,000 acres, cultivated as in 1801, supported 3800 as against 6000 in 1841, whilst 32 acres had been reclaimed for every 100 of population. But if in agriculture the productive power of the country was not quite doubled, there can be little doubt that with very moderate estimates in other industries it was more than doubled. This was certainly the case in the manufactures of cotton, wool, silk, linen, paper, and soap; and it is instructive to note that the tonnage of shipping, and the number of bricks and of carriages, was doubled. I think, then, we may safely say that the productive power of the nation had at any rate doubled during the period. Thus m would become, by considering population and efficiency,

$$2 \cdot \frac{18·7}{14·3} = \text{about } \frac{19}{7}.$$

But $\qquad \dfrac{w_1}{w_2} = \dfrac{7}{10}$; $\quad \therefore \dfrac{w_1}{w_2} \cdot m = \dfrac{19}{7} \cdot \dfrac{7}{10} = \dfrac{19}{10}$.

That is to say, the purchasing power of the sovereign in the period had nearly doubled, or general prices had fallen nearly 50 per cent. Roughly speaking, the personal property of the country had increased in quantity nearly three times, but in value only one and a half times.

I have been able to make the calculation only in a rough manner, but I have not exaggerated the items taken; and from other circumstances—*e.g.* durability of many portions—we might suppose that the quantity of wealth had increased more than three times, and thus prices have fallen more than 50 per cent. I have taken only personal property, so as to use Porter's figures, but I may mention that taking also real property into account, by another calculation there is very little difference.

I have made several more calculations on the same plan, and the general result is always the same —namely, that since the end of last century down to 1850 there was a great appreciation of gold, the purchasing power of the sovereign having almost doubled even between 1821-41.

Even between 1848 and 1868—the period during which the great gold-discoveries took place, and are supposed generally to have depreciated gold to a great extent — I find that the purchasing power of the sovereign (calculated by this method) rose probably a little, and that in fact, instead of depreciation, there was on the whole appreciation. In this calculation I have used the figures which Mr. Giffen [*] adopted for his calculation by quite a different method. The income of England assessed to income-tax at the two dates was about £230,000,000 in 1848, and £365,000,000 in 1868.

We may assume with Mr. Giffen that $\frac{w_1}{w_2}$ was also in this proportion. Now, in finding m or the increase in quantity, we have Mr. Giffen's assertion that "the population is one-quarter more numerous, and, man for man, their industry is nearly twice as productive."

If we take m as 2, we get appreciation in the proportion of 6 : 5.

In this case—

$$\frac{w_1}{w_2} = \frac{230}{365} = \frac{46}{73} = \text{roughly } \frac{3}{5}.$$

So that if we assume that $m = \frac{5}{3}$, or that the quantity of wealth was increased in the proportion of 3 to 5, there would have been neither appreciation nor depreciation.

If, again, we assume that the quantity of wealth had increased simply in proportion to the population, we should have $m = \frac{5}{4}$, and thus the coefficient of appreciation would become $\frac{3}{4}$. Thus, at the outside, the utmost depreciation of the standard by this method is 25 per cent. But when we look into the history of the times between 1848-68, we find it was a period of enormous production. The new supplies of gold in the way described by Tooke gave

[* *Essays in Finance*, First Series, p. 95.

a tremendous stimulus to labour, and this country, more than any other, felt the effect of the stimulus. For example, between 1848 and 1858 only, the mileage of railways was doubled, the value of the exports trebled, and the tonnage of shipping increased 35 per cent. Now if we assume that the wealth per head of the community had increased in this twenty years only by 20 per cent, then by 1868 the effects of the new gold had been neutralised, and the standard had regained its former purchasing power. I am inclined to think, however, having regard to the enormous increase in the activity of production, that an actual appreciation had occurred.

It is this calculation which will probably create most surprise or doubt, as the general belief is, that the effects of the gold discoveries were much greater, and lasted much longer, and by the method of index numbers (Jevons) there seems to be a depreciation of from 26 to 30 per cent at least.

I propose, then, to make some remarks on this matter, using a more recent illustration. The most elaborate calculation recently made in this method is that by Mr. Sauerbeck, formed on a list of forty-five articles of the kind mentioned, including all important food-products, minerals, raw materials of manufactures, and a number of other articles, such as hides, leather, petroleum, and timber. Now the total value of all these articles (and a certain proportion was re-exported) was on the average 1872-74, £577,000,000, and in 1883-85, £482,000,000.

Using the formula $\dfrac{w_1}{w_2} \cdot m$, we obtain m from figures quoted by him as $\frac{617}{525}$ (that is, for the articles in question).

Thus, $\frac{w_1}{w_2} \cdot m = \frac{617}{525} \cdot \frac{577}{482} = $ about $1\cdot37$ as the co-efficient of appreciation, or a fall in prices in the proportion of $137 : 100$, or a fall of about 26 per cent.

Now, when we turn to the national inventory, we find that in 1875 it was calculated by Mr. Giffen as £8,500,000,000,—land being reckoned at about £2,000,000,000, houses at about £1,400,000,000, and movable property not yielding income (furniture, etc.) at £700,000,000 ; these three items alone being about seven times the value of the articles used for the index numbers, which contribute about one-fifteenth only of the grand total. It must be observed, also, that Mr. Giffen's calculation is only of capital, and would thus exclude, apparently, all commodities consumed within the year. This leads me to observe that one of the most important consumable commodities is the labour of the country, the amount annually spent on manual labour being reckoned at £620,000,000, and on professional labour £180,000,000. How much of this should be reckoned I shall consider later.

Now, as regards the index numbers, it is evident at once from the figures quoted that, as regards bulk, the amount is not sufficient, and therefore the measure obtained in this way can only be justified by assuming that the movement in other commodities will be fairly represented by that in raw materials.

But on analysing the causes of difference in relative values, this assumed representative character of raw materials does not seem reasonable, whether we take long periods or short intervals. Take for example the rent of agricultural land and the price of agricultural produce. It is easy to show that if the yield remains the same, and there is a fall in prices, but a less fall in the expenses of working, then rent will fall more than in proportion to the fall in prices.

Then, again, as regards houses. We must distinguish between the building-rent and the ground-rent. Over any considerable period the rise in ground-rents in large cities has been relatively the greatest of any commodity. So far as the cost of building, however, is concerned, the movement of prices in the case of building-rents might easily be in the opposite direction, and any change in the cost of building indirectly affects old buildings. If houses can be built cheaply, people cannot let old houses at their former rents.

It is, however, principally in articles in which machinery has taken the place of manual labour that the movement in raw material fails to be a correct measure of the fall in prices. Any economy in labour, any more effective combination or division of labour, acts in the same way as machinery. Speaking generally, over a long period the cost of production of raw materials admits of much less diminution reckoned in labour than is the case with other commodities.

This leads me to notice in passing that it is this improvement in the efficiency of labour which makes it impossible to take labour as the unit of measuring value.

If all articles were produced by unskilled labour, paid at uniform rates, then changes in these rates would be the best possible measure of change in purchasing power. Roughly speaking, if money wages doubled all prices would be doubled, and the standard would have half the purchasing power; but if the efficiency of labour has doubled, money wages might be doubled and prices remain the same. If we could allow for efficiency, so as to make a quotation for wages for work done, wages would be the best possible measure of a very large group.

Now in any very short period it may be said there can be no great change in the efficiency of labour, and consequently if the hours remain the same, the average rate of wages would be a good practical measure for short periods. Between 1850 and 1856 Tooke calculated that there was a rise in the average of wages of 15 to 20 per cent in unskilled labour: the rise was in many cases 40 per cent.

But even in such a short period we find that, as regards cotton goods, the raw material was about the same, and the price of the cheaper forms of cloth the same, whilst the better cloth had fallen in price 25 per cent. Thus the rise in wages in this industry of 20 per cent must have been accompanied by more than that increase in efficiency. Still, if the rise in average wages was, as computed, 20 per cent in six years, we may assume that at first there was a depreciation of gold to about that extent.

But fascinating as this method of calculation seems

at first sight, through its apparent simplicity, it is really practically of very little value. There are thousands of rates of wages for various kinds of work, and the efficiency of labour and capital is constantly changing, and the average of the change can only be roughly measured.

I give, however, one other example. Mr. Giffen calculates that in fifty years the wages of skilled labourers have risen 50 per cent: in a previous calculation he supposed that between 1848 and 1868 the efficiency of labour in general was doubled, so that it does not seem unreasonable to say that in fifty years skilled labour became three times as efficient. If this is allowed, then the commodities produced by skilled labour must, on the average, have fallen at least one-half in price (for profits have also fallen). On the whole, however, it seems best to consider wages only in so far as paid for services rendered, and not to count them in the national inventory when the result of the labour appears in a material form. We should then only include the value of the wages of domestic servants and of various professional people who produce nothing material—*e.g.* doctors and lawyers.

This examination, however, of the rate of wages, shows clearly enough the insufficiency of the index numbers founded on raw materials as a measure of appreciation. In the first place, the improvement in efficiency of labour has been much more marked over any considerable period in other industries than in the extractive and agricultural group. Skilled labour obtains higher nominal wages reckoned in time, but produces more cheaply. The rise in skilled labour, however, has raised proportionately the wages of unskilled labour, in which the increase in efficiency has not been so great. Thus agricultural labour in this country costs more, and therefore the fall in produce due to foreign sources of supply has a still greater effect on the rent and the price of agricultural land.

In the same way, the relative cost in the other extractive industries has risen. Again, in America and our colonies, and in all countries in which there is a considerable element of skilled labour, the cost of unskilled labour compared with skilled, regard being paid to efficiency, has increased, and thus the relative cost of raw materials has risen. This rise will be greater still if it is assumed that in all fully peopled countries the stage of diminishing return has been reached, owing to the necessity of resorting to inferior sources of supply, and more costly methods of production and extraction. Eventually, at any rate, the tendency to a relative increase in the cost of raw material on this ground must also operate to make raw materials a still less accurate measure.

At the same time it must be allowed that at any particular time, owing to great improvements in communication, and the opening up of new countries, some kinds of food products may fall more rapidly than manufactures, in which case the fall, if general, would be less than the usual index number; and if the value of the raw material compared with the labour in manufactures is small, manufactures may fall less rapidly than the raw material (*e.g.* fine lace).

The general method which I have described cannot at present be used with any degree of accuracy, owing to the want of statistics. In the United States, when the census is taken, a careful estimate is made of the national wealth.

If the authorities were to calculate the value of the old items at the new figures, then a good approximation might be made to the general coefficient of appreciation. It would, however, be a much more simple task in this country, where the conditions of industry are not subject to such violent changes. As it is, all estimates of the national wealth, even for nominal value, rest on the income-tax returns, and for quantities we must resort to still vaguer measures.

Even, however, when used in this very rough manner, some very useful qualifications of the method of index numbers may be obtained.

Speaking generally, I should be inclined to say that over a long period—say, more than twenty years —the index numbers based on raw materials are likely to give too low a measure of appreciation. That is to say, if we were to take the purchasing power of the standard as regards things in general, we should find it greater than as regards raw materials. But, on the other hand, in any short period,—and the shorter it is, the more the tendency is marked,—the index numbers may make the appreciation appear greater than it is when the wider basis is taken. This is nearly equivalent to saying that raw materials, and the like, feel appreciation much more quickly than the derivative products.

If, for example, we compare 1875 with 1885, the *Economist* index numbers give a fall of about 30 per cent, or the purchasing power of the sovereign has risen very steadily until £100 will purchase as much as £130 before.

Now, by the method of coefficients, taking the gross returns of all kinds of property and profits assessed to income-tax, and allowing for increase of population, we have (Sauerbeck) a nominal income of £17·5 in 1875 as against £17·9 in 1885 per head of population. This, it may be remarked, is an increase of 2·3 per cent, compared with an increase of 32·6 per cent in the former decade.

This great fall in the rate of increment of itself would point to an appreciation of the standard in the second period, and this is confirmed when we endeavour to estimate m in the formula or the increase in quantities.

We find that the production and imports into the United Kingdom of all the great staples in Mr. Sauerbeck's list has increased by 525 to 617, or nearly 18 per cent, and the tonnage of steamers has become doubled.

The fact that the rental of houses has increased more than 30 per cent, whilst population has only increased 11 per cent, would point to the conclusion that a great amount of building must have taken place, and that the quantity of house accommodation, regard being paid to the size and convenience of the houses, must have largely increased.

It is said the returns for the second date were taken much more strictly; but the general conclusion, after making all allowances, is that on the wide basis of national wealth the appreciation cannot at present be so great as indicated by the index numbers. Since

1880 the gross rental of lands in the United Kingdom has fallen about 5 per cent; but from 1875 the fall is only 3 per cent. In Scotland, where leases prevail, the figures are nearly the same; and in Ireland, the land of no rent, there is actually a slight increase during the last ten years. These figures show not merely the danger of trusting too much to the income-tax returns, but they show also that the gross rental of land, and thus the value of land, responds slowly to the general movements of prices.

The same is probably true of houses, for unless there has been a very great change in the quality of houses, it would seem that house-rent, like land-rent, has not felt the appreciation so quickly as raw materials,—in fact, it has done so less quickly than land.

Then again, as regards Schedule D, it seems highly probable that the absolute decrease between 1876 and 1880 was due to a fall in the profits of producers owing to the fall in prices of commodities, and that the rise which has taken place since is mainly due to the increased profits of the middle-man, who is a very imperfect conductor of the fall in wholesale prices. If this view is correct, we again find that the actual appreciation, or general fall in prices, is much less than indicated by the index numbers. This view is con-firmed by the slight fall in money wages.

If, however, it is true that over a long period the true appreciation is more than that marked by the index numbers, we must expect the nominal value to consumers of lands, houses, and commodities to fall much more, and although the official returns as yet

hardly give evidence of this, there are abundant signs
of the fall being in progress. The disturbance caused
by the readjustment of rents is in full operation, the
payment of the same nominal wages to the higher
class of domestics is only possible by restricted employment, and any attempt at readjustment in other
employments is resisted to the utmost.

The inquiry in the present paper is however purely
statistical, and in the main an inquiry on the theoretical side. The only assumption made is that the
price of every saleable commodity, and the prices of
larger and larger groups, are the resultant of two sets
of causes — one special and the other general : the
wider the range and the more diversified the prices
chosen, so much more do the special causes tend to
neutralise one another, and to lay bare the influence
of the general causes. If all kinds of raw material
and simple products show a downward movement
on the whole, we may presume that this is due to
some very general causes ; but such causes may be,
although general, such as affect this large group of
commodities principally. If, however, the downward
movement is found in the mass of the wealth of a
great country, we must go further in search of causes ;
and if the same tendency is observed over all countries
using the same standard, still more general causes must
be sought for. We can no more discover these general
causes by analysing the movements of particular prices,
than we can discover the velocity of the earth in its
orbit by analysing the movements of the creatures
upon it. In comparing relative velocities on the
earth's surface, we assume that surface to be at rest ;

and in analysing any number of particular prices and their relative movements, we always assume that the value of the standard remains the same.

I hope to discuss at a future time the causes and consequences of these changes in the value of the standard.

CAUSES OF MOVEMENTS IN GENERAL PRICES

*READ BEFORE THE ROYAL SOCIETY OF
EDINBURGH, JANUARY 30, 1888*

IT was shown in the preceding paper that if we take the total mass of purchasable commodities in any country, and allow for variations in quantity, the nominal monetary value will not vary exactly with the quantity of those commodities at different times, —in other words, that the monetary unit will at different times purchase more or less, on the whole, of all things that bear a price. From the nature of the monetary standard, this result seemed certain to ensue, and history confirms the theory, whatever method be adopted to measure the variations in the standard. In the present paper I propose to investigate what may be considered as the *veræ causæ* of such variations.

As this is probably the most difficult problem in economics, I do not anticipate that the inquiry will be exhaustive, but I hope it may prove to be on the right lines, and thus prepare the way for a more complete solution.

The most common error is to imagine that a general movement in prices can be explained by considering the causes of changes in relative values.

The point may be made quite clear by an illustration. Suppose that a number of yachts are racing with a steady breeze,—then to explain the greater speed of some compared with others, we should look to the build, to the sails, to the seamanship, and so on : we should, in short, simply compare the sailing power of one yacht with another, and in that way explain why one was gaining and another losing.

But if the wind gradually and equally declined in force, or if the tide began to operate in a uniform way, we should, so far, simply get an increase or decrease in the absolute speed of all, and not a change in relative positions. And surely there is no need to point out that we could not discover the strength of the tide or of the wind by examining the build of the various yachts and the seamanship of their crews ; and thus that the facts which are of the utmost importance in explaining the relative speed, throw no light on the most important causes affecting the general speed of all.

Now that is precisely the way in which we must consider the effects of gold in the gold-using countries.

Gold is the wind of commerce and the tide of trade, and its abundance or scarcity raises and lowers general prices just as the wind or tide raises or lowers the speed of vessels. But we shall never discover the influence of gold simply by observing relative changes in various articles.

A concrete example may perhaps still better express

the nature of this fallacy. In the fourteenth century in England, silver was the standard; and about 1300, an ounce of silver would purchase roughly the work of three common labourers for a week, or about three bushels of wheat, or a quarter of an ox, or one and a half sheep, or about a quarter of an acre of good arable land. At the present time, if we take the nominal value of silver in gold, an ounce of silver (*i.e.* 5s.) would purchase one-ninth as much labour, half as much wheat, one twenty-fourth part as much meat, and one-fiftieth as much land as six centuries ago. Thus wheat is twice as dear, meat is twenty-four times as dear.

By considering conditions of supply, etc., we can tell why the value of meat has risen so much compared with wheat; but how in the world, without bringing in silver, can we tell the relation of both to the standard ?

It is easy to see that, taking these important commodities as samples, the value of the monetary standard has decreased very much,—in other words, that there has been a great rise in prices. But it ought to be equally plain that no account of the causes of changes in the relative values of the various commodities *inter se* would explain their average relation to silver or gold.

And yet no error is more common than to suppose that the recent fall in prices can be explained by simply showing the causes of changes in the relative demand and supply of particular commodities. We are constantly told that the fall is due to a fall in freights, which is a cause only adequate *directly* to

explain the fall of sea-borne produce relatively to commodities produced at home (*e.g.* unskilled labour); or
that it is due to improvements in production by the
adoption of particular processes which, as stated, is
only adequate to explain directly the relative fall compared with things to which the processes do not apply.
Yet no one would be so foolish, in the case of the
American greenbacks and the French *assignats*, as to
attempt to explain the rise in prices by shortness of
supply of, or increase of demand for, commodities, or
a falling off in mechanical ingenuity.   Every one can
see, when it is magnified, that the quantity of the circulating medium compared with the transactions to be
effected is fundamental.   Yet when gold and silver
money are the basis of circulation, it is thought that
the quantity is of no importance.   Prices fall, it is
said, because of the greater power of man over nature,
with the fact striking us in the face that the Dakotah
farmers, with prairie soil and American machinery,
cannot raise wheat at so low a price as in England in
the Middle Ages.

The "quantity" theory of money, after being long
considered the best established proposition in political
economy, has found opponents recently on two plausible
grounds.

1. It may be said that, unconsciously, perhaps, but
still effectively, we have in the course of time really
adopted, in place of gold, a different standard of a
vague composite kind.   To make this view clear, for
it is difficult to grasp, an example may be taken.
Suppose next year that by law the wages for a certain
type of unskilled labour are fixed at so much money,

no more no less, and that thus the money price of a large mass of labour is directly determined. Then, by industrial competition, other wages must be adjusted, and eventually commodities must be similarly proportioned in price. When the process is complete, money would no longer be the real standard, but only the medium of exchange. If there were not enough for circulation, there would be inconvenience or a use of substitutes; and if there were too much, it would be melted and sold as old metal.

Now it seems to be imagined that custom, operating over a mass of commodities, has silently effected what this example supposes might be done by law. It is thought, apparently, that there is a customary level for very important groups of prices, that other prices are adjusted in accordance therewith, and thus that the quantity of money is simply adjusted to the level of prices, and not the converse.

A sufficient answer to this theory seems to be found in the easy manner in which the immense additions to the stock of gold, through the Australian and Californian discoveries, were put in circulation. A complete refutation would demand a restatement of the quantity theory.*

2. The accepted theory has also been attacked from another point. For many years it has been observed that nearly 99 per cent of the wholesale transactions in this country are effected without the actual intervention of metallic money, and from this fact it has been argued that the amount of metallic money is of the smallest importance. Now, on examination, this

* Compare p. 54.

theory reduces either to that just noticed—namely, to
the assumption of a customary level to which credit
documents, just as much as gold, must be adjusted;
or else it must mean that the quantity of credit, instead
of the quantity of gold, determines the level of prices.
But this second interpretation overlooks the fundamental distinction between convertible and inconvertible
paper; it implies that banking can be conducted without real reserves; and it practically assumes that the
level of prices in one country is independent of the
level in other countries.   If it were true, there would
be no limits to the rise in prices.

At the same time, it must be allowed, and indeed
it has long been admitted, that within certain limits
credit does influence prices in the way suggested, and
the history of commercial crises confirms this view.
And there is also truth in the position so well stated
by Sir James Steuart, that nearly any form of wealth
can be "melted down into bank money"; and thus,
by means of cheques, a circulating medium of the most
elastic kind can be obtained.   But it is none the
less true that the quantity of metallic money, *taking
the whole system of gold-using countries*, is the real
basis on which the whole superstructure of credit
rests.

If, then, it be granted that in gold-using countries
gold is not only nominally but really the standard of
value, and that it is not merely a convenient medium,
directly and indirectly (through banks), for exchang-
ing commodities the values of which are determined
in relation to some other standard, it must follow that
movements in general prices can only be explained

by taking into account the causes which affect the demand for, and the supply of, gold.

Causes affecting the supply of gold for coinage.—The principal causes affecting the supply require little more than a bare enumeration. (1) We must consider the existing *stock in the hands of man*, and must estimate the rate of waste by wear and tear. In this respect an observation by Tooke is worth repeating—namely, that the larger the stock the greater the absolute waste. (2) It follows from this that the larger the stock, so much greater must be the annual production simply to replace the waste. Thus the *amount annually produced*, the second factor, even if all devoted to coinage, does not constitute so much positive addition to the stock in hand. (3) The supply of gold may be increased by the release of hoards; and (4) by the melting down of plate. (5) By the *substitution* of *notes* or other *credit instruments*, the effective supply of coinage may be increased. Thus, if England were to adopt £1 notes, and were only to keep one-fifth of the gold withdrawn as a reserve, more than £70,000,000 probably could be added to the world's gold coinage in other places. Similarly, when any great country adopts inconvertible paper, a great part of its gold may be driven abroad to other gold-using countries. (6) The stock available for coinage may be *lessened* by being *hoarded*, or *converted into plate*, or *exported* for either purpose to countries with a different standard. It has been found convenient to place some elements, especially (6) under supply, though occasionally they are treated of under demand, because a demand for gold as a commodity is directly equivalent to lessening the amount available for coinage.

Causes affecting the demand for gold as coinage. Some of the causes affecting the demand are equally obvious; but in considering others, most of the difficulties of the subject arise. It is easy to see that (1) if a nation *substitutes gold for silver* or for *paper*, it at once increases the demand for gold. In this case, however, it might be advisable to consider the demand as tantamount to a contraction of supply, so far as the other gold-using areas are considered. (2) It is easy also to see that, as *new countries* become *more thickly peopled* and *more wealthy*, whatever economies in banking and the like they may adopt, they will, if gold is their standard, increase the demand. (3) Similarly, as *out-of-the-way districts in old countries*, in which low customary prices had been the rule, and in which the circulation had been feeble and sluggish, come under the influence of competition, they will require more gold than before, unless they happen to supply it from hoards. (4) It is also obvious that even in the *great centres of old countries*, other things remaining the same, every increase in population and trade will lead to a greater demand for gold.

In all these cases the general result is, that more gold is required if prices are to remain at the same level; and, consequently, if an additional supply is not forthcoming in any of the modes mentioned above —*e.g.* by the increased use of substitutes—the general level of prices must fall.

At this point the first serious difficulty arises in

the question, How does the increased demand relatively to supply really operate in reducing prices? "General prices," it may well be said, is but an expression for the sum total of an infinite series of particular prices, and the meaning of the question is, How are these particular prices affected?

In the first place, it must be observed that the problem will be solved if we can show how any important group of valuables may be affected by this pressure on gold. For it *must be admitted as fundamental and preliminary, that relative values will be adjusted when they are reckoned in money, just as they would be if money did not intervene.* The adjustment will take time, and may be productive of real disturbances of relative values for the time being; but if one great group of things falls in price, at once there will be a tendency for the other groups to bring about again the same relation of net advantages to the respective producers as before. In other words, all the causes embraced in industrial and commercial competition operate to make a new level of prices express the same relative values (other things remaining the same) as before. Therefore, just as we explain the emptying of a cistern by the discovery of one leak, without entering into all the causes of movement of all the particles, so we may explain a general fall in prices by the pressure on gold, if we can discover one place in which the pressure may break down the old system.

Now there appear to be two distinct modes in which a pressure on gold or a relative scarcity of supply may affect prices. In the *first* place, the pressure may make itself felt at the great commercial centres through the banking reserves; and with the present interdependence of nations, a great pressure on one bank may disturb all the rest. Every commercial crisis furnishes an example of this species of pressure. A period of buoyant credit and high prices is suddenly broken by some great failure; this failure leads to others; the banks are drawn upon; to protect themselves, they raise their rates and check their advances, and a general fall in prices ensues. The real force which brings down prices is the necessity of having a certain amount of real reserve. As prices rise through credit influences, more gold is needed for currency, and the higher level attracts imports, the payment for which may cause a foreign drain.

There is, *secondly*, the more fundamental method of reducing prices through a contraction of the currency, which, before the institution of banking, was the only method by which a pressure on gold could operate on prices. We find examples on a large scale in history of this direct connection of prices with the quantity of money; but at present the power of credit may seem so great as to neutralise this influence. It is, however, a great error to suppose that this mode of action of gold upon prices can no longer operate, simply because in great cities and populous districts banking is highly developed.

For we must consider, also, the new and undeveloped countries in which credit has only a feeble existence, and in which prices can only rise by an actual increase of currency, and conversely, must fall if the currency is contracted. Accordingly, it is quite possible that with the reserves at the centres of commerce increasing, with rates of interest low and credit good, a fall in prices may occur and be really due to a pressure on gold. For, if a contraction of currency has occurred in out-of-the-way places, the great staples of these countries may fall in price, and thus by commercial competition drag down other prices. Suppose, for example, that the old countries have in a period of prosperity advanced large amounts of capital to more backward countries. A commercial crisis intervenes, and it is necessary to realise and to call in the advances, or at least further lending is stopped. In this way a balance is due to the old countries, and can only be met by a contraction of the currencies of the debtor States. It follows, then, that with every appearance of abundance of gold in this country, a fall in prices may take place owing to the contraction of currency in other countries.

Every one can see that foreign competition lowers prices at home in numbers of particular articles, which, again, operate indirectly on other commodities. It is strange that so much difficulty should be felt in seeing that wherever the pressure of gold operates first of all, its influence will be transmitted throughout the gold-using areas. If the pressure can be relieved from other stocks, the depression of prices due to this cause will be temporary; if, however, no relief is obtainable, the fall will be permanent, and for the future values will oscillate about a lower level.*

* The reader will observe that this argument is only a restatement of the old orthodox position. For a fuller statement, with modern instances, compare Mr Giffen's *Essays in Finance*.

On some obscure causes affecting the value of gold compared with commodities.—There remain to be noticed some of the more obscure causes affecting the general level of prices in a system of gold-using countries. Nothing is more common than to hear the recent fall in prices in this country ascribed to *improved methods of production* of various kinds of commodities. It is quite clear that an improvement in the production of one thing—other things remaining the same—will cause its value to fall relatively to other things; and in general this fall in value will be expressed by a corresponding fall in price. And obviously a large number of commodities may be affected in the same way.

But the effect on the *general level* of prices of this disturbance of relative prices is by no means so clear, and is, in fact, indeterminate. Let it be supposed, for example, that there is a great improvement in the production of all kinds of clothes, so that, relatively to other things, they fall in price. The great body of consumers of clothes will then have a surplus money income, if they still use only the same amount and quality of clothes as before. In this case there would probably be an increased demand for other things, and, according to the conditions of production of these things, they might rise or fall in price. If they are produced according to the law of diminishing return,— if they can only be increased at an increasing cost— they will rise: but if they can be produced more cheaply on a larger scale, they will, of course, fall in price. Thus, as the indirect consequence of this improvement in production, some things may rise and others fall in price.

But it is also possible that, attracted by the greater cheapness, people will spend more of their income than before on clothes, and thus that there will be a lessened demand for other things, and then the converse of the effect just noticed will be observed.

In a similar manner, the effect of *improvements and reductions in freights* is also indeterminate. In fact, it is best to assume that the act of production is not complete till the commodity is in the hands of the consumer, and thus this case reduces to the former.

It is worthy of remark that, in general, any *real improvement* in production is, in the first place, accompanied by an *increase in profits*, which is, indeed, the proximate cause of the adoption of the improvement. Thus, if a large group of commodities fall in price owing to improved processes, and if, as usually happens, there is more to spend on other things, which, again, causes a fall in some things owing to the extension of division of labour, then the *apparently* general fall in prices will be characterised by an increase of profits, and a rise in the price of articles produced at an increasing cost. Conversely, it may be suspected that a so-called general fall in prices, not marked by an increase of profits, nor by such a partial rise in prices, is not due mainly to improvements in production.

Agricultural produce and the *produce of mines* follow in general the law of diminishing return. Consequently any permanent fall in the *relative value* and *price* of such produce, if the amount consumed is the same or greater, must be due to improvements in production or freight. But if there is a fall in *price* in these things, which is not merely indicative of a fall in

relative value, the fall must be attributed to general
currency causes, because the natural tendency is for
the relative value of such produce to rise, which would,
but for such a disturbance, be marked by a rise in
price.

A great *increase in production generally*, or a greater
addition to the chief staples than the markets can
carry off, will tend to make their values, and thus
their prices, fall. This fall will be accompanied by a
loss of profit, and, as a consequence, production will
be checked until the prices again become remunerative.
*Thus a fall in prices, due simply to over-production,
tends to correct itself*; and commercial history furnishes
many examples. Neither theory nor history lends
support to the idea that over-production involving a
loss of profit can be both general and permanent, and
thus cause a general and permanent fall in prices.

A *change in the distribution of the real wealth* of
the country may lead to important changes in relative
values. A rise in real wages, for example, or the
growth of a large middle class, founded on the split-
ting up of larger incomes, may lead to an increased
demand for certain classes of things, and according to
the conditions of production, these things will rise or
fall in value; and thus there may be an effect on
prices similar to that due to improved processes in
production. We should in general expect some things
to rise and others to fall owing to this agency. Similarly, a change in the habits of the people as regards
consumption may produce effects analogous to those
just described.

If we regard the whole system of gold-using countries, the various *methods of taxation* adopted in different States, and their *mutual obligations*, will affect general prices. By an extensive protective policy, a country may keep up a high level of prices compared with that in a free-trade country. But this higher level of prices will make a greater demand on the world's stock of gold.

Again, according to the state of credit, a drain of gold may be met with a much less effect on prices by some countries than by others.

If one country has a *permanent tribute* to pay to another, an adjustment of general prices will take place of the nature described by Mill,[*] *if we consider these two countries as the only countries.* But if there are more countries to be considered, it is clear that the general level of prices cannot be higher in one than in the rest, simply because it receives a tribute. Suppose A owes a tribute to B, and that there are five other equally important nations trading with both of these and with one another. Obviously the level of prices in B cannot be permanently higher than in the other five countries. For these countries would increase their exports to B and diminish their imports, and thus lower the level of prices. Consequently, the effect of a tribute will be spread over a very wide area, and seeing that *general* prices must be affected, according to this theory the effect will be small.

In any actual case, since the effect on prices must be spread over the whole world, it is probably inappreciable. To take a particular example, the United Kingdom has due to it every year large sums in the

* *Political Economy*, book iii. chap. xxi., § 4.

shape of interest, which partly account for excess of imports over exports. But it is doubtful if the general level of prices is in consequence raised; for in all the great staples of manufacture we undersell other countries.

Thus, on the whole, it would appear that these obscure causes of variation, although *veræ causæ*, are comparatively of small magnitude—that is, compared with those formerly enumerated. Of course, if we take only a few commodities as representing the total mass, there is always a possibility that one or more of these minor influences may vitiate the result; and that was the principal reason for adopting the more elaborate and difficult method described in my former essay.

Commercial history appears to support this conclusion as to the comparative unimportance of these minor causes. During the last fifty years, for example, the methods of production and of communication have been greatly and continuously improved; but during the first part of the period prices were falling, during the second they were rising (or at least the rate of the fall declined very much), and during the third they have again fallen rapidly. There can be little doubt that the principal cause of the change in the middle division was the great gold discoveries.*   In the same way the great silver discoveries in the sixteenth century were coincident with great improvements in industry and commerce, and yet they caused a great

---

* Compare the Essay, p. 165, on "The Effects of Great Discoveries of the Precious Metals."

rise in prices. In both of these cases the rise in
prices would probably have been much greater but for
the great extension of trade requiring more money.
Thus a disturbance of *relative values*, owing to particular improvements, seems of very small importance
compared with an increase in the quantity of transactions, and the growth of trade and population.

In the same way it appears that during the last
fifty years the changes in the distribution of wealth,
the changes in fiscal policy, and the changes in the
relation of exports to imports, have been of relatively
small importance—that is to say, no general movements in prices can be mainly attributed to any of
these causes.

If, then, we wish to account for the recent fall in
prices in gold-using countries, we must look for more
general causes than those connected with various
changes in relative values. There remains one of
much importance in addition to those already noticed.

On the interaction of gold and silver prices.—So far
the argument has proceeded on the assumption that
only one metal, gold, is used for standard money. If,
then, we wish to examine the causes of movements of
prices in silver-using countries, we have only to substitute silver for gold in the reasoning. It is, however,
of course possible, and recent experience seems to afford
an example, that silver prices may remain steady or
rise whilst gold prices fall; and under different circumstances the converse might happen.

The explanation of the causes and consequences
of such a divergence in movement is one of the most
difficult problems of the present time. For we have

very little actual experience which throws light on the present situation. Before the end of the eighteenth century the trade between gold- and silver-using countries was carried on under very different conditions; and from that time up to 1874 the variations in the gold price of silver were comparatively very small. A sudden depreciation of silver of the kind and extent recently experienced is a new fact, especially when coupled with the keener competition and greater sensitiveness of international markets, due to the extension of telegraphs, banking, etc.

Assume that there are two systems of countries with a considerable trade, and that in the one gold alone is the standard and silver a commodity simply, whilst in the other the converse is the case. Suppose now, that, owing to causes of the nature explained above, gold prices move downwards, whilst silver prices, being under different influences, remain the same. For example, it is possible that a rapid growth of trade and population, with diminished supplies of gold in gold-using countries, might be coincident with an extension of credit and banking in silver-using countries. At any rate, let it be assumed that a divergence takes place of the kind indicated.

If the ratio of gold to silver changes in exactly the same proportion as the general level of gold to silver prices, there will be no disturbance of trade. The exports from the gold countries will sell for the same amount of silver; but this silver, being depreciated, will be worth so much less gold than before, and thus these exports will share in the general movement of gold prices. Similarly, the exports from silver coun-

tries will obtain less gold, but it will command the
same amount of silver. The only disturbance will be
as to old monetary obligations.

In this case the natural course of trade would
remain the same as before, a variation occurring simply
in the relative values of the two metals.

It must, however, be observed, by way of qualification, that the assumption of a general movement of
prices of a *perfectly uniform* character in the two
systems of countries is extremely hypothetical, for
some prices may move more quickly than other prices,
and thus temporary disturbances of various kinds may
be caused before the adjustment is completed.

But *ultimately*, as economists are too fond of saying,
the price levels will leave relative values unaffected,
and if the ratio has been adjusted in the precise degree
supposed, international trade will take its normal
course.

The question then arises, *Will the ratio be so adjusted as to correspond exactly to this divergence?* Seeing
that silver is simply a commodity in the gold-using
countries, we may assume that ultimately it must fall
in its gold price, just as other things. If all other
competing substitutes have fallen in price, the demand
for silver will be lessened until it also falls to an equal
degree.

But then, conversely, gold is simply a commodity
in the silver-using countries, and thus, if general silver
prices remain the same as before, the silver price of
gold ought to remain the same by parity of reasoning.
It is, however, quite obvious that, with inter-communi-
cation of markets, an ounce of silver cannot fetch in

London (say) only one-sixth of a sovereign, whilst in India it fetches still one-quarter of a sovereign.

How, then, will the adjustment be made? So long as this divergence exists, there will be a profit in exporting silver to India and exporting gold from India. An ounce of silver, bought for a sixth of a sovereign, exported to India will obtain a quarter of a sovereign; and similarly, a sovereign, exported from India, will obtain six ounces of silver instead of four. Eventually, the rate of exchange must become the same (allowing for carriage, etc.) in both countries. But this may happen, either through silver rising in price in the gold countries, or the gold rising in price in the silver countries.

Suppose now that gold, relatively to commodities, has appreciated 25 per cent, and that silver prices have remained constant. Illustrating the above argument by this figure, we should find that the gold price of silver in London had fallen 25 per cent, whilst the silver price of gold in India had remained the same; or the gold price of silver in London would be 45d. an ounce, and in India 60d. These prices cannot be stable, and apparently it depends simply on the relative demands for the two metals, as commodities, what the resultant price will be. Suppose (taking a mean) it becomes 52d. in both countries, then general gold prices have fallen 25 per cent, and silver about 12. Then exports to India will sell for the same silver as before, which is equivalent to 12 per cent less gold, but these same commodities in the gold countries will only fetch 25 per cent less gold. Conversely, exports from India will obtain 25 per cent less gold, and this will obtain only 12 per cent less silver. Thus exports to India increase and from India diminish, and this condition is again unstable.

It thus appears that unless the ratio of gold to silver is adjusted so as to correspond exactly with the change in the levels of gold and silver prices, a real disturbance of trade will take place, until the levels of gold and silver prices are adjusted to the new ratio of gold and silver.

Next, let it be supposed that there is established a certain level of prices in gold-using countries, and a certain level in silver countries, and that the ratio of gold to silver is suddenly and greatly changed. Silver is simply a commodity in the West, and if large stocks are thrown on the market the price (reckoned in gold) must fall. Suppose that the price of silver falls 25 per cent, and remains low for a considerable period. Then if gold prices remain the same, and also silver prices, a great stimulus would be given to exports from the silver countries, whilst exports thither would be checked. Accordingly (since this condition is not stable) the general levels of prices must be adjusted either by gold prices falling or silver prices rising.

The assumption generally made by English economists of the last generation was that, in the case supposed, silver would be exported to the East, and thus that silver prices would tend to rise, and also the gold price of silver in the West would partly recover from its fall. But it seems probable, in the light of recent history, that this theory is incorrect, and that the adjustment is more likely to take place by a fall in the gold prices proportionate to the fall in silver.

It is easy to see that to produce a rise in silver prices over the vast area of the East, where credit is still in its infancy, and custom not yet in its dotage, enormous masses of silver must be put in circulation. But if these masses of silver have first to go through Western markets, the price of silver will fall, and the state of general gold prices will be adjusted to this fall before the silver can influence the Eastern markets. The point is, that prices in silver-using countries cannot be forced up simply because gold ornaments have become dearer. Depreciated paper implies a rise of prices consequent on excessive issues, or simply through taking gold as the real basis, but general silver prices will not move in the same easy manner according to the gold price of silver.

By the adoption of a very simple formula, a general argument may be stated, of which the above are particular cases.

It must be assumed, as before, that whatever changes take place in the general levels of prices in gold-using and silver-using countries respectively, or in the relative values of gold and silver *inter se*, after sufficient time to make the adjustment, the *relative values* of commodities generally must, so far as these changes are concerned, eventually be unaffected.

Thus, if a general fall in gold prices becomes definitely established, the articles exported to silver-using countries, and also the articles imported from those countries, must share in this fall.

Similarly, if silver prices remain steady, the exports from silver-using countries must obtain the same amount of silver, and the silver price of the imports to them also must remain steady.

Again, seeing that in actual trade the exports from gold-using countries are sold for silver, and those from silver-using countries for gold, it follows also that variations in the ratio of exchange of the metals (taken in connection with the general levels of prices) must leave relative values the same.

It will be observed that these postulates contain no more than is implied in effective industrial and commercial competition. Suppose, for example, that owing to a sudden and extensive contraction in the supply of gold, or an increase in the demand, a general fall of prices sets in in the gold-using countries. Some commodities may not be so soon affected as others, and no doubt the fall will be irregular; but obviously those articles which happen to be exported to silver-using countries must also share in this tendency to fall— that is to say, the tendency will be for the relative *prices* of commodities to be adjusted to their former relative *values*.

Similarly it must be assumed that a mere change in the relative values of gold and silver as metals cannot neutralise the general effects of competition; although, until competition has done its work, exceptional advantages or disadvantages may ensue in particular cases.

Apart from these assumptions, however, the postulates imply that a disturbance of a general kind may arise in three distinct ways—namely, *first*, with causes primarily affecting the general level of prices in gold-

using countries ; *secondly*, with causes primarily affecting
the general level of prices in silver-using countries ;
and *thirdly*, seeing that silver in gold-using countries
and gold in silver-using countries are simply commodities, with causes primarily affecting the ratio of
gold to silver (as metals).

The object of the following analysis is to show the
various ways in which equilibrium may be restored
according to the origin of the initial disturbance, and
further, to show the nature of the stimulus or the
check, as the case may be, to the trade between gold-
using and silver-using countries, until equilibrium is
reached.   It has been found convenient to take the
first two cases together.

It may further be remarked that, in any practical
case, causes of the three kinds indicated may begin to
operate simultaneously, or at any rate that before one
has completed its effect another may come into play.
Thus the recent demonetisation of silver might at the
same time have tended directly to cause a disturbance
in the ratio of gold to silver, and also an appreciation
of gold (through greater demands upon it) relatively to
commodities—that is, a fall in the general level of
prices in gold-using countries.   But no solution seems
possible without a preliminary analysis of the effects
of the various causes in isolation.

With these postulates, suppose that G_1 means the
number of ounces of gold which a given mass of exports
(say E_1) to silver countries will command at the rates
current in the gold countries (say at English ports).

Similarly, let S_1 mean the number of ounces of silver
which a given mass of exports E_2 (of equal value with

E_1) to gold-using countries will command at the rates current in the silver-using countries (say at Indian ports). [The general argument, it will be plainly seen, is unaffected by the cost of carriage, which may accordingly be neglected.]

Let r_1 be the ratio of gold to silver, such that one ounce of gold is equal to r_1 ounces of silver.

Then, when trade is in equilibrium, that is to say, in the absence of any artificial impulse, $\dfrac{S_1}{G_1} = r_1$.

CASE I.—(a) Now assume that, owing to *general causes operating in gold-using countries, gold becomes definitely appreciated.* Then the mass of commodities which formerly obtained G_1 ounces of gold will now obtain less (say G_2). Therefore, for the restoration of equilibrium, either S_1 must fall proportionately (say to S_2, r_1 remaining constant), or else r_1 must rise in proportion (S_1 remaining constant), or a change in both must occur, S_1 falling and r_1 rising, until $\dfrac{S_2}{G_2} = r_2$.

Until equilibrium is thus brought about in one or other of these ways, commodities worth G_2 in gold-using countries will be worth more gold than G_2 in silver countries, after being sold at silver prices and converted into gold; and commodities exported from silver countries will obtain less than at home. Thus there will be a stimulus to exports from gold-using countries (and the converse for silver-using countries).

(b) In a similar way it may be shown that if *gold becomes depreciated relatively to commodities*—that is, if G_2 becomes greater than G_1—then either silver prices must rise or else r_1 must fall, or both; and until equilibrium is reached, there will be a stimulus to exports from silver countries and a check on exports thither.

(c) If *silver prices rise, owing to causes operating in silver-using countries*, then equilibrium will be restored either by gold prices rising, or r_1 rising, or both—the stimulus in the meantime being to exports from the gold-using countries, and the converse for the silver-using countries.

(d) If *silver prices fall*, then either gold prices must fall or r_1 must fall, or both—the stimulus being in the meantime to exports from the silver-using countries, and the converse for the gold-using countries.

(e) If silver prices were to move one way and gold the opposite way, then the case would reduce to one of those already considered, according as $\frac{S_2}{G_2}$ was greater or less than $\frac{S_1}{G_1}$.

CASE II.—Now let it be supposed that, *whilst S_1 and G_1 remain the same, r_1 suddenly changes and becomes greater*—that is to say, the metal silver becomes depreciated relatively to the metal gold, whilst there is otherwise nothing to change the general levels of prices. Let r_2 be the newly established rate, then $\frac{S_1}{G_1}$ must become $\frac{S_2}{G_2}$, so that $\frac{S_2}{G_2} = r_2$.

(a) Thus, if S_1 remains the same (*i.e.* $S_2 = S_1$), then G_2 must be less than G_1, in the proportion r_1 to r_2. In other words, if silver prices remain the same, gold prices must fall proportionately to the fall in silver.

Until equilibrium is restored, under this hypothesis there will be a stimulus to exports from silver countries (and the converse for gold-using countries).

(b) If G_2 is equal to G_1, and S_2 becomes proportionately greater than S_1, so as to make $\dfrac{S_2}{G_1} = r_2$, then, until equilibrium is restored, with this kind of movement there will again be a stimulus to exports from the silver-using countries (and the converse for gold-using countries).

(c) If, on the contrary, r_2 *becomes suddenly less than* r_1—that is, as metals, gold becomes depreciated relatively to silver—then $\dfrac{S_1}{G_1}$ must be similarly adjusted.

If S_1 remains the same, G_1 must rise. In the meantime, exports from the gold countries will feel the stimulus.

(d) With the same hypothesis, if S_2 becomes less, G_1 remaining the same, then, until equilibrium is reached, exports from the gold countries will again feel the stimulus.

The correctness of the general analysis is confirmed by the case (I. b) of the great gold discoveries, for there appears to have been a stimulus to exports from silver-using countries, the balance being met by the export of silver thither. (Tooke's *History of Prices*, vol. vi. p. 718, etc.)

The use of the formula may be illustrated by the case of inconvertible paper (in place of silver) compared with gold.

In this case, substitute P for S, and let r_1 be the

number by which the gold currency must be multiplied to obtain the equivalent paper, r_1 in general being
a fraction greater than unity.

Then when equilibrium is established :—

$$\frac{P_1}{G_1} = r_1.$$

Case (a).—Suppose that, by *excessive issues* of the
paper, P_1 rises in the first place. Then also, since in
this case G_1 may be considered steady, r_1 must rise ;
and until $\frac{P_2}{G_1} = r_2$, there will be a *stimulus to exports
to the paper country.* In other words, they will obtain
higher prices in paper, which will command more gold
until gold obtains a corresponding premium.

Case (b).—But if r_1 *rises first through the paper
becoming discredited* before the general level of prices
has been much affected by excessive issues, then P_1
must also rise if G_1 remains steady ; and until the
corresponding rise in P_1 takes place, there will be a
stimulus to exports from the paper country.

Light may be also thrown on the problem whether
the premium on gold is the *exact* measure of the
depreciation of the paper relatively to commodities,
by considering the possible changes in G_1, owing
indirectly to the issues and depreciation of the
paper.

As this analysis is of great practical importance at
the present time, and also leads to a considerable
modification of a well-known theory, some further explanation may be offered of the symbols used and of
the assumptions implied.

The given mass of exports E_1 might be taken to mean the aggregate of exports from gold-using to silver-using countries; but for the sake of simplicity it has been found convenient to take only such an amount of E_2 (supposing E_2 is greater than E_1) as in normal conditions is equal in value to E_1.

It is also assumed in the analysis that what is true of E_1 and E_2, is also true of all the exports which, under any circumstances that arise, may be made from gold- and silver-using countries respectively. Thus, under actual conditions, any change in S_1 and G_1 implies a change of prices in groups of commodities of such magnitude that this change may be held to involve a corresponding change in other commodities.

It is easy to see, for example, if wheat falls in price, that indirectly, through the effects on agriculture, a wide range of prices will become affected, and the commodities in the aggregate of international trade between gold and silver countries are of such importance that any considerable fall in their prices must operate very widely. It should also be observed that a great rise in r_1, S_1 remaining steady, would give a proportionate profit on every exportable article from silver-using countries unless there was a corresponding fall in the gold price.

It will be observed in every case of the formula that whenever through any change in either S or G or r the equation $\dfrac{S}{G} = r$ becomes $\dfrac{S}{G} > r$, then there is a stimulus to exports from the gold-using to the silver-using countries (and conversely a check on exports from the latter to the former); whilst if the equation becomes $\frac{S}{G} < r$, the stimulus and check will act in the opposite way.

For the convenience of those who are unfamiliar with or distrust symbolical reasoning, this general conclusion may be stated as follows :—If for any reason, whether from a change in gold prices or in silver prices or in the ratio, articles exported from the gold-using to the silver-using countries obtain *relatively* more gold (on conversion) than when retained in the gold-using area, there will be a stimulus to exportation ; and similarly, if articles exported from the silver-using countries obtain *relatively* more silver than if retained in the silver area, exportation will be stimulated.   And this is only a particular example of the moving principle in all international trade.

As regards the nature of the stimulus, it must be observed that the whole train of reasoning depends upon the assumption that a stimulus due to purely monetary causes will bring into play counteracting forces, and will tend to be converted into some change in silver prices, or in gold prices, or in the ratio of gold to silver.   The practical difficulty is that the adjustment takes time, and that the further adjustment of contracts and customs takes still more time, so that before one disturbance has been neutralised another may begin to operate.

There will, of course, be a strong disinclination on the part of those who hold that Ricardo and Mill have said the last word on the theory of international values and the distribution of the precious metals, to admit that a mere change in the relative values of gold and silver can have such wide-reaching consequences. It is then of the utmost importance to observe that with the demonetisation of silver a new set of conditions arose, and furnished a case to which the accepted theory does not apply. In discussing the question of the effects of money on international trade, the old theory constantly takes the " precious metals " as a unit. Mill, for example, entitles his chapter : " Of the distribution of the *precious metals* throughout the commercial world"; and it is on the "*precious metals*" that the quantity of " *money* " is based.

Now, according to this view, all countries have only one monetary system (which practically was the case when Mill wrote), and, consequently, the question of the interaction of two monetary systems never comes in sight. Thus it is quite possible that Mill's theory is right under his hypotheses, and yet inapplicable to a totally different case. According to Mill's theory, the depreciation of silver can only be a mere incident of exchange, such as might occur if two trading countries had the same currency. The whole theory really implies that there is a stable par between gold and silver, whilst the present problem arises from the fact that the stability has vanished.

It is interesting to treat Case II. according to Mill's theory. Silver becomes for some reason depreciated, which in this view simply means that the exchanges become unfavourable for the silver-using countries— that is, their form of the " precious metals " obtains less than usual of the other form; or, to take a particular example, a mass of rupees or the corresponding bill obtains a less amount of sovereigns;

and, conversely, sovereigns obtain more rupees. Thus there will be a stimulus to exports from the silver countries to get sovereigns wherewith to buy rupees; and, conversely, there will be a check on exports to the silver countries, because the rupees fetch less sovereigns. Consequently, the exports to the silver countries will no longer pay for the exports therefrom, and a balance of the " precious metals " will be due. When this balance arrives, it will, by the quantity theory, tend to raise prices in the silver countries, and thus to encourage exports thither, and to check exports therefrom. Then the exchange will right itself, and possibly go to the other side of the old par.

That is the pure theory; and, given a stable par between gold and silver, the theory is sound in principle, though a less direct application of the quantity theory is required with telegraphs and banks in full operation. No better proof could be given that this account of the accepted theory is correct, than the treatment of the question in Mr. Goschen's standard work on the *Foreign Exchanges*. In discussing the limits of the fluctuations in the exchanges between gold - using and silver - using countries, he commences by saying: " Either gold or silver will be at what may be called the *par value* between the two, or, as is more generally the fact, the one will be at a premium as compared with the other." Clearly this assumption of a par value between the two metals must have been made under very different conditions from the present.

The inadequacy of Mill's theory may, however, be best shown by a somewhat startling deduction. If

England and India had the same currency (say gold), would any one believe for a moment that a fall of 30 per cent could occur in the exchange value of the gold rupee against a gold sovereign, or if it did occur, that it would continue for years? And yet those who say that the fall in the rupee is simply *a consequence of a readjustment of trade*, must be prepared logically to make this admission. Hitherto such a fall in the exchange has only taken place with depreciated paper, and the movement in paper prices has usually responded to the premium on gold; but to put silver on the same footing with paper, the Governor-General of India must be an alchemist with unlimited powers of producing silver rupees.

The essence of the present argument is, that silver may fall first of all in the gold-using countries, apart from any disturbance of international trade (except as a consequence); and those who admit that in these countries silver is only a commodity can hardly deny this position. " Gold is simply merchandise in such countries as have a silver currency, and silver is merchandise in such countries as have a gold standard; and according to the price of the merchandise in a given moment, so will the exchanges fluctuate." *

There can be no doubt that the price of silver and the exchanges fluctuate together, and that if silver falls, a sovereign or its equivalent will so far command more rupees.

And if this fall were due merely to an excess of exports from the gold-using countries, or diminution of imports from the silver-using countries, so that

* Goschen's *Foreign Exchanges*, p. 76.

there was a less demand for silver than usual for
export, then no doubt there would be a recovery, and
the fall would only temporarily inconvenience or
benefit those who had to buy or sell silver or its
equivalent.

But if silver is simply merchandise in the gold-
using countries, can we say that its value depends
*entirely on the demand for export to the silver-using
countries for trade debts*, and that no other causes
can make its value fluctuate? Obviously there are
several other causes which may be of importance, as,
for example, the increase of production, the release of
the hoards of French peasants, the suspension of the
Bland Act, the sale of old stocks by Germany, and
further demonetisation by Western nations.   And
even apart from all these causes, does not the demand
for export itself depend upon the general balance of
indebtedness, and not only upon trade debts?

But once let it be granted that the ratio may
change apart from the course of trade,—once let it be
admitted that it is not only the demand for silver
for export to silver countries for *trade debts* that
determines its value,—and there is no escape from
the second case of the analysis. If the metal silver,
for example, falls (say) 30 per cent, either silver
prices must rise or gold prices must fall, or both.
Hence, if silver prices remain fairly steady, the fall
must be entirely in the gold prices; and to suppose
that this fall in gold prices can be confined to the
great staples of trade with silver countries, is to
surrender all the principles of industrial and commercial competition.

It thus appears that, if we assume the *variation to occur first in the ratio*, and if silver remains depreciated, there is a stimulus to exports from silver countries, and a check on exports thither until equilibrium is restored, either by gold prices falling or silver prices rising. Reasons have been given elsewhere * for the belief that gold prices are more likely to fall than silver prices to rise. The latter could only take place by large exports of silver.

If through direct causes at the same time gold prices are falling, equilibrium will be sooner attained and the stimulus neutralised.

Now, as regards recent history, we know for certain that silver has depreciated relatively to gold; and it seems probable that silver prices have remained fairly steady, whilst gold prices have fallen. This fall in gold prices may be due partly to general causes of appreciation, and partly to the *prior* depreciation of silver. The suddenness and rapidity of the fall seems to point to the latter as, at any rate, an important factor, and the anti-silver policy of various nations accounts for the depreciation. This view also seems confirmed by the course of trade, for if the depreciation of silver were (as in Case I. *a*) simply the *effect* of the *general appreciation of gold*, it would have been accompanied by a stimulus to exports to silver-using countries and a check on exports therefrom.

It is possible that, owing to general causes, silver prices have fallen to some extent. In this case the fall in gold prices must be even greater than is

* *Treatise on Money*, p. 102.

indicated by the depreciation of the metal silver, if equilibrium has been restored, and part of the fall must be ascribed to general causes of appreciation.

It is worth observing that, so far as the fall in gold prices is due to the depreciation of silver, there would be an apparent abundance rather than a scarcity of gold in the great commercial gold-using countries.

In order to illustrate further the practical uses of the analysis, some possible changes in the immediate future of gold prices may be indicated.   As soon as the depreciation of silver as " merchandise " has reached the limit of its fall, there may be a reaction in gold prices which will tend also to force up silver. So far as the fall in gold prices is due to the prior depreciation of silver, it will imply rather a superfluity than a scarcity of gold, and with speculation wearied with watching and ready to expand credit on the slightest pretence, there may well be a sufficient " quantity of money " to support a higher level of prices.   Again, if silver were to rise owing to its increased use in America, gold prices would also tend to rise.   And if silver were sent in large quantities to the East, and the long-looked-for fulfilment of Mr. Bagehot's prophecy were to occur, then also a rise in the ratio and in gold prices might take place.   The persistent fall, however, since 1874 shows how tedious the process may be, and so far as this fall is due to general causes of appreciation there is no natural tendency to recovery.

But whether the particular application is correct or

not, the bearing of this general analysis on the question of bi-metallism is most important. If the ratio
of gold to silver is left to what are termed market
influences solely, then an alteration in the ratio may
have as a consequence a disturbance of prices and
trade, and unless the alteration is temporary such a
disturbance must ensue. Silver prices being more
steady than gold prices, the latter are more likely to
be affected. Thus great discoveries of silver in the
West, or a further demonetisation, might cause a
further fall in the metal silver, and indirectly a further
fall in general gold prices.

Again, if silver prices and gold prices remain
subject to different influences, the metals being independent, then the ratio must be adjusted to these
changes, and this change in the ratio may react on
general prices, and will in any case disturb the monetary obligations of gold- and silver-using countries.

But these disturbances in the ratio, whether they
are, according to circumstances, the cause or the effect
of changes in the levels of gold and silver prices, can
only be mischievous. It is of the smallest importance
to the world at large whether the gold price of silver
or the silver price of gold is much or little. If silver
falls in value relatively to gold, more silver and less
gold may be used in the arts; but that is only a
matter of interest to jewellers and to the very small
class who spend a large part of their wealth on ornaments made of the precious metals. A movement in
the price of coal or iron is of much more importance
to the world of *consumers* than a movement in the
price of silver. But when a movement in silver has

the indirect consequences indicated in this analysis, then the movement becomes of interest not only to jewellers, but to Governments—not only to a few lovers of ornament, but to nations.

If, on the other hand, gold and silver were linked together, discoveries of either metal would act as a stimulus to trade; both metals would replenish the general stock; the general level of prices throughout the world, so far as the metallic currency is concerned, would be governed by the same causes, as there would be practically only one monetary system; and instead of changes in the ratio, with the consequent disturbances of prices and contracts, the principal result would be that silver would be more largely used as the basis of note issues in the reserves of banks.

MR. GIFFEN'S ATTACK ON BI-METALLISTS

THE "NINETEENTH CENTURY," DECEMBER 1889

UNDER the innocent and modest title of "A Problem in Money,"* Mr. Giffen has in reality discussed the most fundamental questions in the theory of money and prices. He has not only challenged positions of the bi-metallists (*e.g.* the fixed ratio) which, since the publication of the Report of the Royal Commission, most people had begun to suppose might be taken for granted, but he has attacked the theory of the relation of money and prices which is generally accepted in economic text-books, and which has become familiar to the general public in recent years through the arguments of Mr. Goschen and others who are not bi-metallists, in explanation of the fall in prices or the appreciation of gold. Not content with this extended assault, Mr. Giffen has substituted a new theory of money which, if it survives its birth, will probably be known as the "merchandise" theory. This theory should, perhaps, rather be described as prehistoric than new, but at any rate it is essentially different

* See *Nineteenth Century*, November 1889.

from the theory which has been generally accepted by economists since the time of Ricardo.

It is to be regretted that not only in substance, but also in style and manner, Mr. Giffen should have thought fit to return to the old-fashioned mode of treating bi-metallists. There is nothing to be gained, even in vigour, by calling a theory "rotten" which is held, for example, by Professor H. Sidgwick, the author of the most recent standard work on political economy; by Mr. A. J. Balfour, "the philosophic doubter"; by Sir David Barbour, Finance Minister for India and author of an excellent book on bi-metallism, and by others whose business it has been for many years to teach the principles of economics; and Mr. Giffen might have had a little more regard for his opponents than to accuse them of holding a "palpable delusion—very far from creditable to its originators and adherents." It will strike most people, too, as rather odd that, in an essay on a current controversy, Mr. Giffen makes no allusion to the Report of the Royal Commission, which on all sides was acknowledged to give, at the least, an admirable statement of the principles and theories advanced, and the most accessible and reliable information on matters of fact. The only advantage in Mr. Giffen's style of treating opponents with the silence of contempt, or the abuse of a professional politician, is that there is obviously no need for them, out of respect to his feelings and reputation, to soften down his contradictions and to gently insinuate a slight disagreement with his conclusions. With such a sturdy opponent one can, at least, speak bluntly without fear of offence.

It is, however, with Mr. Giffen's arguments only that I propose to deal, as I quite agree with him that no question can be settled by authority—living or dead.

The first and avowedly principal object of the essay is to destroy the quantitative theory of money, which is " at the root of the bi-metallic theory, so far as bi-metallism is based on any consistent and substantial theory."

To begin with, Mr. Giffen states the theory in a form in which it never was held, and is not now held, by any one, bi-metallist or mono-metallist.

" It is said or assumed," he writes, " that every portion of the precious metals not wanted for any other purpose becomes ' money'; that the ratio of exchange with other articles rises or falls as there is less or more ' money,' the fall or the rise being proportionate to the change in the quantity of ' money,' and that this money use is also so much the preponderant use that nothing else is material in settling the ratio of the exchange between the precious metals and other commodities." That is to say, according to Mr. Giffen, the quantity theory only takes into account the quantity of metallic money, and assumes that general prices—for that is the meaning of the ratio of exchange with commodities—rise and fall simply in proportion to this quantity. But, as a matter of fact, every advocate of the quantity theory of money—and that is practically every economist of repute since Ricardo—has pointed out many other conditions which must be considered besides the mere quantity of metallic money. Amongst these, the most important are the rapidity of circulation, the volume of trade, the influence of barter, the use of the metals for other purposes besides coinage, the cost of production of the precious metals, their great durability, and the effects of credit or representative money. I have elsewhere * examined these influences at length, and have also discussed the effects of other more obscure causes of variation, such as improvements in production of other commodities, over-production, etc. There may be differences in the number of qualifications and the degree of importance assigned to them by different writers, but assuredly the quantity theory in the bare form given to it by Mr. Giffen has been supported by no one.

The most puzzling thing, however, in the whole paper is the next position in which Mr. Giffen states in a preliminary manner his own view of the relation between money and prices. For here he flatly contradicts the opinions which he himself had expressed on this very quantity theory over and over again for years, and even so lately as last autumn. There is, of course, no reason why a writer on currency should not change his opinion just as Mill changed his opinion on the wages question, although it is both usual and convenient to make, as Mill did, a frank acknowledgment. But Mr Giffen is content with saying that he still admits there is " a " relation between the quantity of money and prices. Surely the indefinite article in inverted commas never implied so much, and never was a complete change of view indicated with such an appearance of consistency. The whole sentence must

* *Money and Monetary Problems*, pp. 54-106 and 286-323.

be quoted for comparison.   Mr. Giffen now maintains
that " there is ' a ' relation between the quantity of
money and prices, but it is rather one in which prices
assist in determining the quantity of the precious metals
to be used as money, and not one in which prices are
themselves determined by that quantity."   The change
in his opinion may be indicated by a simple illustration.
It is as if he had formerly maintained that Henry the
Seventh was the father of Henry the Eighth, and now
held that there was indeed " a " relation between them,
but that it was one in which Henry the Eighth was
rather the father than the son of Henry the Seventh.

One example, though hundreds might be given,
of this remarkable change of attitude must suffice.   In
his work on *Stock Exchange Securities* (chap. ii.) Mr.
Giffen discussed *ipso nomine* " the connection between
prices and the quantity of money."   One sentence may
be quoted : " An addition to the circulation raises all
prices, a deduction from it lowers them."   This
sentence is not a merely incidental remark, but fairly
represents the whole argument of the book.   The relative prices of securities and commodities are worked
out entirely on the basis of the accepted quantity
theory of money, and the same theory is constantly
appealed to in all Mr. Giffen's previous financial essays.
But in this last paper he suddenly turns round and
says : " It is the range of prices as part of a general
economic condition which helps to determine the
quantity of money in use, and not the quantity in use
which determines the prices."

Mr. Giffen's consistency is, however, a matter of no
importance except to himself and those who trust to

his authority and not to his reasoning for their opinions. But if his present general position is sound, there is an end of bi-metallism, and not only of bi-metallism, but of the greater part of the received theory of money from Adam Smith to Mr Goschen. The new position, then, deserves examination, on the ground that it will at any rate serve to test the strength of some important economic principles.

Those who are familiar with financial history* will recall the opinions which were held by the Directors of the Bank of England during the restriction of cash payments, and which, as Bagehot says, "have become almost classical by their nonsense." The Directors acted on the principle that the state of prices and trade generally required a certain amount of currency, and they imagined that so long as they issued notes only at 5 per cent, and only in the discount of good bills, those notes could not be depreciated. They thought, like Mr. Giffen at present, that the quantity of money, so far as prices were concerned, was an effect and not a cause; but, as every one knows, their notes became depreciated, and prices rose in response to the increase in issues. The justice of the comparison may be seen from the following statement by Mr. Giffen: "The paper (and this is true of *inconvertible* as well as convertible paper) is very nearly a fixed quantity per head in such countries, or rather a quantity varying between fixed points according to the seasons, and it hardly seems to vary with prices within very wide limits indeed."

When the Bank Directors found that there was a

* *Cf.* Bagehot's *Lombard Street*, chap. vii.

premium on gold, they maintained that gold had appreciated, that its price as "merchandise" had risen; they
could not believe that their notes were depreciated
owing to excess when they had only supplied the
legitimate demands of commerce. The fallacy of this
reasoning was exposed by Ricardo in his essay on the
"High Price of Bullion," and again in his "Reply to
Mr. Bosanquet"; and its reappearance in all its original
simplicity at this time of day is exceedingly curious and
instructive.

Mr. Giffen may of course reply that he is referring
only to notes of "small denominations," and that
inconvertible notes are only mentioned to illustrate
the use of metallic money. But it is precisely with
such small notes that the theory of depreciation,
depending wholly on the quantity theory, is worked
out; the notes first of all displace the coinage and then,
being issued in excess, become depreciated.

We may now examine Mr. Giffen's "merchandise"
theory of money, which is advanced as a substitute for
the old quantity theory. The object aimed at is to
show that "the precious metals all through, whether
used for monetary purposes or not, are merchandise,
and the ratio at which they exchange with other
articles is determined in precisely the same way as the
ratio between any other commodities, as the ratio, for
instance, between copper and wheat, or beef and shoes."
The method of procedure is to advance from the simple
case of gold and silver used for purely industrial
purposes in the arts, through less and less obvious
cases—hoards, "token" money, standard money, and
reserves—until by an induction by simple enumeration

we arrive at the paradoxical conclusion that the precious metals are " all through " merchandise.

The first case does not demand much attention, and is only of interest as illustrating Mr. Giffen's powers of perverting the opinions of his opponents and converting his own. He alleges that bi-metallists have not allowed for the enormous use of the precious metals in the arts. On the contrary, however, the growing demand for the use of the precious metals, especially gold, in the arts has always been one of the strongest arguments of those who ascribe the fall in prices largely to the diminution of the gold available for money. The point has been admirably brought out by Sir David Barbour. But the conversion is more interesting than the perversion. Mr. Giffen is anxious to put his merchandise theory on the best footing, to begin with, by making the quantity of regular merchandise as great as possible, and he appears to be as bold and ready in changing his facts as his opinions. In the *Essays on Finance* (2nd series, published 1886), he complains that Soetbeer's estimate of nearly £10,000,000 as the industrial demand on the annual production is too high, and forthwith reduces it to £5,000,000, which is about a quarter of the annual production. In the present paper, however, we are told, without any reference whatever to any authority, that about two-thirds of the gold annually produced is taken for the arts. But whether it is two-thirds or one-quarter, the amount of the new gold used in the arts may no doubt be described as merchandise, and no one will deny that the sum-total of the precious metals used as plate, ornaments, etc., must be very great. As will be shown presently, however, gold is in many respects a very peculiar form of merchandise, even when regarded apart from its monetary uses.

The next use of the precious metals which Mr. Giffen takes up is the case of hoards—whether private as in the East, or public as in governmental banks "beyond any strict requirement of monetary circulation," and in military chests. The way in which these hoards are brought under the "merchandise" theory and excluded from the "quantity" theory must be described in the words of the writer: "Whatever the motives may be which determine these hoards, the hoards themselves are not *money in circulation* in any form, and the demand to replenish them is not a demand for 'money,' and the supply of these demands is not a supply of 'money,' which can help to make any such relation between the quantity of money and prices as the quantitative theory of money, and with it the bi-metallic theory, assume."

That hoards are not in circulation is a verbal truism, but that the demand for hoards and the supply of hoards have no place in the quantity theory of money is obviously not true. The locking up of large quantities of gold in recent years has always been regarded as an important factor in the appreciation of gold on the quantity theory. The absorption of metallic money in hoards diminishes the quantity in circulation as effectively, for the time being, as if it had been destroyed.

Mr. Giffen next proceeds to "money" in circulation, and states that there is "money" and "money," and that it is convenient to make distinctions. It is doubtless convenient to make distinctions, but it is highly

inconvenient, to say the least, to give a new and
arbitrary meaning to such a well-defined term as
" token " money. The precious metals are employed
first (says Mr. Giffen) " for token or *quasi*-token coinage, *i.e.* for the retail payments of society." It is true
that " token " coins are used for retail payments, but it
is a gross misuse of language to say that all money
used for retail payments is " token " money, or even
" *quasi*-token " money. The vital distinction between
" token " and " standard " money cannot be slurred
over with a *quasi*, however much virtue you put in it.
Mr. Giffen actually speaks later on of that part of the
gold money in a country like England which is
" *explicitly* token money." In the proper meaning of
the term there is no such thing as " gold token-money "
in England, though (as every one knows) Mr. Childers
recently tried to make some. If the question were one
of words only, no more need be said ; but, as too often
happens, the confusion of language leads to a confusion
of thought. Taking " token " money in the accepted
meaning of the term—that is, as money the nominal
value of which, even after allowing for cost of coinage,
is above the metallic value—it follows at once that
the quantity issued must be limited, and also that the
amount of such money as legal tender must also be
limited. Obviously, then, so far as token money is
concerned, it is the duty of a Government to adapt the
issues to the demands of trade and the convenience of
the people. Properly managed, token money ought
not (except indirectly as economising the use of the
precious metals) to act upon prices—and this is pointed
out in every work on the subject (*e.g.* Walker's *Money*).

The precise connection between the amount of token money and prices presents some difficulty. It is possible, for instance, that with a lower range of prices people would use less standard money and more tokens— a point brought out by Lord Herschell on the Commission. But any difficulty of this kind Mr. Giffen evades by a very short and easy method—namely, the dogmatic: "Apparently, then, for a community of given numbers in a certain state of civilisation and economic development, only a definite amount of such small money is required, *whatever the range of prices may be.*" We are then told that "the statistics of copper coinage show that it is a machine whose size is increased automatically as population increases—more rapidly *perhaps* in good times (when prices rise) than in bad times when prices fall." The " perhaps " throws a strange light on the appeal to statistics which are not quoted.

But the copper coinage is only introduced by way of preparation for the precious metals. Mr. Giffen next takes silver "in such a country as England," where of course it is, properly speaking, "token" money. Here we have the amazing statement that as regards the amount of the silver money in circulation " the determining factor is a *custom and habit* of the people which requires so much silver money *per head.*" This reminds one of the old cure for impecuniosity— namely, to make a habit of always keeping sixpence in your pocket. Again, it is interesting to compare Mr. Giffen's views in the *Essays* (published in 1886) with his present position. There he says: " Cash is wanted in the complex system as small change, the amount of the small change required *depending in turn on the rate of wages and profits*—i.e. *on nominal values.*"

It is really astonishing to find that Mr. Giffen should go about painfully to prove that "token" money does not act upon prices, and should after all push his case to an absurdity, when he might have taken for granted all that the argument requires. If bi-metallists supposed that "token" money would act on prices as well as standard money, they would not propose the adoption of silver as standard money as a remedy for falling prices. Every one admits that the demand for silver to make "token" money is simply a demand for silver as merchandise in the first place.

The truth, however, is, that Mr. Giffen has paid the natural penalty for a gross perversion of language, and has fallen into a hopeless confusion of facts. He tries to show that gold, which is standard money, follows the same laws as "token" money, properly so called, because it is used in *retail transactions*, and is thus, according to his peculiar use of the term, "token" money. This attempt to regard "standard" money as on the same footing with "token" money necessarily leads to the omission of vital differences. In the first place "token" money is confined to a particular country and its value is arbitrary, but the value of "standard" money depends upon world-wide causes. As Ricardo showed once for all, we cannot, as regards standard money, take a country in isolation. If, owing to abundance of standard money, the level of prices in one country rises above the general level, the money will tend to flow abroad, but token money could not be exported. Secondly, standard money can be coined to an unlimited extent, and is only full standard money when this is the case. Thus any amount of gold could at once be converted into English "pounds sterling." Thirdly, standard money can be used to purchase anything immediately, because it is unlimited legal tender.

As regards " token " money, in the proper sense of the term, it must from its nature depend upon the will of the Government of any particular country. Sometimes Governments have permitted the abuses of private tokens, and sometimes they have issued too many and sometimes too few token coins. But no one will deny that, when properly managed, the quantity of token money—so far as it is related to prices—depends upon the prices, and not the converse, although the assertion that a fixed quantity is required per head of population is unproved and is also opposed to Mr. Giffen's former opinions.

The case of standard money is however utterly different, although it is easy to see the origin of Mr. Giffen's confusion. He has taken one country, when he should have taken all the countries with the same standard. He has argued that what is true of one country is true in the same sense of all taken together. It is perfectly true to say, and indeed it is an essential part of the quantity theory, that, *given a certain range of prices* and certain general economic conditions in any particular country, this country will only require a certain amount of standard coin, and will not retain more in circulation. But it is one thing to say with Adam Smith and Ricardo that the precious metals are distributed through the nations proportionately to their wealth, trade, and requirements, and quite a different thing to say with Mr. Giffen that the sum-total of these requirements determines the quantity in circulation in the world. The distinction has been put in a nutshell by Ricardo * :—

If the quantity of gold and silver in the world employed as money were exceedingly small or abundantly great it would not in the least affect the *proportions* in which they would be divided among the different nations—*the variations in their quantity would have produced no other effect than to make the commodities for which they were exchanged comparatively dear or cheap.* . . . If in the progress towards wealth one nation advanced more rapidly than others, that nation would *require and obtain a greater proportion* of the money of the world.

Here we have the accepted quantity theory and the theory of national requirements in perfect harmony. The general level of prices is first determined by the quantity of money in circulation (with the qualifications mentioned before), and the quantity which each nation requires depends upon general economic conditions.

Mr. Giffen does not appear to see the real meaning of this international character of standard money, even when he comes to the reserves of banks and the bullion required for foreign remittances. He simply asserts that the reserves, when not hoards, tend to become a fixed quantity, a quantity oscillating between fixed points, here as elsewhere contradicting his former opinions with perfect unconcern. How he could miss the essential point of the Ricardian quantity theory after writing the following sentence, is a mystery : "The whole reserves and precious metals in course of remit-

* " High Price of Bullion."

tance in the civilised world may be considered a single
fund, which varies even less as a whole than the
particular parts of it in individual countries." Precisely
so; and if the demands on this single fund increase,
owing to the growth of commerce and population, will
nothing happen to prices ?

We are now in a position to consider Mr. Giffen's
main result—that gold is simply "merchandise," and
that its use as standard money does not make it differ
from other forms of merchandise as regards the laws
regulating its value. This conclusion was reached by
considering standard money as "token or *quasi*-token
money," and by practically assuming that the quantities
required, whether for circulation or reserves, are fixed
by custom and habit. In fact, Mr. Giffen has abandoned the quantity theory to such an extent that he
will hardly allow that there is even "a" relation at all,
or any dependence whatever, between money and prices.

Prices apparently move up and down according to
credit waves, demand and supply, cost of production,
and the like, but even general prices do not depend in
any sense on the quantity of money.

But every one allows—even Mr. Giffen must still
allow—that the average level of prices determines, or
rather is the same thing as, the value of gold, and that
the only meaning of the value of gold is its exchange
value in terms of commodities. If, however, this is the
case, how can its value depend directly, like that of
ordinary merchandise, upon its cost of production ? In
the generally accepted view, which Mr. Giffen now
professes to combat, the cost of production operates
through the quantity of "money"; if the cost rises, for

example, less is produced annually; but if that method is excluded, how can cost operate at all?

The difference between the old quantity theory and the "new" merchandise theory may be put in another way still more clearly. The usual way of estimating the exchange value of gold is to take "index numbers"—in other words, the average prices of a number of selected commodities. And although the price of gold reckoned in gold money is of course fixed, the exchange value reckoned in commodities varies. Now, can we say that the movements in these "index numbers"—the movements, that is to say, in the prices of cotton, coffee, copper, etc.—depend upon gold as "merchandise"? Who, except a goldsmith, looks upon gold as mere merchandise in making a bargain? Who can say that all sales are, in effect, the barter of particular commodities against gold bullion? Yet barter of this elementary kind is the logical outcome of this merchandise theory.

The truth is, that standard money is a medium of exchange and a measure of values, and can only be considered as merchandise when converted into bullion, and even then it is merchandise of a most peculiar character owing to the monetary use. What other merchandise can be disposed of instantly in unlimited quantities at the same money price per unit?

The second part of Mr. Giffen's paper is hardly deserving of notice, after the unanimous finding of the Royal Commission on the fixed ratio. Two glaring mistakes may, however, be pointed out. In the first place, when he tries to prove that Sismondi, in a passage quoted, is the real founder of the theory of the

fixed ratio, he fails to observe that Sismondi referred
to one country only, and not to a convention of
nations; and, further, that he supposed that the ratio
would not be permanently fixed, but must be changed
from time to time.   It is surely a most singular
perversion of thought and language to ascribe the theory
of a ratio fixed permanently by a group of nations to a
writer who makes no mention either of fixity or of
international action.   Mr. Giffen's second mistake is
to suppose that gold and silver are required for such
different monetary uses that they would not be interchangeable if bi-metallism were adopted.   Yet in the
same passage he maintains, according to the orthodox
view of Gresham's Law, that the metal which is over-
valued by the legal ratio will drive the other out of
circulation.   But this really means that the two metals
are, as money, so readily interchangeable that the
slightest difference will serve for displacement of one
by the other.   The very foundation of Gresham's Law
is that the kind of money-material—the mere substance—is a matter of utter indifference.

In conclusion, Mr. Giffen attempts to crush his
opponents by the weight of authority :—

> Not only are there no exponents of the bi-metallic theory to
> set against the exponents of the mono-metallic theory, which has
> a greater array of economic authority on its side than almost any
> other conclusion which can be named, but there is no consistent
> exposition of principles and facts anywhere which can be
> appealed to at all by the bi-metallic rank and file.

It is important to observe that the opinions paraded
by Mr. Giffen are at the best only applicable to the
isolated action of various countries, and have no bearing

whatever on *international* bi-metallism, which alone holds the field.

The audacity of the appeal to authority by a writer who has set himself to disprove the theory of money which forty years ago Mill described as the best-established proposition in political economy, which Ricardo eighty years ago professed to derive from the most approved writers on the subject, and which the most recent standard work * on currency describes as generally accepted with or without qualification by the whole body of economists—is only equalled by the audacity of the charge of inconsistency by a writer who has deliberately contradicted every opinion on money and prices which he had hitherto maintained. Mr. Giffen's present opinions are many centuries older than the writers whom he professes to honour by irrelevant quotation; they are, in fact, the opinions of those prehistoric traders who had not invented "money," and who made all their exchanges by barter of "merchandise" against "merchandise."

* Professor Walker's *Money*.

MR. ALFRED DE ROTHSCHILD'S PROPOSAL TO THE MONETARY CONFERENCE

"SCOTSMAN," DECEMBER 3, 1892

As the proposal made by Mr. de Rothschild to the Monetary Conference has been published in full in the press, and as the Conference cannot be regarded as a merely judicial body, there does not seem to be any objection to a public discussion side by side with the secret deliberations of the members of the committee of experts. The proposal is remarkable not only in itself, but far more so on account of the very strong language in which it refers to the monetary situation—" I need hardly remind you that the stock of silver in the world is estimated at some thousands of millions; and if this Conference were to break up without arriving at any definite result, there would be a depreciation in the value of that commodity which it would be frightful to contemplate, and out of which a monetary panic would ensue, the far-spreading effects of which it would be impossible to foretell." It does not require any great knowledge of the silver question to deduce some obvious consequences that follow from this admission.

In the first place, it is plain that the Conference, in the opinion of this eminent banker, has not been called together for an academic discussion, or even for the sifting of evidence in the manner of the late Royal Commission. On the contrary, it must devise some practical remedy, or at the least some temporary palliative to prevent a gigantic catastrophe. It follows, secondly, that the position hitherto most strongly maintained by most mono-metallists has been abandoned. No one can assent to this emphatic warning, and yet at the same time argue that silver is a commodity like other commodities, and that if we only leave things alone it will find its natural level, and all will be well —ultimately. Ultimately—it may be; but in the meantime—the deluge. The third consequence is that if Mr. de Rothschild's proposal is found to be impracticable or useless, some other remedy must be tried, unless the resources of civilisation are declared to be at an end. In this way international bi-metallism and other remedies have been brought nearer the sphere of practical politics than they ever were before.

In the meantime, however, Mr. de Rothschild's proposal holds the field, and it may be worth while to discuss some of the more obvious difficulties which it presents. The essence of the scheme is that Europe should follow the example of the United States and purchase a certain amount of silver annually. At present America purchases 54 million ounces per annum, and the proposal is that the European Governments should buy silver to the extent of, say, £5,000,000 so long as the price of silver is below 43d. an ounce. At 40d. an ounce there would be just

30 millions of ounces against the 54 millions of America. At first sight, the most curious feature of the scheme is the recommendation to follow the example of America. Authorities on currency are not conspicuous for unanimity, but the condemnation of the American plan has been almost universal, and the present difficulties of America form one of the principal arguments for a solution of some kind. From the passing of the Bland Act of 1878 up to October 1892, silver certificates and Treasury notes had been issued to the extent of 433,000,000 dollars. It is stated that the whole of this was in active circulation except some 4,000,000 dollars.

The silver certificates, however, are not on the same footing as full legal tender notes redeemable in gold, and although in ordinary transactions they circulate as if they were, the banks take good care to get rid of them as soon as possible. If, then, America goes on coining silver at its fixed minimum, and no other vital change occurs, there seems to be no escape in that country from a premium on gold in the near future, followed by the adoption in time of a silver standard pure and simple. If, on the other hand, America stops coining silver, the depreciation of that metal must be sudden and severe, and the pressure on gold will lead to a further fall in general prices. It may, of course, be objected that the experience of fourteen years, from 1878, is sufficient to prove that there is no danger of a premium on gold; but it is generally understood that if the silver certificates had not recently received a stimulus to circulation through being issued for smaller sums, the premium would already have arisen.

What Mr. de Rothschild's scheme really amounts to is this : If America will go on as before, then the European Governments will follow her example in the mildest degree that will be accepted.   They also will buy a certain amount if the price is not more than 43d. per ounce.   But if America goes on as before, and the European palliation stops at 43d. per ounce, the progress of events in America must, as before, be through a premium on gold to a silver standard.

As regards Europe, unless the price of silver remains above 43d., her Governments must follow the lead of the United States, although more slowly and reluctantly.   It is of no avail for them to purchase silver to sell again ; they must either hoard it in banks or put it in circulation to have any effect on the price. Take the case of England : the amount of silver used, being token coinage, can only be increased artificially by making the silver more convenient, or by raising the limit of legal tender to, say, £5.   Practically this would mean, in either case, the issue of silver certificates.   A ten-shilling note based on silver would no doubt circulate very largely if it were allowed to do so, and would probably drive a good deal of gold from circulation.   The States forming the Latin Union have already in circulation as full legal tender large quantities of silver, the nominal value being some 33 per cent more than the metallic value.   What are they to do with the new silver that falls to their share ? Are they to coin it at the old ratio, and thus add to their depreciated stock, and run the risk of a premium on gold being recognised internally ?

It is not necessary to pursue the difficulties of M. de Rothschild's scheme into further detail, for, as indicated in the original statement, certain modifications might be adopted. One other point, however, of general interest may be noted. The United States, taking coinage and use in the arts together, is said to consume silver annually in excess of its production, and yet its heroic efforts to check the fall in the price of silver have failed, the price having reached its lowest limit this year. What hope can there be that the additional action of Europe on the same lines, but in a modified degree, will convert the failure into a success? Even such a moderate success as a permanent, steady 43d. in putting a stop to the severe fluctuations in exchange would be of great advantage; such a ratio might even be said to secure the greatest advantage under the actual circumstances; but at the best—and this is doubtful—all that the scheme seems likely to achieve is that the price of silver would never exceed 43d., whilst the minimum would be as doubtful and fluctuating as before.

In conclusion, attention may be directed to the evils that the Conference is called together to remedy, if possible.

First of all, there are the fluctuations in exchange, especially felt by the Government of India and its officials, and by those trading with silver-using countries.

Secondly, there are the special difficulties of those countries which have masses of over-rated silver. English bi-metallists have generally maintained that any fixed ratio would be better than none, but other

States may naturally desire a rehabilitation of silver. England has no silver coins, but tokens.

Thirdly, there is the general fall in prices reckoned in gold; that is to say, there is not only the depreciation of silver relatively to gold, but the appreciation of gold relatively to commodities. It is this part of the fog which most people find densest and most bewildering, but it hides some very real dangers.

The question is: Will the purchase by Europe of £5,000,000 of silver annually when its price is not above 43d. remedy these evils, or most of them, in the best way practicable? At the time of writing, the answer from Brussels has not arrived.

THE MISSING LINK BETWEEN GOLD AND SILVER

"SCOTSMAN," APRIL 15, 1893

THOSE who thought that bi-metallism was killed by the adverse vote in the House of Commons must have received a rude shock from the article in the *Nineteenth Century*, in which Mr. Leonard Courtney announces his conversion to the faith. On the Gold and Silver Commission Mr. Courtney was certainly the keenest cross-examiner on the mono-metallic side; and he had the advantage of being thoroughly imbued with the orthodox political economy, and was an expert in the art of putting questions in the irritating manner of Socrates. He gave one witness at least the idea that his opinions on the subject were petrified in a very jagged form. It is evidence of remarkable courage and most reasonable sweetness on the part of Mr. Courtney to announce his recantation in what may be considered the official organ for converts of various kinds, and to take the trouble to polish his sentences till they shine with epigram and good humour. Mr. Courtney has, besides, the great merit of a pervert;

other people have drawn the line at fixing a definite ratio. They would leave it to Parliament, or Conference, or Commission; but Mr. Courtney stamps his foot and says twenty-five to one. His audacity is to be admired and imitated. At the same time there is a deep gulf between fifteen-and-a-half and sixteen to one—the ratios at which silver is in France and the United States legal tender—and this new proposal for twenty-five to one.

If international bi-metallism is ever to be adopted —and it only waits for the conversion of a hundred members of the House of Commons—and if Mr. De Rothschild's prophecy as to a gigantic monetary catastrophe is to be prevented, some method must be discovered for reconciling the divergent interests on the ratio. As regards this country and India, any fixed ratio would be better than the present uncertainty; but countries which have large masses of legal tender in silver that is rated in our money at about 60d. an ounce, will naturally think once or twice before they consent to accept Mr. Courtney's ratio of (about) 38d.; it would seem like a definite absolute loss of so many millions of hard money. The worst of it is, too, that perfidious Albion would lose nothing in proportion.

In the Middle Ages—when people were supposed to know nothing of finance—it was the habit of Governments, when a depreciation of the coinage had *de facto* taken place, to recognise the fact. The English coinage, for example, by natural wear and tear dwindled in weight, and the Government time after time recognised the fact, and altered the definition of the standard coin accordingly. Except on one occasion—curiously enough under the original Defender of the Faith—the fineness of silver was not tampered with; but the weight of the coins became less and less, and the best explanation is, not that the kings were thieves, but that they recognised facts. In these days, with all our knowledge of finance, we prefer the policy of the ostrich: we are ready to eat anything and shut our eyes to anything—the "we," of course, including our ancient enemies as well as our noble selves.

Nobody denies that, compared with gold, silver has suffered a great depreciation; the fact is written down every day in every newspaper with a money article: silver used to oscillate about 60d., it now oscillates about 38d. In any ordinary business, if some part of the capital had depreciated in value, something would be written off; and even in the management of the currency, when the coins become so worn as to be a nuisance, the Government calls them in and rehabilitates them at its own expense. But in this case of the depreciation of silver—with consequences of the greatest magnitude—the Governments of the civilised world do nothing; the fact stares them in the face, but in this case, at any rate, they are provided only with patience. Consider, first, the position of the United Kingdom. By the Coinage Act a troy pound of standard silver is coined into sixty-six shillings, and the other silver coins are in the same proportion —that is to say, silver coins are rated as if silver were worth about 66d. per ounce. It is, of course, quite in accordance with sound monetary principles that our silver coins, being tokens, should be overvalued; but if the original policy was sound which overvalued the

silver 6d. an ounce, the present policy by which it is
overvalued 28d. can hardly be sound also. It is a
dangerous thing for a country to have its silver coinage of large denomination so much overvalued. The
premium on private coining is now between forty and
fifty per cent, and it is quite possible that the glut of
silver of which bankers complain is partly due to this
cause. At the same time, the Government is tempted
to force the issues of silver on the public, and the
Chancellor of the Exchequer, in a speech that was
meant to be conservative, boasted that the profits
on the mintage of silver had recently been nearly
£1,000,000 a year. If the original ratio of Lord
Liverpool, which had the good fortune to become
sacred in about half a century, was wise and prudent
and honest, the present ratio of coining silver is precisely the opposite. If the spirit of the law were to
be observed, we ought not to coin our standard silver
into more than forty-eight shillings the troy pound at
the outside. Accordingly, instead of the jejune offer
of Mr. De Rothschild, this country might well agree
to encourage the others by making its silver coins
heavier. The sacrifice would be simply the sacrifice
of a windfall. As regards our friends the enemy who
have masses of silver—full legal tender—it is still
more politic and honest for them to recognise the fact
of depreciation, and adjust their coins accordingly.
If they are afraid of a loss, evident, palpable, and dis-
agreeable, they might adopt the old English method
and reduce the weight of their gold coins; if they
prefer to recognise the fact that gold is *de facto* the
standard, and that prices have been partially readjusted,

they also might add to the weight of their silver coins,
and in response India might make the rupee heavier;
if they choose the middle way of compromise, they
might take from the gold coins what they add to the
silver.   In any case, however, the fact of the depreciation ought to be recognised.   If the United States
continue to coin silver as at present, no possible regulation of Government can prevent the adoption of a
silver standard.   That, indeed, would not be a bad
solution, but it would be rather undignified, and
national pique would make the transition difficult.   On
the whole, then, it seems the best policy to recognise
the fact of depreciation and weight the silver coins.
The consequent demand for silver would, of course,
raise its price, and ,the result would be a compromise
between the present and the old price of silver.   The
key to the solution of the problem is undoubtedly to
be found in the recognition of an accomplished fact.
So long as we plume ourselves on making a million a
year out of our tokens, and a few other millions out
of our foreign debtors, foreign countries are not likely
to move: the lure of Mr. De Rothschild was no better
than a big salmon-fly; the offer to give up the *Con-
junctive* profits of mintage, and to exact only the pound
of flesh from our debtors, would seem much more like
common business.   The central idea of this argument,
though arrived at independently, has in its favour the
authority of Dr. Soetbeer, by far the most eminent
statistician on the subject; but, alas! he now has the
authority of the dead.   His plan, however, was complicated by many niceties, and he assumed that gold
would remain the sole standard.   The plan here

suggested is intended as a practical transition to bi-
metallism. If the United States were to make their
silver dollars heavier, they would do a much better
stroke of business than by making a gold loan— they
would really lead the way towards an international
agreement.

THE LIVING CAPITAL OF THE UNITED KINGDOM

"ECONOMIC JOURNAL," MARCH 1891

ALMOST all systematic writers on Political Economy have discussed the question whether or not the skill of the artisan, credit institutions, the national organisation of industry, and other intangible elements in the social fabric should be included in the wealth of the individual or the nation. Adam Smith boldly places under " fixed capital" the acquired and useful abilities of all the inhabitants or members of the society, on the grounds : *first*, that the acquisition of such talents " by the maintenance of the acquirer during his education, study, or apprenticeship always costs a real expense, which is a capital fixed and realised as it were in his person "; and, *secondly*, because the improved dexterity of a workman may be considered in the same light as a machine or instrument of trade " which facilitates and abridges labour, and which, though it costs a certain expense, repays that expense with a profit." J. S. Mill, on the other hand, insists at the outset that " in propriety of classification the people of a country are not to be counted in its wealth. They are that for the sake of

which its wealth exists. The term 'wealth' is wanted
to denote the desirable objects which they possess, not
inclusive of, but in contradistinction to, their own
persons." It is true that at a later stage in his work
Mill attempts to distinguish between the skill and the
personality of the artisan, and to include the former
under wealth and not the latter, but in doing so he
destroys the value of his first position. For just as
there are close analogies between the living instrument
and the dead, as clearly expressed by Adam Smith,
there are also differences of vital importance. To take
but one example : the interest derived from dead capital
must for many purposes be contrasted with the wages
obtained for skilled labour.

Without entering further into this very thorny
subject of accurate definitions, it may be premised that
the application of the term "capital" to skill and the
like will be justified or not according as we wish
to emphasise resemblances or differences. In many
inquiries we certainly ought to draw a sharp line
between capital and labour in the narrow and popular
senses of the terms, especially in cases where ethical
considerations cannot be altogether excluded. At the
same time, however, there are other occasions upon
which analogy will be more useful than contrast, and
such an occasion is offered by the problem I propose to
discuss in the present paper.

Briefly stated, that problem is to find the money-
value of the "living capital" of the United Kingdom—
that is to say, the "capital" fixed and embodied in
the people as distinguished from the lands, houses,
machinery, and the like.

The problem is by no means new, and is, in fact, old enough to possess the interest of a revival. It was a favourite topic with Sir William Petty and his followers in " political arithmetic." It may be worth while to quote Petty's general description of his method, and also to give a particular example. The principle is explained as follows [*]: " Suppose the people of England to be six millions in number, and that their expense at £7 per head be forty-two millions ; suppose, also, that the rent of the lands be eight millions and the yearly profit of all the personal estate be eight millions more ;—it must needs follow that *the labour of the people* must have supplied the remaining twenty-six millions, the which being multiplied by twenty (*the mass of mankind being worth twenty years' purchase as well as land*) makes five hundred and twenty millions as the value of the whole people : which number, divided by six millions, makes above £80 sterling to be the value of each head of man, woman, and child, and of adult persons twice as much ; from whence we may learn to compute the loss we have sustained through the plague, by the slaughter of men in war, and by the sending them abroad into the service of foreign princes." The concluding sentence indicates the uses of the method : but a more interesting example may be given—no less than the most " thorough " solution of the Irish problem ever attempted, so "thorough," indeed, that Petty is careful to explain that it must be looked upon rather as a " *Dream* or *Reverie* than a rational Proposition." [†] He begins by saying that he has heard

many wise men, " when they were bewailing the vast
losses of the English in preventing and suppressing
rebellions in Ireland, wish (in such their melancholies)
that the people of Ireland being saved that island were
sunk under water." This is the key to the position.
The people of Ireland are " living capital" in a dis-
advantageous situation. If they were transported to
the *more populous* districts of England and Wales and
the Lowlands of Scotland their labour would be worth
so much more, and the value and strength of this really
" United" Kingdom would be so much greater. The
example is amusing by its grotesque detail, and it is
interesting to note that the same argument is applied
also with relentless logic to the Highlands of Scotland.
The principle, however, on which it is based is perfectly
sound, and has recently been much insisted on by
American economists. Up to certain limits the increase
of population in a given area more than proportionately
increases the productive power of the people. The
principle is, in fact, one of the main elements in the
advantages of division of labour.

Following Petty's example up to the end of last
century most writers who made estimates of the
national wealth included as the principal item the value
of the " living capital." In recent times, however,
this element has been altogether dropped from the
calculation. The omission is, I think, unfortunate in
many ways, and especially in that it unconsciously
leads people to exaggerate the importance of the
material wealth of the nation in the narrowest sense of
the term. Some years ago a thrill of gratified pride
passed through the country when Mr Giffen calculated

that its material wealth (or capital as he called it) was accumulating at the rate of some two hundred and forty millions per annum. A more recent calculation by the same statistician to the effect that, in spite of depression and low prices, accumulations were still going on, though not so rapidly, was also received with undisguised satisfaction—especially by the owners of dead capital. Mr Giffen, it is right to bear in mind, took great pains to explain, especially on the last occasion, that his estimate was necessarily made in a very rough manner. The essence of his plan is to begin with national income as the basis, and to capitalise the various kinds of incomes at different numbers of years' purchase. This income is partly obtained from the income-tax returns (and is so far reliable as a minimum), but apart from this calculation a number of arbitrary and conjectural elements are introduced. There are important classes of income which do not pay income-tax, and there are items of property which do not yield income at all, e.g. the furniture in houses and public buildings. Again, of some important classes of income only a certain portion is supposed to be due to capital in the strict sense of the term,—that is to say, as distinct from labour. Thus only one-fifth of the incomes of trades and professions (in Schedule D) is accounted for in this way—the remainder being, in the language of the economists, "wages of superintendence." Of the income of the lower middle class and the labouring classes a still smaller proportion is set down as due to capital proper. It is plain also that the number of years' purchase selected in different cases is somewhat arbitrary, and

in every case must depend partly on the rate of
interest. It is necessary that these qualifications
should be borne carefully in mind, for there is something so pleasantly definite about two hundred and
forty millions per annum that the steps in the calculation are liable to be forgotten.

It is well, also, that some of the teaching of the
older economists should be remembered—that capital,
although saved, is always being consumed, and that,
as Adam Smith says, "the annual labour of every
nation is the fund which originally supplies it with all
the necessaries and conveniences of life which it
annually consumes." If this learning is somewhat too
musty, at any rate the American statistician, Mr
Atkinson, may be heeded when he states that the
richest nation has never more than the value—all
told—of two or three years' production in hand in a
concrete form, and that the whole world is always
within a year of starvation. The recent accumulations
of dead capital, when regarded in this manner, will
assume somewhat less startling proportions.

A far better way, however, of restoring the due
economic perspective seems to be to revert to the
method of Petty and the early masters, and to assign a
value to living, as well as to dead, capital. In order
to make the comparison as fair as possible, I shall first
of all take Mr Giffen's figures for the various classes of
income, and also for those parts of the various incomes
supposed to be derived from the possession of capital
in his sense. In this way a first approximation will be
made to the income derived from "living" capital, and
greater accuracy may be then attained by considering

in more detail certain kinds of income, and also certain comparatively permanent sources of " wealth " (personal) which do not yield income.

The fundamental difficulty, which has probably thrust this problem into the background, is to pass from income to capital. We are all familiar with capital valuations of lands, houses, etc., based upon the revenues which they yield, but since the abolition of slavery in civilised communities we are not familiar with the capitalisation of wage-earning power. The short and simple dogmatism of Petty, already quoted, as to the mass of mankind being worth twenty years' purchase *as well as land*, seems, at any rate, to require elucidation. Why should the mass of mankind, it may well be asked, be worth neither more nor less than land ? If land becomes worth thirty years' purchase, will mankind rise in value in equal proportion ? and if land falls in value, will humanity fall also ? The " indestructible and original powers of the soil " are, by implication, as immortal as man is mortal, and, unlike him, require no care or labour for their preservation ; and the points of contrasts between land and mankind might be indefinitely increased.

This preliminary difficulty, however, must in some way be surmounted before the comparison between " dead " and " living " capital can be effected ; and a few facts may be noticed which serve to show that the valuation of human beings is not so remote from ordinary thought as at first sight appears. Constantly, for example, cases are occurring in the law courts which recall the methods of compensation adopted by our Saxon forefathers. A money-value is placed upon husbands, wives, sons, and daughters, and even upon their component parts. The loss of a leg has its value appraised equally with blighted affections and shocks to the system. Again, to look at the question from another point of view, every father of a family knows that it costs a considerable sum to rear children to a self-supporting age, and the higher the trade or profession selected so much the greater is the cost.

Estimates were recently given in a newspaper, expressly for the guidance of parents, of the total cost of qualifying for various employments.

These instances, however, do not at once suggest any practicable method of valuing the total human stock of a nation, with its infinite variety of ages, occupations, and abilities. A simple enumeration and summation is plainly impossible. The difficulty involved in the ages alone, from this point of view, seems at first sight almost insuperable.

We must exclude the very old and the very young, so far as earning-power is concerned, or even regard them as of negative value—but where shall we draw the line?

The clue to the solution seems to be given in the practice of insurance companies, based on the principle that whilst the individual dies the race remains, and not merely the race, but the classes and divisions of the race remain to a great extent uniform. Life insurance is mainly concerned with age and mortality, but a similar principle may be applied to the occupations of the people. The individual lawyer or carpenter perishes, but the profession or the trade survives, like a Platonic idea. In a stationary economic condition of a people, we might suppose that every trade and profession is an immortal, unchanging corporation. In this way we can see that Petty was justified in valuing the people as he valued the land —both are permanent sources of income. If the society under consideration is progressive, we are still more justified in this method of procedure in arriving at a minimum valuation. If wages are rising and the number of workers is increasing, we may be certain that after an interval of, say, ten years, the value of the "living capital," however estimated, will be greater than at present, and this living capital may be regarded as of the most permanent kind.

When this principle is once admitted, the only difficulty is to separate that part of the total income of the community, due to living labour in every shape and form, from that part due to capital in the narrow sense of the term. As the main practical object of this paper is to supplement Mr. Giffen's familiar estimates, it will be convenient, as already indicated, to take his figures to start with.

In an essay * on the progress of the working classes, Mr. Giffen states:—"The capitalist as such gets a low interest for his money, and the aggregate return to capital is not a third part of the aggregate income of the country (which may be put at not less than £1200 millions), and is, as I should estimate, not much more than a fourth part." It follows at once from this that the value of the "living capital" is, at any rate, nearly three times the value of the dead.

* *Essays in Finance*, 2nd Series, p. 403.

If it be objected that this simple method of valuation is illusory, I reply that it is actually less illusory than Mr. Giffen's own calculations, for the living capital of the race is less perishable than much of the so-called material capital.

But the full strength of the case can only be seen when the details of Mr. Giffen's method are examined. Take, for example, the table quoted in his recent work on the *Growth of Capital* (p. 11). The object of this table is to give the amounts of the principal classes of income, and to capitalise those parts of these incomes which are supposed to be derived from capital proper. Now it will be found that of the total income of the trades and professions for 1885, namely, £180 millions, only one-fifth part is supposed to be derived from capital, and this is capitalised at only fifteen years' purchase. But the curious thing is that in the other items of income no such corresponding division is made. The largest item in the national inventory is the value of the houses. This is obtained by simply capitalising the return of rental under Schedule A in the income-tax returns at fifteen years' purchase, by which a gross value of nearly £2000 millions is obtained. But it is perfectly plain that houses would not yield a return of between 6 and 7 per cent unless a certain portion were actually earned by the constant expenditure of labour. Similarly as regards the income from lands, farming capital, railways, waterworks, and all kinds of companies, a division ought to be made in the same way as in the income derived from trades and professions. The value of the dead capital would in this way suffer a corresponding diminution.

Some idea of the importance of this point may be obtained from considering the *aggregate* figures of incomes (paying income-tax) and the corresponding capital—the former, taking Mr. Giffen's figures, being (roughly) £429 millions, and the latter £7620 millions. This gives he average of years' purchase at 18, or, in other words, the yield to the capital is about $5\frac{1}{2}$ per cent.

Now it is plain that if the pure rate of interest, as indicated by railway debentures and corporation stocks, is only about 3 per cent, this extra return to capital must be considered as mainly due to the labour involved in maintaining and employing the capital. The element of risk when the question is considered from the national point of view is obviously of comparatively small importance.

Passing now from the capital owned by those paying income-tax to the other principal items in the national inventory, the first in importance is the "movable property not yielding income, *e.g.* furniture in houses, works of art, etc." This valuation is made by simply taking half the value of the houses, and reaches the round figure of £1000 millions or thereby. For the purpose in hand it is only necessary to observe that even to make a proper use of this movable property involves a large amount of labour, which is unrepresented in the wage-earning or profit-earning classes. The musical and artistic skill, for example, "fixed and embodied" in young ladies should be included in an estimate of living capital, just as much as their pianos and paint-boxes are included in the dead capital. It is plain that the value of the greater part of movable property would vanish but for the acquired abilities of the inhabitants. A simple example will make this point clear. The more widely spread the love of art of the highest kind, so much greater will be the value of old pictures. In the ancient world, when slaves were trained in all kinds of accomplishments, a very high value was placed upon natural abilities and education, and the mere fact of personal freedom cannot be held to destroy the meaning of an economic estimate. But this argument must, if valid at all, be carried further.

In order to make an adequate estimate of the value of living, on the same basis as in the case of dead, capital, the men, women, and children must be considered not merely as creating or giving value to so much material wealth, but as in themselves constituting, like the movables of the inanimate inventory, more or less permanent sources of enjoyment. Domesticated humanity may properly be considered to have a money-value—*first*, because it costs a very real expense to produce and maintain; and, *secondly*, because it furnishes pleasures which common experience shows rank very high in the scale of limited and desirable things. This second ground of valuation is of importance qualitatively, as showing the real basis of the comparison, but it is plainly unworkable quantitatively, and it therefore seems necessary to fall back upon cost of production for a measure, as in the case of public property, which also is not directly exchangeable.

Take, first of all, a simple hypothetical case to illustrate the principle. Five shillings a week for fifteen years is about £200, and this does not seem an extravagant estimate for bringing up the child of a superior artisan or tradesman. The value of the house in which the child is reared would probably be something less than this sum; in other words, an "economic man" could more easily purchase a house in fifteen years than rear a child during that period.

The example is plain enough, but to advance from the particular to the general is by no means so simple. Several distinct difficulties are involved—difficulties of age, sex, and social position, for example. Seeing that only very general results are aimed at, something like Mr. Giffen's simple method of halving a known item seems very attractive; if the dead movables are half the value of the houses, why should the living not be roughly estimated in the same manner? As the object of the present inquiry is mainly comparative, in default of any better plan the value of the house may provisionally be taken as the basis of the valuation of the people in it, just as it is taken as the basis of their expenditure for purposes of taxation.

It only remains, then, to determine this quantitative relation of the two valuations—the cost of producing the people compared with the cost of producing the house. The principle applied must be simple and general; it is impossible to make a summation of problematical figures for different classes. The best clue to the selection seems furnished by the example already taken. We may compare roughly the rental of the house with the expenditure on the persons it contains. Now, according to Mr. Giffen's tables, the total rental of houses is about £128 millions, whilst the total income of the nation is about £1300 millions,

from which it follows that ten per cent is spent upon
house-rent. If we take the usual figure of five persons
to every house, and further assume that ten per cent
of income is spent upon the complete maintenance of
each person and ten per cent on rent, we shall still
have four-tenths of the income left over. Accordingly
it does not appear beyond the mark, taking the family
as a permanent institution in the sense already explained, to consider every "person" as of equal value
with the house in which he lives, and every family of
five times the value of the house. As this part of the
estimate of the living capital presents most difficulty,
and is most liable to be misunderstood, some further
explanation or justification may be derived from the
following considerations. In the first place, in the
Census Returns nearly 60 per cent of the population
are placed in the "unoccupied" class. On analysis,
however, it appears that this class comprises children
and young persons who are preparing for occupations
of various kinds, and women who, as wives and
daughters, are occupied with household duties. Now
a child has as just a claim from the present point of view
to valuation as a colt, and the employment of domestic
servants and governesses shows that the unpaid work
of women of the class described ought to be considered
of at least equal value. But secondly, even the
"occupied" classes must be considered not merely as
earning income, but as furnishing in their private
capacity utilities to the community or to their families
on which a value may properly be placed. There is
no difficulty in seeing that in an estimate of "living
capital" some allowance must be made for the people

themselves (apart from their wealth-producing power)
—the difficulty is to determine the most reasonable
measure.   Cost of production or of maintenance (if
we consider the various classes as immortal species)
has the advantage of simplicity, and may also be supported by various analogies, e.g. public works, light-
houses, roads, breakwaters, would naturally be valued
by their original cost and the additional annual outlay.

It is not necessary to enter into particulars regarding all the items in Mr. Giffen's table of material
wealth.   The general result is perfectly plain; the
closer and more critical the examination, so much the
greater appears to be the relative importance (taking,
as far as possible, the same basis and method of calculation) of the " living " to the " dead " capital.   It
has already appeared in the course of this inquiry that
the method of calculation adopted by Mr. Giffen is,
in some respects, inconsistent.   There seems to be no
sufficient reason discoverable for the precise figures
adopted for turning income into capital, nor for deciding what part of income ought to be considered as
derived from capital proper, and what part from the
management of the capital.   Farmers' capital, for example, is calculated on the basis that it yields over
12 per cent *per annum*—

O fortunatos nimium, sua si bona norint, Agricolas !

In conclusion, after this reiteration of the necessity
of caution, an attempt may be made to give the appearance of numerical precision to the estimates of the
national capital, living and dead.   For the latter, Mr.
Giffen makes a grand total of some £10,000 millions.

Of this amount, however, the movable property in houses, etc., and the Government and local property in the shape of buildings, docks, etc., to the amount of nearly £1500 millions do not yield income, whilst another £500 millions of capital is invested abroad. Thus the dead capital in the country *yielding income* is about £8000 millions, and the income yielded (deducting that from foreign investments) is about £500 millions.

Now it will be observed that the pure interest on £8000 millions at 3 per cent is £240 millions only, or not quite half the amount (*i.e.* £500 millions) put down as derived from dead capital. It follows, adopting the principle examined above, that the other 3 per cent, or thereabouts (or the other half of this income), must be put down to the "living capital" associated with the dead capital; in other words, if the capital (in the ordinary sense) of the country actually yields 6 per cent, whilst the rate of interest, pure and simple, is only 3 per cent, half this total yield is due to the labour of the capitalist. Now the capitalist (*i.e.* the species, not the individual) *qua* labourer, remains as much a permanent factor of the industrial resources of the country as the land itself, and therefore we may fairly assume that the aggregate value of the living capitalist (considered as an enduring species) is, on Mr. Giffen's showing (adequately interpreted), about equal to the aggregate value of his capital, *i.e.* about £8000 millions.

In giving, however, an estimate of the national "living" capital, it will be best to take the items in the order of their importance. The figures, as Mr.

Giffen says of his comparatively small "dead" capital, are so large that a million or so is of no consequence, and the calculation must be made in a very rough manner.

Assume, then (following Mr. Giffen as already quoted), that the income of labour in the ordinary sense is £800 millions per annum. At thirty years' purchase this gives the value of labour *qua* labour as £24,000 millions. Next consider the capitalist as an employer and worker and not merely as the receiver of interest. Mr. Giffen assumes that four-fifths of the income under Schedule D (trades and professions) is really not interest but earnings of management. This, however, amounts to upwards of £140 millions, and capitalised as before extends beyond £4000 millions. To this amount must be added the £8000 millions derived, as already explained, from considering the management of the aggregate national dead capital. The total is thus £12,000 millions. Next we must consider the people of the country not as mere producers, labourers, or employers, but as "things in themselves," or rather superior domestic animals reared for their affectionate dispositions and intellectual and moral activities. Here, as already explained, it seemed best to take a rough empirical rule founded on "cost of production." For the present purpose it has been assumed that every "person" is worth, or rather costs, at least as much as every "house." Without stopping to expand the meaning of the inverted commas we reach at once a sum-total of £10,000 millions.

Lastly, taking the income of those who return under

Schedule E (official salaries and the like), and capitalising in the usual way, we conclude the inventory of the national living capital with the modest item of £1000 millions.

The results, arranged in order, are: Living labour (ordinary), £24,000 millions; living labour (trades and professions), £12,000 millions; domesticated humanity (all kinds*), £10,000 millions; professional salaried officialdom, £1000 millions—in all, a grand total of £47,000 millions.

Thus, the living capital of the United Kingdom is, taking the estimate given above, about five times the value of the dead !

Or, to illustrate the general by the particular, the just ransom, appraised on commercial principles, of the men, women, and children, would be five times as great as the market price of all the material wealth— lands, houses, railways, mines, furniture, pictures, and the infinite variety of instruments of production and objects of consumption !

This estimate of living capital is no doubt open to question, both as regards the principle on which it is based and the actual figures adopted. But the important point to observe is, that it is as well founded and as useful as the corresponding estimate of capital in the narrower sense of the term.

It may be well to restate the general principle in the light of the conclusion. There are two main positions. First of all, the people of the country are

---

* As explained above, this item is obtained by considering the people as valuable "things in themselves," and not merely as wage-earners.

regarded (like the dead capital) as earning so much income. There can be no question whatever that the part of the national income due to personal exertion of all kinds is far larger than that derived from the pure interest on previous accumulations, or from the rent of appropriated natural agents. The relative proportions assigned, it may be remarked, might have been set down still more in favour of "living" capital if other considerations had been allowed for, as, for example, the "abstinence" involved in saving. It seemed best, however, not to carry the analysis beyond the point already accepted in the corresponding estimate of "dead" capital, which has always been kept in view.

Exception may, no doubt, also be taken to the method of capitalising this income; but in a stationary, and still more in a progressive, state of society, it seems legitimate to look upon this income as derived from permanent sources—in short, to acknowledge that life is as permanent as land. Now, in capitalising permanent kinds of income, where, from the national point of view, risk may be omitted, the rate of interest must obviously be the basis, and at present thirty years (or even thirty-three) may be fairly taken.

But secondly, just as Mr. Giffen and others give a value to that part of dead capital which does not yield income (e.g. the furniture in houses), so a value must be given to "living" capital simply as a permanent source of enjoyment. Here the natural basis (seeing that exchanges of this kind of capital are not now made) seems to be cost of production. As regards the precise method to be adopted, opinions may differ;

my own choice was influenced largely, apart from the
reasons already given, by the idea of making the comparison with the dead capital as close as possible. A
more accurate method, however, might with some
difficulty be founded upon aggregate national estimates
of various kinds of annual consumption, expenses of
education, and the like.

The uses to which the general result may be applied,
after making every possible allowance for correction,
are so various and far-reaching, that they demand a
separate investigation. It is sufficient now simply to
allude to such problems as Socialism and the relations
of labour and capital (in the narrow sense); national
education of all kinds; and, finally, the nature of the
progress of civilisation in its historical aspects, as
indicated by the growth of "living capital."

CAPITAL AND LABOUR: THEIR RELATIVE STRENGTH

"ECONOMIC JOURNAL," SEPTEMBER 1892

In the first number of the *Economic Journal* I published a paper entitled the "Living Capital of the United Kingdom." The central idea was to estimate in terms of money the value of the people of this country, *i.e.* the living capital, by methods similar to those which had been used for calculating the value of the material wealth or the dead capital: the lands, houses, railways, etc. At first sight, no doubt, there is something paradoxical in saying that a man as such, not being a slave, apart from his possessions is actually worth so many pounds sterling; and the paradox seems to be magnified as we ascend from the individual to the whole nation. Yet there is after all a very real meaning in an estimate of this kind. The living capital, like the dead, costs much to produce and keep in a state of efficiency: there is a very real expense in rearing and educating children before they are capable of earning their own living. Capital (in the ordinary sense) must be sunk in them just as in coalpits or ships; there is probably no machine that takes so long to bring to working order as a human being—the average man is the most costly of animals.

And from another point of view also humanity may be said to possess value: man not only costs much wealth, but produces much wealth. In the last resort all wealth is due to the manipulation by man of the forces of nature, or, without going so far, man earns an income in the shape of wages, just as land, houses, and machines earn rent and interest. Thus then on examination the paradox disappears, and it seems theoretically possible to estimate the value of mankind on the grounds both of cost and of earning capacity.

A good many things, however, are theoretically possible but practically impossible—we may know how to do sums, but we cannot do sums without figures; and where are we to find the figures the summation of which will give us the value of a nation? The answer is that, as in the case of the material wealth of a nation, we can only obtain our results indirectly. In material wealth we start with the income-tax or succession duties, or some other official estimate of certain portions of income or capital, and then we make very rough estimates for the remainder, as, for example, when we assume that the movables contained in houses are of half the value of the houses.

Computations of the national wealth—even in a country like the United States where some attempt is made at an enumerated valuation—are necessarily very rough and, considered absolutely, untrustworthy. But one of the most important principles of statistics is

that for relative purposes—for purposes of comparison—
if we adopt the same methods, the proportions may be
sufficiently correct to be valuable in spite of original
errors in the absolute amounts. Take, for example,
the question of the comparative growth over a period
of ten years in the wealth of the various parts of the
United Kingdom—England, Wales, Scotland, Ireland.
We may be wrong—far wrong—in the absolute
amounts assigned, but if we adopt the same methods
and apply them under the same conditions the comparative results may be quite trustworthy or at any rate
worthy of consideration for practical purposes.

In the same way if we apply the same methods to
estimate the relative values of living and dead capital,
valuable results, though only proportionate and relative,
may emerge out of aggregates which in themselves
make no claim to strict accuracy.

The object of the present paper is to draw some
practical conclusions, and not to reassert or justify the
methods and results of my previous calculations. At
the same time, one part of the theoretical method
adopted may be adverted to on the ground that it has
directly an important practical application. In estimating the value of various kinds of labour I proceeded
on the assumption that although the *individual perishes
the species survives*. Take, for example, a stationary
state of society; assume that the population, methods
of production, and general distribution of wealth remain
practically the same for a hundred years. In such a
society there will probably be not a single individual
alive throughout the period, and yet under the conditions assumed there will be all the time about the

same number of people of various ages and about the same number engaged in various occupations. The individual carpenters, drapers, lawyers, etc., will have passed away, but their places will have been taken by others.   In fact, just as we used to be told that every particle of the body was changed in seven years, whilst the body was still supposed to be the same, so we may assume that the body of carpenters, etc., remains the same though the component elements have changed. It follows then at once that we may look upon the various species of labour in a stationary state as practically immortal or, what is more to the point, may consider labour as durable as land.

If then we are justified in taking the capital value of land at thirty years' purchase, we ought to estimate the capital value of labour at the same rate.   It is true that to get wages labour must do work ; but it is also true that to get rent land must also do work.

Now it seems to me that this very idea of the permanence of labour,—and for the present I use labour in its ordinary sense, and not, as later on, as inclusive of all grades between the prime minister and the shoe-black, —this very idea apart from any quantitative expression is fruitful of practical results ; for the idea which makes the labourer immortal makes his wages or reward also continuous.   Much harm has been done by considering the living labourer as an individual, and dead capital as a species—the former as liable to all the accidents of life and to the certainty of death, the latter as indestructible and immortal.   People speak of the conflict between capital and labour, and by capital they mean what they say, but by labour they mean individual labourers, and the conflict seems something like that between an express engine and a tunnelful of navvies, where the engine must always get the best of it.

But if we regard labour as meaning labourers, we should regard capital as meaning the various concrete capitals of various individuals—if the one is perishable so is the other. The owner of a ship or a factory or any other form of capital can get no profit unless his capital is employed, and if it remains unemployed and uncared for, it loses value, and in many cases the value may disappear altogether. A man who cannot employ his capital loses his income as surely as the labourer out of work loses his wages; the former likes it no more than the latter, and it is notorious that the capitalist will carry on his business even after profit has disappeared simply to keep up his capital. It is well known that in several cases lately in England farmers were allowed to stay on rent-free—in some cases even the landowners in addition undertook certain repairs. Was this charity? Possibly to some extent, but certainly business also, for otherwise the farms would have been ruined.

Instead, however, of regarding both capital and labour as equally perishable let us consider both as equally permanent. We are thus able to confer on labour some of the advantages which are generally only ascribed to capital. No complaint is more common in regard to ordinary labour than the uncertainty of employment owing to fluctuations in trade. We are constantly reminded that most wages are paid by the week, and that a labourer is liable to dismissal, and thus indirectly to starvation and death. But though this may be true of *a* labourer it is not true of labour. To say that all the labour of a country, or even a considerable part, could be dismissed by capital into starvation is palpably absurd. I am not forgetting that lock-outs may occur. But they are not so common as strikes, and at any rate they are only for differences —for a relatively small percentage of wages or some relatively small change in the conditions of employment. I never heard of a capitalist dismissing all his hands as an offended lady may dismiss her cook; still less would a body of masters meet together and agree to dismiss all their men simply to show their authority. The losses involved in the stoppage of the employment of capital are too serious for amusements of this kind.

Accordingly if we regard labour as a whole, and consider a sufficient period, we find that the uncertainty of employment is reduced to moderate dimensions. I see from official returns * made as to the state of the skilled labour market that when about 4 per cent are out of employment this is described as indicating only a moderate demand for labour. But if, when 96 per cent are employed, the demand is only moderate, what, I ask, becomes of the uncertainty of employment? It must be remembered also that many of these unemployed are on strike. Surely a moderate degree of thrift and a very little foresight ought to keep the wolf from the door.

I trust I have not made my point so clear as to appear a truism—if I have, a particular example may serve for the obscuration necessary to interest. The

* *Board of Trade Journal*, October 1891.

advocates of a peasant proprietary, and generally the *laudatores ruris*, dwell on the uncertainty of the wages, and thus of food and shelter, of the dweller in the cities compared with the happy peasant. No doubt in many respects the peasant has the advantage, but hardly in the matter of certainty of income if we compare classes. Consider, for example, the present famine in Russia, the potato famine in Ireland in 1846, and the periodic returns of scarcity in Scotland under the old crofting system.

The truth is, that the wage-earners of this country as a whole—I refer to the great mass of ordinary labourers —have a much more stable income than the mass of peasant proprietors in other countries; the yield to labour on the large system of industry is more *certain* than the yield to land of the *petite culture*. Apart from this it must also be observed that the former is greater in amount and therefore leaves a larger margin for saving or insurance in case of need.

Apply now this idea of permanence to the family. It is true that the family is not now so emphatically the unit of society as in ancient times, but for the sake of clearness a reference may be made to simple conditions of society. At one stage of development—for many centuries—the family was actually regarded as permanent. The permanence of the family was the most prominent element in the practical religion of early societies. Bequest outside the range of the family was unknown, and there was practically, though not technically, common holding of the property. Now although in modern societies the individual is accentuated, the institution of the family has not disappeared: parents support their children in necessity, and children their parents. In many countries such support is compulsory by law: I believe I am right in saying that in Scotland a man is liable for the support of his mother-in-law, even if his wife is divorced. At any rate there is no doubt still a sufficient cohesion in the individual members to justify the practice of many economists of taking the family as the unit in considering the capacity for earning wages. Now from the point of view of investment of earnings, an ordinary labourer cannot do better than give his children a sound education— physical, moral, intellectual. The peasant proprietor in many cases starves and overworks his family to feed his land; from the point of view of national economy there could be no greater mistake—the living capital should feed upon the dead capital, and not the dead upon the living.

But the idea of the permanence of life is not yet exhausted. Hitherto labour has been regarded as consisting only of the lower grades of labour, but the peculiarity of a modern industrial society as compared with the simple ancient agricultural societies is the great complexity and variety in labour in the true sense of the term. Consider the " unoccupied " class of the Census.* If we put aside children under fifteen who may be assumed to be " occupied " with their education; women, who are occupied with domestic duties; old men about sixty-five years of age; and if we assume further that of young persons between fifteen and

* *I.e.* those returned by rank, property, etc., and not by occupation: nominally for England and Wales 57 per cent of the population. (*Census of* 1881.)

twenty in the so-called "unoccupied" class many are preparing for professional life, then the "unoccupied" class—in the sense of the really idle portion of the community (England and Wales)—is reduced to very small dimensions: out of 25,000,000 it does not amount to 200,000. Of these again many are engaged in managing their estates, in scientific or literary pursuits, and various forms of social work. Thus of men between twenty and sixty-five the vast majority are engaged in some form of labour in the extended sense of the term.

Now in the permanent stationary society we are considering, it is true that the groups of workers remain relatively the same, but it is not true that there is a system of oriental castes. There must always be hewers of wood and drawers of water, but the curse, if it be a curse, does not descend unto the children or children's children. Just as in his imaginary Republic Plato provided that if a golden child happened to be born of iron parents he should be promoted to the golden rank, so also in the actual system of industrial competition and natural liberty the strong rise and the weak sink in the social scale. All of us know cases of men in the highest stations sprung, as we say, from nothing, and also cases in which before the third generation the children of the great capitalist have dropped to a low level. And the more education is spread so much the more effective does this competition become. And here I may remark parenthetically that the best economic justification of free education and of assisted education of various kinds is that the strong may have opportunities for showing their strength, or in other words, that the workers of the nation shall be occupied according to their capacity.

To resume then : We couple with the idea of permanence the idea of permutation—the permanence of occupations with the permutation of individuals—and thus we narrow at once the chasm between so-called capital and labour, or between classes and masses. Of course I do not mean to imply that at present all have equal opportunities—that would only be possible under an omniscient, infallible, and absolute despotism. It is enough to say that those who speak of the tyranny of capital and the slavery of labour make a very ill use of language, and overlook what is unquestionably the most important fact in the history of civilisation— namely, the break-up in progressive societies of slavery and serfdom.

It is time, however, to pass from the meaning and method of computing living capital to the *comparative* results and their consequences. The principal result obtained in the calculation was that for the United Kingdom, the value of the people—the men, women, and children—was £47,000 millions, compared with about £10,000 millions, the value of the dead capital— the lands, houses, furniture, etc. Now I confess that to me this result seemed rather startling, and some of the consequences, although obvious, seemed startling also. But unfortunately I forgot that with the vast majority of people anything expressed in terms of millions is expressed in terms of unknown quantities. I made out the value of the people of the country to be £47,000 millions sterling, but if the result had been instead one million or a hundred thousand millions, to most people it would have been as interesting and as intelligible as the distance of some fixed star. For ordinary reasoning anything above a million is practically infinity. But although the magnitude of the absolute amounts of living and dead capital eludes the intellectual grasp, it is not so with the relative amounts. Forget then the millions and consider only the proportions. Regarded in this way my result was that if we reckon up the value of the people in the same way as we reckon up their possessions—that is, if we take the principles both of earning capacity and of cost of production and maintenance—then the value of the living capital is about five times the value of the dead. We have got rid of our millions—even savages can in general count five fingers on one hand. There is certainly no doubt that, whatever methods we adopt, this general proposition is true—the value of the people of a community, whether considered as earning income or as involving cost, is much greater than that of their material wealth, including productive capital and objects of enjoyment.

We have again approached the clear and watery lucidity of the truism, yet it seems to me that this very general proposition is a most potent economic instrument both for the destruction of fallacies and the extraction of truth. Consider just one or two fallacies. We are told that the wealth of the community is gradually being concentrated in a few hands, and that in the natural evolution of society we shall have ultimately—just before Socialism is established—if I may again use figures, an upper ten thousand possessing all the wealth, and a lower ten millions doing all the labour, and doing all the labour for their masters the upper ten. Now apply the truism at which we arrived. The great mass of the labour of a nation is devoted to satisfy the wants, not of a few individuals, but those of the mass of the nation itself. Instead of labour being used mainly to pile up heaps of dead capital in the hands of a few, it is used mainly in the creation and maintenance of living capital embodied in the labourers and their families. Take a rapid survey of the production and consumption of the material wealth of the United Kingdom. We have the most productive agriculture in the world, and practically none of that produce is exported. We may indeed assume that at present we grow hardly half the food we consume. Now it needs no demonstration that the upper ten thousand could not, even with the aid of their servants, horses, and dogs, consume this wealth. It must go to the bulk of the people, it must be converted into the living capital of the nation. Consider our manufactures, in which our supremacy is still greater. Does a fraction of society wear all the cotton and cloth, use all the pots and pans, all the boots and shoes, all the blankets, and, in a word, all the produce of manufacture on a large scale? It is utterly absurd; production on a large scale is only possible with a market on a large scale, with consumption on a large scale. Thus again the great bulk of our manufactures must go to the great bulk of the nation. It is true a large part is exported, but then exports are paid for by imports, and the most important part of these is again food and the raw material for more manufactures. We might in this way go through all our great staple industries, but one more example must

suffice. Consider the enormous capital sunk in railways.
People are too fond of looking simply at the interest
obtained by the shareholders, which is generally exaggerated, and wages obtained by the workers for their
work. But look at railways from the national standpoint. It is notorious that as regards passengers the
great majority are third-class, and the passenger service
of the great railways would not pay unless they were
used by the mass of the people. Similarly with the
goods traffic: there again we see even more clearly that
the service is conducted not for the few, but emphatically
for the many—not to pile up luxuries in the houses of
the rich, but to minister to the physical wants of the
great mass of the people.

To resume then: If we look upon a nation from the
standpoint of the permanence of various classes, we see
from the very nature of modern industry that the great
mass of the annual produce must be consumed by the
great bulk of the people.*

Let us now consider the question more directly
from the point of view of production, so as to discover
the relative importance of living and dead capital
considered as parts of modern industrial organisation.
The chief results of my calculations were that if we
take the dead capital which yields income as the basis
of comparison, then ordinary labour, considered as living
capital also earning income, is three times as valuable,

---

* "The whole consumption of the inferior ranks of the people, or of
those below the middling rank, it must be observed, is in every country
much greater not only in quantity but value than that of the middling
and of those above the middling ranks. The whole expense of the
inferior is much greater than that of the superior ranks."—*Adam Smith*,
book v. chap. ii.

and the labour of the employers and of all the various professions is about one and a half times as valuable as the dead instruments of production (including land). Thus on the whole, for carrying on the various employments of the nation, labour of all kinds, from the highest to the lowest, is four and a half times as important as land, machinery, railways, etc. Stated quite generally, the result is that the productive powers of the nation depend much more upon its living people than upon its previous accumulations and its material instruments. Consider the question for a moment from the historical standpoint, and compare the productive capacity of the country at the present time and (say) in the fifteenth century. Our present production is greater, not so much because of the accumulations of material wealth, but mainly through the greater efficiency of labour of all kinds, especially the higher grades of labour devoted to practical science and the organisation of industry. In other words, our great inheritance from the past is not to be found in the storehouses of the rich and the treasuries of kings, but in the living brains of the people.*

We have again reached what may seem a truism, but again we have an application to a popular fallacy. It is too often assumed that the inequalities in the distribution of wealth are mainly due to the monopoly by a few individuals of the material instruments of production. No doubt at one time when society, mainly agricultural, rested on slavery or serfdom, a principal cause of inequality of fortune was to be found in the unequal distribution of land and the

* *Cf.* List, *National System* (translation), p. 140.

instruments of production. But with the progress of
society this cause has become of minor importance.
The principal cause now of inequality of income is
not the partial monopoly of the material instruments
of production, but the partial monopoly of brain-power
of various kinds. We must look at society as a whole,
and not be deceived by a few exceptional cases. That
I may not seem to be beating the air, let me give an
extract from a prominent Socialist—Mr. Sydney Webb.
" A fortunate few," he says, " owing to their legal power
over the instruments of wealth production, are able to
command the services of thousands of industrial slaves
whose faces they have never seen, without rendering
any service to them or to society in exchange." *   Apparently from the last clause the writer has in view
especially the owners of land. Take agricultural land.
In this country the great land-owners let their land to
tenant-farmers and receive about as much interest on
their capital as the owners of consols. If a tenant-
farmer has not brains or business capacity—if he does
not look after his farm—he will speedily become
bankrupt. Take manufactories : unless they are properly managed they must be closed. And so through
the whole range of instruments of production ; the
owners as such, by way of rent or interest, may obtain
a moderate return to their capital, but the real management of labour—in Socialistic phraseology the ex-
ploitation of labour—is left to another class. This is
allowed apparently in the next passage I will quote
from the same writer. " A larger body of persons
contribute some labour, but are able from their culti-

* *Economic Journal* for June 1891.

vated ability or special education to choose occupations
for which the competitive wage is high owing to the
small number of possible competitors." Well, take as
an example of cultivated ability or special education
the employers of labour generally. Surely their higher
wages, if they happen to be high, are not due to absence
of competition. The competition is notoriously so fierce
that any initial advantage is soon neutralised unless
there is also initial ability. The men who make money
in business are in the main those who conduct their
business best, and who make or adopt improvements
of various kinds. Take the professions : no doubt
special education is required, but it is certainly not
the small number of possible competitors that makes
wages high. As a matter of fact the competitors are
so numerous that a professional man of only ordinary
ability may often make no wages at all. The most
potent cause of inequality of wealth is inequality in
brain-power. There are a few who in almost any
occupation would rise to the top, and many who would
equally sink to the bottom. There are certain kinds
of brain-capacity, the outcome of a conjunction of
natural ability, education, experience and, it may be,
opportunity, which are comparatively rare, and, like
other rare things, command a scarcity value ; intellects
of this sort also directly or indirectly save much labour,
or increase the efficiency of labour, or more generally
add to the wealth of society, and therefore (taking an
average) deserve this scarcity value. It is to minds
of the creative order that the industrial progress of
society is originally due ; by new ideas they break
through routine, and open up new markets, new in-

dustries, new methods.   There are again men of lesser
creative power, but capable of carrying out these ideas—
men of great force of character and practical wisdom.
For one George Stephenson there are many railway
managers, and for one manager many porters.   It is
not necessary to illustrate further the descending scale
of capacity, but it is necessary to insist on the general
principle ; for the idea is still prevalent that all that
any person requires to rise in the industrial world is
opportunity in the shape of capital, and that in brains,
so far as any are required, all men are equal.   But in
industry, as in science, in war, in literature, in art,
there is no such equality.   It is not merely a difference of degree that may be balanced by greater perseverance.   No amount of perseverance will make a
short-sighted man see so far as an ordinary person, or
an ordinary person so far as a man with a telescope.
· The industrial world is full of opportunities, but the
difficulty is to see them.

It may seem that I have wandered far from my
subject, and that the relative capacities of brains has
little to do with the relative importance of living and
dead capital.   But it seems to me that nothing is
better calculated to illustrate the position that the
mere possession of wealth, the mere ownership of previous accumulations, does not give the owners the
tyranny over labour.   Previous accumulations may
obtain 4 per cent interest, but this is relatively a
small part of the national income.   Four-fifths of
what is called profits is simply wages of one form of
labour, or rather of many forms of labour of a highly-
skilled character.

We are now in a position to see that the question as to the relative strength of labour and capital is ambiguous, and the answer must depend on the meaning ascribed to the terms. Take first the general question. If we mean by labour simply manual labour, and we throw all the mental labour into the scale of capital—if every one who does not work with his hands is considered as a capitalist, or is conjoined with capital against labour—then in any general conflict—if such were conceivable—capital must be victorious. The destruction of such an intangible thing as credit, the mere closing of all banks, would of itself stop business, as surely as the refusal of the captains and officers of ships to navigate must stop foreign food supplies. A general revolt of this kind of labour (*i.e.* ordinary manual) against this kind of capital (*i.e.* including all above this class) might produce anarchy for a time, but then its power would cease.

If, however, we throw into the scale of labour all those who make their income by some form of work, and confine the term capital to the dead instruments of production, then no doubt labour is stronger. But with this wide meaning of labour, and narrow meaning of capital, a general conflict between labour and capital is still less conceivable, for the obvious reason that in this sense we are all labourers.

The simple truth, however, is that, wherever we draw the line between the capitalist and the labourer, anything in the nature of a *general* conflict is impossible. In modern industry the two are inextricably mingled, the two factors are necessary to the result, and that result includes not only the satisfaction of the most urgent physical wants, but also, in part at least, of all the highest needs of civilisation.

It follows from the same line of argument that the nearer we approach to a general conflict between labour and capital—again, wherever you draw the line—the more speedily it must close. For the more you widen the area of conflict, the greater the dislocation of industry, and the greater the discomfort, and even privation, created. A simultaneous strike of all those engaged in transport—by railway, by road, by sea— would at once create a famine worse than any due to natural causes. Astonished at this obvious inference, the less instructed of the New Unionists call on us to fear and tremble before the power of labour. But they forget that the lower you descend in the social scale, the greater would be the misery. So long as any semblance of law was kept up, so long as absolute anarchy was avoided, those with money or credit would be served first from any accumulated local stores.

For a moment let us narrow the area of conflict still more. Let us take the case of an ordinary strike (say) for an advance in wages. In such a case is capital or labour the stronger? The only answer is that it depends entirely upon circumstances which differ in almost every instance. But one thing is certain, if any set of labourers by a fortunate display of strength obtain more than the market for their labour justifies, their triumph will be very short-lived. A monopoly in any form of labour is of all monopolies the most difficult to maintain.

It is, however, impossible in this paper to enter on the question of particular individual struggles between

capital and labour. Throughout I have treated the
subject from the national point of view; I have looked
on the nation as a gigantic organism, the parts of
which are constantly renewed, and in the course of
centuries are not only renewed but developed. From
this standpoint the conflicts between capital and labour
are temporary local ailments; and if the nation is to
remain even stationary—still more, if it is to be progressive—the relations between capital and labour,
and the relations between the higher grades of labour
and the lower, and between the brain-worker and the
hand-worker, must be those of the sound mind to the
sound body. Anything like a general conflict between
labour and capital can only be compared to national
suicide.

THE INDIAN CURRENCY EXPERIMENT

"CONTEMPORARY REVIEW," SEPTEMBER 1893

IT used to be a commonplace with writers on political economy that their science was at a disadvantage compared with some other sciences, because it could not avail itself of experiment. In these days, however, economic experiments of all kinds are being made in such profusion that the parliaments of the world may be compared to chemical laboratories. Before the final explosion has taken place in the great silver experiment of the United States, the Governments of India and Britain have begun to make a very pretty precipitate with the same metal. Just as we are about to learn from America what will happen to the country that coins too much silver, India is preparing to let us know what may happen from coining none at all.

The closure of the Indian mints is essentially an experiment—an experiment, indeed, that looks very like an accident. The melting-pot has been turned over to see what will happen.

The procedure, considered as the act of a responsible Government, is based on the Report of the Committee on Indian Currency, and this Report again is based partly on facts and partly on principles. As regards facts, there are unfortunately too many unknown quantities—too many unanswerable questions—*c.g.* What will the natives of India do with their hoards of rupees? How will they like the fall in the price of their silver ornaments? As regards principles the Report is uncertain and vacillating: it fails to distinguish between the immediate effects of a disturbance and the ultimate effects of a new equilibrium. It relies too much on a simple appeal to facts without analysis. It proclaims a truism with great boldness, but is suspicious of *media axiomata*. It is afraid of the simplest deductions from principles, but is content to rest inductions upon very scanty observations.

It will save time to begin at the beginning, and it will conduce to clearness to make a sharp distinction between the difficulties in the way of giving an artificial value to the rupee and the ultimate benefits, provided these difficulties are overcome; and to separate the immediate effects of the actual closure of the mints from the effects of the adoption of a gold standard which at present is problematical.

The beginning of the experiment is the hard and solid fact that the Government of India has to pay to the Home Government some seventeen millions of pounds sterling annually. But the revenues of India consist not of so many millions of pounds sterling, but of so many tens of millions of rupees. So long as ten rupees were about equal in value to one pound (Rx. = £1) all the Indian Government had to do was

to set aside a third or a fourth of its rupee revenue
for Home charges; so far the Indian Budget was quite
simple, and there was no uncertainty.   But when
silver began to fall in value, and with it the rupee,
more and more rupees were required to make up a
pound.   Unfortunately, however, the revenues of India
did not show the same elasticity, and the proportion
to be remitted to England became greater.   The
Indian Government contrived in some way to contend
with the fall of the rupee from about 2s. to below
1s. 4d., but the prospect of a further sudden and
aggravated fall, through the action of the United
States, brought the Governments of India and England
to the point at which, according to the English tongue,
"something must be done."   In the usual course a
Committee was appointed, and, after the usual delay,
reported, and then, with the most unusual promptitude
—in the twinkling of an eye—something was done.
Without debate in Parliament or discussion in the
press the Indian mints were closed to silver.   The
Report was acted on before it was published; so
great was the hurry that the course of post was too
slow : it was a case of legislation by telegraph.

It is most important to observe that the key to the
whole situation is to be found in the Government
remittances from India to England.   The recommendations of the Committee are based upon the facts or
assumptions that India cannot increase its taxes nor
diminish its expenditure, and therefore cannot, with a
further fall in the exchange, make its annual payments
to England.   If the evils to be remedied had been
merely the uncertainties of trade, or the complaints of

civil and military officers, *laissez-faire*, time, and the *vis medicatrix naturæ*, would have done service as before, at any rate so far as the British Government is concerned.

The closing of the Indian mints must of course indirectly affect many commercial and financial interests; but, in the first place, the success or failure of the experiment must be estimated solely from the point of view of the Indian Government. If India can by a mere edict avoid further taxation or increasing indebtedness, and even convert a deficit into a surplus, the policy must so far be regarded as successful. If, on the other hand, the experiment fails in the accomplishment of this definite, limited object, and in addition aggravates the evils of the general monetary situation, the condemnation must be doubly severe.

First of all, however, the procedure must be considered simply as a financial expedient of the Indian Government. Thus narrowed down, the question becomes: Will the closure of the mints to the unrestricted coinage of silver, with the announcement that fifteen rupees will be given for a sovereign, and a sovereign accepted for fifteen rupees in payment of taxes, suffice to maintain the rupee at this ratio, or, in other words, keep it at 1s. 4d.? More simply: Will the Government of India be able to make its remittances to England at this rate?* The answer must of course be made under the assumption that

---

* It is true that the rate of 1s. 4d. is said to be only provisional, and that the ratio to be eventually adopted when the gold standard is definitely introduced is to be determined by the circumstances of the time. But if this rate cannot be maintained, the whole policy is so far nugatory, and the difficulties of the Indian Government will remain.

there is a fall in the value of silver, so that the metallic value of the rupee is below 1s. 4d. It was the fear of such a fall, consequent on the anticipated change of policy in the United States, which was the real cause of the suddenness of the measure; and as a matter of fact, on the announcement of the closure, silver fell severely.

The Report of the Committee, on which action was taken, relies on two sets of arguments—one general and the other special. In the first place, an appeal is made to the policy of other nations, with the view of showing that it is possible to maintain a gold standard and a substantial parity of exchange with gold-using countries under monetary systems very different from that of the United Kingdom. The array of examples is imposing, and the summary of methods seems to include nearly every possible case. This substantial parity of exchange has been maintained under all the following conditions:—

(a) With little or no gold, as in Scandinavia, Holland, and Canada.

(b) Without a mint, or gold coinage, as in Canada and the Dutch East Indies.

(c) With a circulation consisting partly of gold, partly of over-valued and inconvertible silver, which is legal tender to an unlimited amount, as in France and other countries of the Latin Union, in the United States, and also in Germany, though there the proportion of over-valued silver is more limited, the mints in all these countries being freely open to gold, but not to silver, and in some of them the silver coinage having ceased.

(d) With a system under which the banks part with gold freely for export, as in Holland, or refuse it for export, as in France.

(*e*) With mints closed against private coinage of both silver and gold, and with a currency of inconvertible paper, as has been temporarily the case in Austria.

(*f*) With a circulation based on gold, but consisting of token silver, which, however, is legal tender to an unlimited extent, as in the West Indies.

" It would thus appear," is the conclusion, " that it has been found possible to introduce a gold standard without a gold circulation; without a large stock of gold currency; and even without legal convertibility of an existing silver currency into gold."

This elaborate account of the monetary policy of the principal nations of the world is extremely well done, and considered as a statistical abstract is most valuable for reference and comparison. Its value, however, as an argument in support of the new Indian policy, is by no means as great as may appear at first sight. If, as is probable, it leads people who profess to be guided solely by facts to the conclusion that it is the easiest thing in the world to establish a gold standard, it will prove altogether misleading.

It is to be regretted that the Committee did not emphasise the fact that in every one of these cases the same general principle is exemplified, the principle, namely, of limitation, first definitely established by Ricardo. Any kind of currency can be maintained at an artificial value, provided only that it is strictly limited, and the degree of depreciation (if any) will depend upon the excess of its quantity, although, of course, the variation is not one of simple proportion.*

* The treatment of the case of Brazil (par. 92) would almost imply that this principle of limitation was not firmly grasped. "The case of Brazil is perhaps the most remarkable of all, as showing that a

Inconvertible notes are the best example, but Ricardo himself gives metallic instances from English history. It may then be taken for granted that if the number of rupees in India can be effectively limited, they may circulate at an artificial value; in other words, they may exchange for a greater value of gold, or any other commodity than would the corresponding weight of silver. The crucial test must be found in the actual conditions of India. References to foreign countries, except for illustration of the general principle, are irrelevant. It would be equally in order to prove that the plan is impossible by references to the numberless cases of failures to maintain an artificial ratio, e.g. Bank of England notes during the restriction.

Unfortunately in this part of the question—the vital part—the Report is by no means so clear, and the information is largely conjectural. The admissions made are, however, in themselves serious enough to have caused a little greater hesitation. Assume, as is the fact already, that the silver in the rupee is worth

---

paper currency without a metallic basis may, if the credit of the country is good, be maintained at a high and fairly steady exchange, although it is absolutely inconvertible, and has been increased by the act of the Government out of all proportion to the growth of the population, and of its foreign trade. The case, it need hardly be said, is not quoted as a precedent which it is desirable to follow. The Brazilian standard coin is the milreis, the par gold value of which is 27d. A certain number were coined, but have long since left the country, and the currency is, and has since 1864 been, inconvertible paper. The inconvertible paper was more than doubled between 1865 and 1888, but the exchange was about the same at the two periods, and very little below the par of 27d." Depreciation, however, eventually occurred through excessive issues.

less than 1s. 4d.—the official rate. It can be maintained at this rate only by rigid limitation of supplies. The supplies from the mints may indeed be effectively cut off unless the Government is tempted to make profits in the manner of the English mint in recent years by coining cheap silver. But *per contra* we have the following ugly facts. In the *first* place the channels of circulation in India are already full to the brim. On this point the evidence of the Report is conclusive.* *Secondly*, there are in circulation outside the borders of India large and unknown quantities of rupees. As the artificial value can only be obtained in India, whereas elsewhere they pass by weight, they will naturally seek the Indian markets. The Report does not attach to this fact the importance usually assigned, and in the absence of the evidence an estimate cannot fairly be given. *Thirdly*, there is the danger of the illegal coinage of silver in the native States, or in foreign countries, or in India itself. Here, again, the Report seeks to minimise the danger, and relies mainly on the experience of other nations, *e.g.* England and France; but the circumstances are different, and the differences do not receive sufficient emphasis. *Fourthly*, there are the hoards of silver, coined and uncoined, in India itself. At the time of writing, the evidence given to the Committee is not available, but the general treatment of this difficulty in the Report seems very unsatisfactory. Under the system that has just been superseded, the metallic value of a mass of rupees was the same as that of the corresponding weight of silver; under the new system (if effective)

* Par. 29-32.

the coined metal will be worth so much more than the uncoined. Accordingly, any one who has a hoard of rupees will be able to get for them a greater weight of silver. It is of course difficult to enter into the secret thoughts of a Hindoo miser, but it seems natural that, under the new conditions, great encouragement would be given to the substitution for the coins of silver ornaments or ingots. According to Gresham's Law, the worse coin drives the better from circulation; the heavy coins are hoarded, the light are used for payments. Conversely then we should expect that, as regards hoards, over-valued coins would be replaced by under-valued metal; in the concrete, that a person would prefer to hoard five ounces of silver in place of four ounces of rupees, and would certainly be glad to exchange the latter for the former. If, however, we have to place against the cessation of coinage the absorption of hoards into the circulation, the rise in value through limitation must be indefinitely postponed. The difficulty of the matter is confirmed by the fact that Sir David Barbour,* probably the best living authority, formerly believed that rupees would be largely brought out of hoards when they were given a value exceeding that of the metal contained in them, but now thinks that the existing hoards would practically remain unaffected. He appears to have penetrated into deeper recesses of the native mind than is possible for the unsophisticated. But, after all, in the absence of evidence can it be said that his second thoughts are best?

* "Correspondence between the Government of India and the Secretary of State," p. 9.

On the whole, then, it seems probable that it must take a considerable time to raise the value of the rupee effectively above its metallic value by limiting the coinage. In time, no doubt, the principle of limitation would operate, but the serious questions are : How long a time will be required ? and What is to happen in the meantime ? The answer to the first depends upon the unknown factors indicated above; the answer to the second depends upon the effect of the new policy on the balance of India's indebtedness.

It may be repeated that the primary object of the whole scheme is to keep up the price of Council bills, or, less technically, to make payments to England, at the rate of fifteen rupees to the pound. The nature and working of Council bills is clearly explained in the Report,* by reference to well-known principles. They are, it is said, only a financial mode adopted as the simplest and best by the Government of India for the purpose of paying a gold debt to England. They are orders for the payment of rupees in India, and the same end would be attained if the Government of India bought sterling bills of the exporting merchants in India and sent them to be cashed on its account in London. In other words, Council bills are simply a mode of payment, and not payment itself.

India (it is stated in the next paragraph) must pay her debts by exports, and the Indian Government cannot in any way avoid whatever expense is necessary in order to pay them. That the exports should ever consist of silver, depreciated as silver is in the Western world, is highly improbable ; but if this

---

should turn out to be the case, it would be because silver was the article which India could best spare.

The principle is admirably stated, and the statement was necessary. Some people suppose that the Indian Government can put a monopoly value on its bills by refusing to sell below a certain price. It can do no such thing. It must sell to those who wish to make payments in India, and if they do not choose to pay the price for that particular form of remittance they can adopt some other mode. Under the old system silver could be sent to be coined, and was sent to a large amount annually. But the bulk of trade exports from India was paid for by trade imports into India. Silver, in fact, was only one of these imports.* The Report insists on the principle that in the last resort the imports of a country and the balance of every other element in its indebtedness must be paid for by exports of some kind or other. If India cannot pay her debts by exporting other commodities, she must export silver or gold; the only other alternative is to allow her debts to increase.

Although this principle, which is at the root of all international transactions, appears to be clearly expressed, it cannot be said that the application is equally clear. As already indicated, the distinction between the immediate or temporary and the ultimate effects of the scheme is not adequately noticed. The primary object of the plan, as so often insisted on, is to prevent a further fall in the Indian exchange—to keep the rupee at 1s. 4d. for foreign payments. Now the

---

* For the three years, 1889-90 to 1891-92, silver was about 14 per cent of the total imports.

foreign exchanges depend not upon the permanent indebtedness of a country, but upon the payments that must be made at a particular time—that is to say, upon a succession of temporary fluctuating causes. If, for example, the closure of the Indian mints were at once to produce an adverse effect on the trade balance of India, the exchange must fall. It is of no avail to say that when the limitation has had time to work its full effect, and that when the balance is again adjusted in favour of India, the exchange will rise. Governments do not legislate by telegraph to provide for the remote future. The proximate cause of the hurry was the fear of a heavy fall in silver, owing to the action of the United States in the coming autumn. If the closure of the Indian mints does not operate, in the way desired, for some years, the object in view will be defeated, and the Indian Government will be forced in the meantime to adopt one or other of the discarded modes of relief.

It is no doubt asserted that part of the plan is eventually to establish a gold standard in India. The consideration of this part of the scheme, however, may be deferred, for it is admitted that it must be postponed, and it presents peculiar and possibly insuperable difficulties. What is of immediate importance is the effect of attempting to give at once a value to the rupee above its metallic value. In other words, we have to consider the effect of a sudden fall in the price of silver on the Indian balance of trade.

The mere announcement of the closure of the mints caused a serious fall in the price of silver, and the action of the United States has still to be taken into account, and it may be assumed that a further fall will take place. In treating this part of the problem not only does the Report not distinguish sufficiently between the present and the future, but the mode of argument adopted is open to objection. Too much reliance is placed on statistics which are not analysed, and on theories that are not proved, although admitted to be paradoxical and not generally received. Figures* of the general course of trade are given, with the view of showing that a fall in the exchange has not stimulated exports relatively to imports, and later on this contention is used as a basis for the argument that a rise in the exchange would not discourage exports and stimulate imports. But the problem is not simple enough to be decided in this rough-and-ready manner. Indian trade has of course during the last twenty years been affected by a variety of causes of which the fall in exchange is only one. It would be absurd to expect that with all these other disturbing elements we should discover exports and imports exactly responding to a fall or rise in exchange in the same way that a thermometer responds to heat and cold.

But that the fall in exchange in recent years has on the whole stimulated exports is evident from another set of figures quoted in the Report, although apparently the connection is not seen. "The above facts"—the reference is to statistics of coinage—"give reasons for believing that the recent fall in silver, coupled with the open mint, has led India to import and coin more silver than she needs, and the worst of the evil is that it is a growing one."† But no one

* Report, par. 27.   † Report, p. 14.

would send silver to India, however much depreciated, unless to receive something in return ; and to say that India has imported more silver than she needs is to say that her exports have been artificially stimulated.

The truth is, that if from causes directly or specially affecting silver in the first place its gold price falls— that is to say, if the fall is not simply part of a general fall in gold prices—until the prices of commodities have been adjusted there must be a stimulus to exports from, and a check on imports to, silver-standard countries.* It may be a matter of dispute how far

* Theoretically, the effect of a fall in exchange on exports and imports is indeterminate. It depends entirely on the causes of the fall. If there is, in the first place, a definite appreciation of gold relatively to commodities whilst silver prices remain the same, then whilst the ratio of gold to silver is being adjusted there will be a stimulus to exports from gold-using to silver-using countries with a falling exchange. I have worked out the different cases in a separate essay (*Money and Monetary Problems*, p. 308 *seq.*).

The following example of the effect when the fall is due to causes affecting silver is taken from the last Blue Book on the trade of British India, p. 5: "The year 1890-91 was marked by extraordinary fluctuations in the exchange value of the rupee. From 1s. 5d. in January 1890, the rate rose to over 1s. 8½d. in September—an increase of more than 20 per cent ; falling again in February 1891 to 1s. 5d. . . . Importers hastened to profit by the rise before prices were adjusted to a new level, and large quantities of goods were shipped to India in the few months during which the rise was in progress. . . . Unusually large quantities of gold also were imported, and on the other hand the export of merchandise was restricted, while the rise was in progress.

" In 1891-92 these conditions were greatly modified. Exchange took a rapid downward course, falling from about 1s. 5¼d. in April 1891, to about 1s. 3₃⁷₅d. in April 1892—a decline of more than 12 per cent ; and though not unaccompanied by fluctuations, these were not so rapid or so violent as in 1890-91.

" The general outcome of the conditions was that, whereas in 1890-91 there was a largely increased importation of merchandise and gold

the fall in silver during the last twenty years has
been due to special causes, such as the closure of
European mints, increase of production, and the like,
and how far to general causes; but in the present case
there is no doubt of the special character of the causes.
The closure of the Indian mints has directly affected
silver, and the cessation of purchases in America must
affect it still more.

It must then be admitted that the closure of the
Indian mints, coupled with the fall in the price of
silver below the rupee value, must stimulate exports
from the silver-using countries and check exports from
India. The Report argues, in the manner familiar to
English law-courts, in the first place, that there will
be no stimulus and no check; and secondly, that the
stimulus and check will be transitory, and can only
last till the inevitable readjustment is made. The
second plea may be accepted, but the success or failure
of the Indian policy depends upon the duration and
the nature of the readjustment.

Suppose that, owing to the closure of the mints, no
silver is sent to India—that it acts in the manner of
a prohibitive duty. For the time being—that is to
say, until the effect on trade has been felt—Indian
Council bills may be kept up to the rate proposed.
But consider the effect on trade.

Either other imports must take the place of silver,
and silver, and a restriction of the export trade, in 1891-92 there was
a restricted import, and an augmented export of merchandise and gold
and silver. The total value of the trade of the year, notwithstanding
the special stimulus given to it by a rapidly-falling exchange and an
abnormal demand for wheat and other food-grains in the European
markets, was smaller than that of 1890-91 "

or exports from India must be diminished, or both events must occur.   If other imports take the place of silver, commercial bills compete with Council bills; if exports diminish there is a less demand for the latter.

Again, the silver refused by India will be sent to other countries.   In this way they will increase their exports at the expense of India.   But India must send something to pay its debts, and if its merchandise is refused it must send gold or silver.

If, in spite of the closure of the mints, India still continues to import silver as a commodity, it will, as before, compete with Council bills, and if it is exchanged for hoarded rupees the rise in value through limitation must be deferred.

Thus, whatever benefits are to be expected ultimately from the gold standard, it seems probable that during the period of transition the closure of the mints will be injurious to India's trade and useless to her finance.

The same result may be obtained by applying the same fundamental principle in a different way.   The revenues of India at present consist of so much silver.   Whatever manipulation takes place, whatever mechanism is adopted, India can only pay a gold debt abroad by selling the requisite amount of this silver. She may sell it to those who in return for goods have payment to make in India, or she may export it and sell it directly for gold.   But one thing she cannot do : if the silver is depreciated on the markets of the world she cannot obtain more than the market price.

When through limitation the rupee has definitely acquired an artificial value, and when India has effectively established a gold standard, the difficulties of exchange will be no doubt remedied. But an effective gold standard means that the Government must be prepared to give gold in exchange for rupees at the rate proposed. At present nothing of the kind is contemplated. The development of events is awaited with anxiety. Accordingly the consideration of the difficulties of this part of the scheme—the gold standard—may be deferred until the Government of India attempts to carry it into practice.

Hitherto the question has been discussed merely as a financial expedient of the Indian Government. As such it is an attempt to avoid an increase of taxation, to meet a deficit due to a fall in value (for remittance) of the taxes at present received. In order that the rupees devoted to the payment of foreign debts may go further, it is proposed to raise the value of all rupees, or, what is the same thing, to prevent a further fall. The method is to stop the coinage, so as to produce by artificial limitation a scarcity value. The result can only be to substitute indirect for direct taxes; or taxes that are not seen for taxes that are seen. As such it may be politically desirable or necessary. Just so may be the issue of inconvertible notes in case of need. But the necessity ought to be extreme.

In conclusion, attention may be directed to the more general aspects of the question—economic and political. However difficult it may be to estimate accurately the economic effects on the trade and development of India during the period of transition, there can be no question as to the general influence

of this new departure on the industries of the gold-
using countries. The closure of the Indian mints to
silver is certain to intensify the evils that followed
on the closure of the mints of Europe. There must
be a further appreciation of gold—in other words, a
further fall in general prices, with an intensification
of the burden of indebtedness, increasing difficulty in
the adjustment of wages, contraction of enterprise
through falling profit, and liquidations on a large
scale. It is equally clear that silver must experience
a further fluctuating fall. Trade with the far East
will be disturbed, and there will be a further
depreciation of capital invested on a silver basis.
If from the point of view of the Indian Government
the scheme were a complete success—if the rupee
could be kept steady at 1s. 4d., and a gold standard
could be adopted with very little gold as a reserve—the
benefit to India could only be obtained with a loss to
the gold-using world, and especially to the United
Kingdom. But the Government of India does not dare
to hope for such complete success. The choice has
been a reluctant choice of evils forced upon it by
political necessity.

The political aspects of the question are as interesting and instructive as the economic. We are told in
an official despatch, dated August 2, 1892, that for
ten years the Government of India had looked for a
solution of their difficulties to international agreement on a bi-metallic basis. It was only on the refusal
of this country to take action at the recent Brussels
Conference that the choice was definitely made. In a
memorandum to the Report, Mr. Courtney has expressed

the opinion that "the Home Government is the greatest obstacle, perhaps the only substantial obstacle, to the establishment of an international agreement for the use of silver as money"; and this was clearly the opinion of the foreign delegates at the Conference. No man living has advocated with more force and clearness than Sir David Barbour the advantages to the world at large, and to India in particular, of international bi-metallism, and he makes no secret of his preference. In the very Minute in which he propounds the plan to be adopted by India for the introduction of a gold standard he concludes with the following remarkable statement:—

I have no hesitation in saying that an international agreement for the free coinage of both gold and silver, and for the making of them full legal tender at a fixed ratio, would be far better for India and all other countries than the establishment of the single gold standard, even if the latter course be possible. Under the former system the worst result that could happen would be the disappearance of one of the metals from circulation, but this would only happen by the other metal taking its place and gradually driving it out, and under such circumstances all countries would have the same standard. The general adoption of the system of double legal tender would be a *perfectly safe measure and would be a final settlement of the question.* The attempt to establish a general gold standard is not without risk.

The Home Government is thus responsible for forcing on India the adoption, or rather the attempt at adoption, of the gold standard. The Council of the Bi-metallic League has done well to emphasise in the declaration just issued the admissions which the policy implies. It is admitted that the fall in silver calls for a legislative remedy, and that such a remedy is possible. It is admitted that the domestic policy of a foreign country regarding coinage may determine the monetary policy of our greatest dependency. It is admitted that an artificial value can be given to the thousand millions of rupees and upwards that constitute the active circulation of India. In short, *laissez-faire* has been abandoned, and the presumption in favour of governmental action has been established, or rather reasserted.

This change of front has led to the abandonment of other positions. In spite of the authority of such eminent financiers as Mr. Goschen and Mr. de Rothschild, the Government apparently no longer believes that a scramble for gold would bring on a financial catastrophe, and that a universal gold standard is impossible. Apparently, also, it no longer believes that silver is the standard naturally adapted to undeveloped countries, that the coinage of unlimited legal tender should be automatic, that the value of the precious metals depends entirely on their cost of production, that gold and silver are commodities like other commodities, that the increase in the burden of gold debts is a fiction, and that the amount of taxation has nothing to do with the standard. The British Government has accepted the principles of bi-metallism, but has not had the courage to carry them to their logical conclusion. It has stopped short at the *étalon boiteux*, and relegated the experiment to its Indian Empire. If the United States follows the Indian example and also closes its mints to silver, the probability is that the British Government may again have to legislate by telegraph, and to take action without consulting Parliament or public opinion.

In the light of the effects on the general situation, the effects of the new policy in Indian finance may be reconsidered. What the Government desired was to prevent a further fall in the rupee, as a consequence of a further anticipated fall in silver. The remedy adopted is to give an artificial value to the rupee by stopping coinage.

In the meantime, however, it is admitted officially that the present rate is provisional; therefore, before the artificial rise is attained, the rupee must follow silver. But the immediate effect of the remedy is to cause a fall in silver, and to hasten the action of the United States. The probability is, that as soon as the full effect on trade has been felt, exchange will be for a time worse than before. Thus, so far as present difficulties are concerned, the remedy can only be compared to relieving a starving man by compelling him to buy an annuity for his old age.

POSTSCRIPT.—Since this article was written I have had the opportunity of reading the evidence given to the Committee, and an account of the proceedings at the introduction and passing of the Bill in India. The weight of evidence appears to be against the recommendations eventually adopted, and to support the views expressed above. The speech of Sir David Barbour brings out very clearly that the measure is a political expedient forced on the Government, and although he defends the plan with ability and spirit, he is evidently very doubtful of success. The rate of exchange is distinctly declared to be provisional, and the adoption of gold as legal tender is indefinitely postponed, so that the necessity for the haste and secrecy displayed does not seem very obvious.

THE END

Printed by R. & R. CLARK, *Edinburgh.*

www.ingramcontent.com/pod-product-compliance
Lightning Source LLC
Chambersburg PA
CBHW032304280326
41932CB00009B/696